MW00559678

Chris Palmer has produced a truly enjoyable book for readers from all walks of life. *Greek Word Study: 90 Ancient Words That Unlock Scripture* is a user-friendly guide to the original language of the New Testament for anyone who desires a better understanding of God's Word. Palmer has "done the work for you" in explaining the use of key words from biblical Greek, in a way that is both clear and simple to grasp. Not only will you gain a deeper understanding of Scripture, you are also likely to discover elements of truth you never knew existed, right there under your nose the whole time!

—*Daniel Kolenda*
Evangelist; president/CEO, Christ for all Nations

CHRIS PALMER

GREEK
μελέτη λόγων Ἑλληνικῶν
WORD STUDY

90 ANCIENT WORDS
THAT UNLOCK SCRIPTURE

WHITAKER
HOUSE

Greek Word Study

90 Ancient Words That Unlock Scripture

Light of Today Ministries
www.lightoftoday.com
www.instagram.com/chrispalmer

ISBN: 978-1-64123-460-3
eBook ISBN: 978-1-64123-461-0
Printed in the United States of America
© 2020 by Chris Palmer

Whitaker House
1030 Hunt Valley Circle
New Kensington, PA 15068
www.whitakerhouse.com

Library of Congress Cataloging-in-Publication Data (Pending)

1 2 3 4 5 6 7 8 9 10 11 ⨆ 28 27 26 25 24 23 22 21 20

This book is dedicated to those committed to the Word of God.

Ζῶν γὰρ ὁ λόγος τοῦ θεοῦ καὶ ἐνεργὴς καὶ τομώτερος ὑπὲρ πᾶσαν μάχαιραν δίστομον καὶ διϊκνούμενος ἄχρι μερισμοῦ ψυχῆς καὶ πνεύματος, ἁρμῶν τε καὶ μυελῶν, καὶ κριτικὸς ἐνθυμήσεων καὶ ἐννοιῶν καρδίας.
(ΠΡΟΣ ΕΒΡΑΙΟΥΣ 4:12)

For the word of God is living and active, sharper than any two-edged sword, piercing to the division of soul and of spirit, of joints and of marrow, and discerning the thoughts and intentions of the heart.
(Hebrews 4:12)

ACKNOWLEDGMENTS

Writing a book is not a venture one undertakes alone. Mark Twain said, "Write what you know," and much of what I know is the result of others who have informed me and guided me along the way. Therefore, it should not be considered unusual that I sensed the influences of these individuals while I was doing research and writing *Greek Word Study*. I'd often imagine I was hearing them caution my treatment of the text, implore me to dig deeper in my research, challenge me to rely on the Holy Spirit, or chide me for overusing the exclamation point, particularly in my first draft. It's a bad habit I still haven't been able to kick. Their wise counsel has given you the book you are holding in your hands, so I'd like to acknowledge them here.

My professors and teachers: J. Brian Tucker, Raju Kunjummen, John Christopher Thomas, Philip Mayo, and John Schwandt; my peers at Moody Theological Seminary and University of Wales, Bangor; my pastor, Bishop Keith Butler; my editors, Mary Achor and Peg Fallon; and my administrative assistant, Luana Minutella.

Beyond writing and research, a successful book project requires the love and support of those closest to you. Here's where I'd like to thank Light of Today Church and, most of all, my loving family.

Finally, thank you to Whitaker House and its magnificent team.

May every investment that has been made into *Greek Word Study* be for the glory of our Lord and Savior, Jesus Christ.

CONTENTS

AUTHOR'S NOTE

I want to take a moment to explain how I have treated the Greek words throughout this book. In most languages, words change depending on how they're used. For example, in English, the verb *cook* can be *cooked*, *cooking*, or *cooks*. This is known as inflection—word changes based on their grammatical function. It occurs even more often in Greek. For instance, the Greek word *legō* (I say) can be *legeis* (you say), *legei* (he/she/it says), *legomen* (we say), *legete* (you all say), or *legousin* (they say). And this is only the present tense, active voice, and indicative mood. The little verb *legō* can change tense, person, gender, and so on in many more ways than these. Sometimes when it does so, it doesn't even look like *lego* at first glance. For instance, "he said" is *elegen*.

Although this isn't a grammar book meant to teach you Greek language construction, I felt it necessary to be pedantic here so you know what's going on as you read each chapter. In *most* of the studies[1], I introduce a Greek word the way you'd find it in a lexicon—and probably how a preacher would bring it up on a Sunday morning. But after that, in the body of the studies themselves, I will give you the inflected form of the word as it is found in the Scripture we are looking at. You'll often notice me saying, "The Greek word here…" That's just me nodding at its inflection. In other places in the New Testament where the word is used, it may not look the same. Should I reference the word again in the study, I will return to using its lexical form.

I really wrestled with whether I should put every mention of any Greek word in its lexical form and hope that those who know Greek would understand and everyone else would not mind. But I decided against this option, choosing to make this work more comprehensive. You may find yourself reading a section and thinking, *Hey, why do some of the words look different?* Now you know why: that's just language for you. And Koine Greek is no exception.

Finally, if you should be curious enough to look these words up in a lexicon, you may notice that many of them take other meanings that I have not indexed or cited. I did this on purpose. Many words have multiple meanings; I have indexed only the definitions used in *Greek Word Study* and nothing beyond that. Doing otherwise would not have benefited nor complemented this particular study.

INTRODUCTION

Albert Einstein once said, "If you can't explain it simply, you don't understand it well enough." That's quite a statement coming from the man who won the Nobel Prize in physics and introduced the world to his revolutionary theory of relativity, $E=mc^2$. Despite the complicated nature and depth of theoretical physics, Einstein never abandoned simplicity. Although a truth might be relatively deep, it is also simple and should be explained as such, especially to a green audience endeavoring to learn the truth firsthand.

It was our own Lord and Savior, Jesus Christ, who happened to exhibit the perfect example of this art of simplicity. Although His teachings contained profound mysteries concerning the kingdom of God, Jesus found ways to place these truths into everyday language that was basic enough for tax collectors, fishermen, shepherds, and poor people to understand. He did this by using concepts of the day to enhance the meaning of the eternal truths He was sharing:

The kingdom of heaven is like leaven that a woman took and hid in three measures of flour, till it was all leavened. (Matthew 13:33)

What do you think? If a man has a hundred sheep, and one of them has gone astray, does he not leave the ninety-nine on the mountains and go in search of the one that went astray? And if he finds it, truly, I say to you, he rejoices over it more than over the ninety-nine that never went astray. So it is not the will of my Father who is in heaven that one of these little ones should perish. (Matthew 18:12–14)

What woman, having ten silver coins, if she loses one coin, does not light a lamp and sweep the house and seek diligently until she finds it? And when she has found it, she calls together her friends and neighbors, saying, "Rejoice with me, for I have found the coin that I had lost." Just so, I tell you, there is joy before the angels of God over one sinner who repents. (Luke 15:8–10)

Truly, truly, I say to you, unless a grain of wheat falls into the earth and dies, it remains alone; but if it dies, it bears much fruit. (John 12:24)

Flour. Sheep. Coins. Wheat. Jesus never abandoned the familiarity of His time even though what He had to say was celestial or deep. Instead, He took advantage of what people already understood and used those concepts to be part of His teaching. In doing so, He didn't just leave us a way of salvation, but also a pattern of teaching to follow. This alone was my inspiration for the method I have chosen to write *Greek Word Study*. It's my prayer that it helps you to better understand the eternal truths from the Word of God that, sadly, are misunderstood all too often.

And, here, I'd like to mention something: I have two different opinions about commentaries. Oh, sure, as a scholar I'm often tucked away in them. Like a mechanic underneath a car, I like to bang together meaning and crank out ideas in order to present truth that can drive people closer to the Lord. *I like commentaries, but I suspect most people don't, so I have certain qualms with them.* While I appreciate commentaries and certainly understand their place, I believe only those who are excessively detail-oriented care to put up with their technicalities. You know—people like me. I'll be the first to say that managing a consistent study within a scholarly work sometimes feels as laborious as probing a long stretch of nighttime sky for a single shooting star. During certain times of the year, you may see one eventually…if you know where to look. But on a typical night, you may be gazing for a long time.

For this reason, I have done the searching for you and have placed my findings alongside ideas you'll understand from the twenty-first century, as well as some everyday examples from my own life. In each study, you'll find insight into key Greek words. These will present you with picturesque examples that will, hopefully, relate first-century living to your own busy, technology-filled life.

You don't need to be scholar to read this book and you don't need to know an ounce of Greek either. In fact, you don't need to know much about the Bible at all. I've gone to great lengths to give you the insight you need to enable your understanding. Just kick back and enjoy.

I've also endeavored to provide enough insights to appeal to veteran Bible students, too.

Start with Study 1, or begin with your favorite number, whatever that might be. There's no order to these studies, although I do think they complement each other in the order I've presented them. If you complete all of them, you'll come away with a solid understanding of important themes in the New Testament. You'll have read portions of most of its books and something from every author. My prayer is that while reading these studies, you'll experience the transforming power of the Holy Spirit, your heart will be drawn closer to Jesus, and you'll be better able to articulate the Word of God…simply, of course.

Maranatha.

μαράνα θά.

Chris Palmer

1

IMITATOR: *MIMĒTĒS*
(μιμητής)

---

*Therefore be **imitators** of God, as beloved children.*

(Ephesians 5:1)

γίνεσθε οὖν μιμηταὶ τοῦ θεοῦ ὡς τέκνα ἀγαπητὰ
(ΠΡΟΣ ΕΦΕΣΙΟΥΣ 5:1)

Memes have taken over the Internet. If you have a smart phone and Wi-Fi, then you know exactly what I'm talking about. They are the backbone of social media and probably the best part of your group texts. Everyone loves them and sends them around, including celebrities, religious leaders, and even the president. The moment news breaks, there's no doubt that the memes will break with it in a matter of seconds. Giant hurricane coming? The president met with the leader of a communist country? A kicker missed a field goal? Worldwide pandemic? A space telescope broke? Memes, memes, and more memes. We've got memes for it all.

It shouldn't come as a surprise that some of the most popular social media platforms—the ones with the most follows, views, and likes—are the ones dedicated solely to nicely curated memes. There are Christian meme accounts, conservative meme accounts, and liberal meme accounts. I even follow a meme account for Ph.D. students. No better way to take a study break than to look at some memes made by others who can relate to my frustrations.

What can I say? I'm a meme-ster[2] and I like to meme.[3]

(For those who've been living off the grid, a meme is simply an image that's embellished with text and makes fun of whatever it's embellishing.)

However, the word *meme* was born long before there were these Internet images that imitated and teased their subjects. It was first coined in 1976 by Richard Dawkins in his book *The Selfish Gene*. Dawkins needed a word to express how culture spreads information—"cultural transmissions," as he calls it—within itself.

Dawkins chose the word *mimeme*, the Greek word for "imitation." Hence, it represents a way that culture is imitated and passed along. Dawkins, however, thought to abbreviate the word to "meme" because it sounded like "gene" and was monosyllabic. Since he invented the word, let's let him define what it means. He says:

> Examples of memes are tunes, ideas, catch-phrases, clothes fashions, ways of making pots or of building arches…memes propagate themselves in the meme pool by leaping from brain to brain via a process which, in the broad sense, can be called imitation. If a scientist hears, or reads about, a good idea, he passes it on to his colleagues and students…If the idea catches on, it can be said to propagate itself, spreading from brain to brain.[4]

Essentially, Dawkins is saying that a meme is cultural transmission spread by imitation. If we buy a pair of upcycled, patchwork jeans, our friends may decide to imitate our fashion sense. When we play a song by a new artist, we imitate what's trending in music and perhaps someone else listening might give that singer a try. Ever come back from a trip to another county and, suddenly, you are appreciating their art, trying out their recipes, and using their figures of speech? They spread it to you through imitation, by "memeing" it.

Believe it or not, before Dawkins was talking about memes, God's Word was already on it. We find this in Ephesians 5:1, where the apostle Paul was urging the church in Ephesus to live like Christ. Paul had just finished talking about how God forgave each of us and imploring the Ephesian believers to do the same for one another (4:32). For them to accomplish this, Paul tells them to *"be imitators of God."*

> Actors in ancient Greece were exalted by society, much like today's Hollywood stars. In ancient Rome, however, actors were slaves and foreigners who were often detested by society for their lack of morals and theatrical political critiques.

The Greek word here for "imitators" in 5:1 is *mimētai*. That's right; it's in the same word family[5] as *mimeme*. It means "a model" or "an impersonator." In antiquity, the word was used to describe actors who imitated their subjects, studying them closely so they could offer their best embellished impersonation. Through this, the subject they were "memeing" was transmitted to those watching.

Paul was telling the Ephesians to meme, or imitate, God. They were to take note of how God forgives and then replicate that forgiveness to one another. This would transmit the concept of God's forgiveness to the rest of the church community so it could become part of their culture. Right there was first-century, Christian memeing for you.

So, you see, memes aren't that new after all. Sure, "Internet memes" are kind of a new thing, but imitating the love of God is not.

Remember that you and I are living "memes" for God. We are called to transmit the love of Jesus and spread the culture of the kingdom everywhere we go by imitating the Lord. There is no better way to communicate the character of God than to impersonate Him in everything we do.

A coworker got mad and cussed you out? Someone borrowed money and didn't pay you back? Your spouse snapped at you? You overheard another parishioner gossiping about you?

Here's an idea: send them a meme. Impersonate the love of God and forgive them instead of trying to get back at them. Now *that's* being a true memester—a memester for the kingdom.

Are you ready to start memeing?

2

WHOLE ARMOR: *PANOPLIA* (πανοπλία)

Put on the whole armor *of God, that you may be able to stand against the schemes of the devil.*   (Ephesians 6:11)

ἐνδύσασθε τὴν πανοπλίαν τοῦ θεοῦ πρὸς τὸ δύνασθαι ὑμᾶς στῆναι πρὸς τὰς μεθοδείας τοῦ διαβόλου
                                                    (ΠΡΟΣ ΕΦΕΣΙΟΥΣ 6:11)

The National Hockey League might have made its best decision ever in 1979: mandatory helmets for every player. I'm a bit shocked that it took them sixty-two years to make this rule...and maybe a little more surprised that players actually chose *not* to wear helmets before 1979. They may not be the most stylish thing in sports, but it just makes sense to wear them when rock-hard pucks are whistling through the air at 105 miles per hour and players are smashing into each other like rivaling bighorn rams during sixty minutes of play.

The NHL's reluctance to require helmets was mainly due to the fact that owners wanted fans to be able to recognize their favorite players. Additionally, fights are common in hockey; it's meant to be a red-blooded, virile sport. And what true savage uses a helmet?

As time skated by, it became apparent even to the hardest-hitting players that without a helmet, they were not fully equipped with the whole armor they needed. With just leather pads and a hockey stick to ward off their opponents, they remained vulnerable. It took five concussions and the death of Minnesota North Stars teammate Bill Masterton to finally convince right-winger Bill Goldsworthy to wear a helmet. It became apparent that protecting the head and face from inevitable trauma was more important than how a player looked or felt about his manhood. One piece of equipment could mean the difference between life and death.

In Ephesians 6:11, we are told something about protective spiritual equipment. This is the armor of God. In describing it to the Ephesian church, the apostle Paul calls it the "whole armor" (*panoplian*). *Panoplian* is a two-part Greek word comprised of *pas* (all; every) and *hoplōn* (armor and weaponry used for military purposes). Together, it means all equipment and weapons required for battle. It is a complete set of weapons, both offensive and defensive. If a soldier had on the whole armor, he was ready for war. Like today's hockey players, they have their stick in hand and are wearing *all* their pads *and* helmet. When they step out onto the ice, they are fortified to stand against any aggressive assault that will inevitably come their way.

There is nuance within the word *panoplian* that we should be careful not to miss: the idea of having *all* your armor on means the alarm has sounded. This is not simply a drill or a team practice. The battle is raging and the enemy is attacking with full force.

I can relate because I played soccer in high school. The rule in practice was absolutely no slide-tackling (one of my specialties) because that would put your teammate at risk. One wrong collision and they could end up injured—and sitting on the sidelines for the real contest. As a result, none of us wore shin pads to practice. Since we had no risk of being cleated, we didn't practice fully equipped. But it was a different story when the big game came, when our opponents would come slide-tackling from every direction. In fact, shin pads were mandatory; we weren't allowed, by league regulations, to step out on the field without them.

In Ephesians 6:11, the apostle Paul was mandating shin pads. He was telling the Ephesian church that the fuming attack of the enemy was underway and the forces of Hell were charging at the Ephesian believers in full force. This wasn't an exercise; they were in the thick of combat. The only way to withstand the assault and live to tell about it was to put on the *panoplian*— *all* of the pieces of armor: the belt of truth, the breastplate of righteousness, the shoes of peace, the shield of faith, and the sword of the Spirit. If they lacked even one piece, they would find themselves mortally wounded and defeated. In fact, having on the whole armor was so central to their gaining victory that Paul says it twice:

> *Put on the whole armor [panoplian] of God, that you may be able to stand against the schemes of the devil.* (Ephesians 6:11)

> *Therefore take up the whole armor [panoplian] of God, that you may be able to withstand in the evil day, and having done all, to stand firm.* (Ephesians 6:13)

In both of these instances, Paul is using the imperative mood, meaning he is speaking quite strongly. He isn't giving the Ephesian church food for thought; he's saying, "Do this and do this now!" The battle depends on *all* their armor. Paul isn't giving them an option.

Paul lists the armor of a Roman centurion. These men were skillful fighters who were expected to demonstrate courage. If a centurion cowered in battle, he could be executed.

It's important to note a crucial implication that God's Word is teaching here: good intentions do not win battles. Many well-meaning Christians have been crushed on the battlefield. A good try doesn't cut it. In the twenty-first century, people want to be optimistic by focusing on what they have rather than what they don't. In other words, if they are wearing 80 percent of the armor, isn't that good enough? No. This verse counters that thought. God is teaching us the importance of being 100 percent in the moment of battle. Therefore, the implication is that if we have a deficiency, it needs to be fixed right away. God wants us to win—and He wants us to have *all* the armor. His grace has made it available for us to put on.

No matter where we find ourselves in the battle, we can put on the whole armor by keeping our relationship fresh with the Holy Spirit. By seeking the Holy Spirit and obeying God's Word, we can be sure that the full power and protection of the Spirit will clothe us in our day-to-day lives.

Wherever you find yourself today, pause and make certain you are fully equipped with the whole armor of God. Don't leave out one piece. Your victory depends on it.

3

WITH: *SYN* (σύν)

---

*On the contrary, I worked harder than any of them, though it
was not I, but the grace of God that is with me.*

(1 Corinthians 15:10b)

ἀλλὰ περισσότερον αὐτῶν πάντων ἐκοπίασα, οὐκ ἐγὼ δὲ
ἀλλ᾽ ἡ χάρις τοῦ θεοῦ [ἡ] σὺν ἐμοί.

(ΠΡΟΣ ΚΟΡΙΝΘΙΟΥΣ Α 15:10b)

I once heard a preacher say, "Every *word* in Scripture is important. Don't
forget about the little words. Slow down and see why God placed them
there." I thought, *Oh, come on, every word? Surely "and" and "the" can't have
much meaning.* Boy, was I ever wrong. It wasn't far into my early studies
of Koine Greek that I saw exactly what that preacher was talking about.
Miniature words can have *massive* meaning. Like the guy who gives his

girlfriend an engagement ring. The box is small, but what's inside has the power to floor her.

We find this in 1 Corinthians 15:10. Here, we see an isty-bitsy preposition, *syn*, which most often means "with." It frequently emphasizes accompaniment, association, and assistance. It links two things for a specific purpose. When two things are "with" each other, they are teaming up and keeping one another company. This may seem elementary, but in 1 Corinthians 15:10, it is hard-hitting.

Here, Paul is writing to the Corinthian church about how he became an apostle. Unlike the other apostles, Paul wasn't yet a believer when Christ rose from the dead, nor was he a believer during Christ's post-resurrection ministry. (See Acts 1:3.) Paul, known as Saul before his conversion, was busy with other things during that time, such as killing and imprisoning those who followed Christ. (See Acts 8:1–3.) In 1 Corinthians 15, Paul tries to explain how he managed to go from killer to conversion to the one who did more than anyone else to spread the gospel of Jesus Christ. He attributed it to *"the grace of God that is **with** me"* (1 Corinthians 15:10).

Paul could have written this in several different ways. He could have said "the grace of God *upon* me," or "the grace of God *in* me," or even "the grace of God *around* me." But Paul selected a more personal word: "with" (*syn*) me. By saying it like this, Paul was linking himself to the grace of God and suggesting that he kept company and was in association with it. It's safe to say that Paul, at times, felt like grace was a tangible person right beside him, assisting him on his journey. Grace was his personal assistant, his ministerial companion, and his partner in the work of Christ. This certainly adds a new dimension to his ministry. Consider Paul's account regarding the challenges of his ministry:

> *…with far greater labors, far more imprisonments, with countless beatings, and often near death. Five times I received at the hands of the Jews the forty lashes less one. Three times I was beaten with rods. Once, I was stoned. Three times I was shipwrecked; a night and a day I was adrift at sea; on frequent journeys, in danger from rivers, danger from robbers, danger from my own people, danger from Gentiles, danger in the city, danger in the wilderness, danger at sea, danger from false*

brothers; in toil and hardship, through many a sleepless night, in hunger and thirst, often without food, in cold and exposure. And, apart from other things, there is the daily pressure on me of my anxiety for all the churches.   (2 Corinthians 11:23–28)

Suffering just one of the hardships on this list is unimaginable, but Paul endured them all. Have you read this and asked yourself how? Paul had a companion to lean on, strengthening and enabling him along the way. God's grace kept Paul company in prison, soothed the wounds of his beatings, bandaged his bruises, kept him afloat when he was drifting at sea, and had his back when danger surrounded him. Grace was a pillow when Paul couldn't sleep, food when he was starving, and a blanket to wrap himself in when he got cold. Like a good assistant, grace fills the gaps and makes up for our weaknesses.

A white marble sarcophagus located under the Basilica of St. Paul's Outside the Walls in Rome is believed to contain Paul's remains. Bone fragments found inside date back to the first or second century. The sarcophagus also contains some grains of incense, a piece of purple linen with gold sequins, and a blue fabric with linen filaments.

I've felt grace this tangibly in my life—like an actual ministry helper beside me—most specifically when God calls me to do something for His purposes. I remember when the Lord began sending me to preach His word to the nations. Doors began to open, but I had no one to accompany me. Before my first international trip, someone said to me with deep concern, "Are you really going...*alone?* What if something happens?" Looking back now, I never went alone. I had the grace of God. And it showed. It was uncanny how quickly I began to assimilate other cultures. Within hours of landing, I would pick up phrases and use them correctly—enough to warm and win the hearts of the people I was preaching to.

Grace even got a hold of my stomach. There has never been an instance where something I ate made me sick. And believe me, I've eaten some weird things. I just noticed how much it meant to the culture for me to try their cuisine with enthusiasm and without hesitation, and so I would go for it—no questions asked. A pastor in Asia once remarked, "It's amazing how you eat whatever you are given. We have never seen anyone from the USA act like this before." All I can tell you is that grace was doing something to my taste buds and my stomach so that the gospel could be preached more effectively.

You may not be called to preach halfway around the world or eat slimy delicacies in faraway places, but you are called to *something*. And when you find out what that something is, you will discover God's grace. Don't fall victim to the idea that you are in this alone. Grace is *with* you. Let it help you and you will accomplish more than you ever imagined.

4

UNSEARCHABLE:
ANEXICHNIASTOS
(ἀνεξιχνίαστος)

To me, though I am the very least of all the saints, this grace was given, to preach to the Gentiles the **unsearchable** *riches of Christ.* (Ephesians 3:8)

ἐμοὶ τῷ ἐλαχιστοτέρῳ πάντων ἁγίων ἐδόθη ἡ χάρις αὕτη, τοῖς ἔθνεσιν εὐαγγελίσασθαι τὸ ἀνεξιχνίαστον πλοῦτος τοῦ Χριστοῦ (ΠΡΟΣ ΕΦΕΣΙΟΥΣ 3:8)

How big is *big*? Google it. Or, I should say, "Googol it." By this, I am not referring to the Internet search giant, but a googol, the number from which it got its name.

To understand this, we have to go back to 1920, when mathematician Edward Kasner's nine-year-old nephew came up with the term *googol* to represent an unimaginably large number—a one with one hundred zeros behind it. That's 10 to the power of 100 or 10^{100}, also known as ten duotrigintillion, or ten thousand sexdecillion, or ten sexdecilliard.

It's a mind-blowingly large number—bigger, mathematicians believe, than the total number of all the subatomic particles in the universe.

When you look up at the night sky and see all those planets and stars in our galaxy, consider that the Milky Way is just one galaxy among billions of galaxies. How about adding up all of the subatomic particles in the universe and figuring out how big that number might be. It is still *not* a googol. Incredible.

The irony is that Kasner's nephew, Milton Sirotta, came up with an even bigger number: a googolplex. That's a one with a googl of zeros behind it! Or 10^{googol}.

Kasner introduced these numbers to the public in 1940 in his best-selling book *Mathematics and the Imagination*. He wrote: "Mathematics is often erroneously referred to as the science of common sense. Actually, it may transcend common sense and go beyond either imagination or intuition."[6] Kasner was saying that there are some things that, even in our wildest imaginations, we cannot comprehend.

In Ephesians 3:8, the apostle Paul tells us the same thing. Rather than referring to the size of a theoretical number, however, he is speaking to the enormity of God's grace.

In his letter to the Ephesians, Paul talks about the wealth of benefits we have in Christ (1:3), the depth and greatness of God's power (1:19), the richness of God's love and mercy (2:4), and the abundant kindness He's shown us (2:7)—all from the grace of God. Paul finds the sheer magnitude of God's grace to be staggering. It is so overwhelming that it often causes him to sink to his knees before God in humble thanksgiving. (See Ephesians 1:15–16; 3:14.)

Paul elaborates further on the vastness of God's grace when he calls it "unsearchable" (3:8). This is an intriguing way to describe it. Here, the Greek word for "unsearchable" is *anexichniaston*. This Greek word is made up of an alpha private (*a*) and two Greek words: *ek* ("from," "out of") and *ichnos* ("footstep," "footprint"). *Ichnos* is an interesting word because in antiquity, it was not only used to denote the physical impression someone's foot made on the ground, but also an entire trail of footprints. When *ek* is combined with *ichnos*, it forms the word *exichniazo* and means "to trace from" or "to track out." It means "to search something out and explore something thoroughly" or "to get to the bottom of something."

In fact, today in the Greek-speaking countries of Greece and Cyprus, *exichniazo* means "to resolve a police case." You see, the idea behind the word is to trace something, follow something, and figure something out like a detective hot on the trail, with intense focus, determined to figure out where all of the evidence is leading.

However, we can't forget the alpha privative (*a*), which negates the entirety of the word that follows it. Therefore, *anexichniastos* means "unable to search something," "unable to figure something out," and "impossible to get to the bottom of something." Like a googol or googolplex, it can't be grasped—it's incomprehensible, impossible to fully understand.

This is the grace of God. Too big to be traced, too huge to get to the bottom of it, and too enormous to figure out. John Newton was spot on: "Amazing Grace."

John Newton, author of the hymn "Amazing Grace," was a profane, slave-trading sailor on the West African coast prior to his conversion. After God spared his life from a storm at sea and a terrible fever, Newton became one of the most influential Christians of the eighteenth century.

When you consider all of God's blessings that have come through His grace, do you find it impossible to comprehend? When you ponder all that God has done for you, despite your sins and failures, are you left in awe and overwhelmed? Does it make you sink to your knees in humble thanksgiving, like Paul?

Why not look back on your life and count all the times that God has demonstrated His unsearchable goodness and kindness to you. Can you think of an instance in particular? How about when He saved you from your sins? Maybe there was a time in your life where He delivered you from death. It could be that you came from humble beginnings, but now, you are wealthy and faring more than just well. Perhaps you did something deserving of serious punishment, but you didn't receive it because God showed you favor.

Whatever the case, you are what you are because of God's unfathomable grace. Grace to the power of googol—grace^{googol}. While we can't fully comprehend the enormity of this, we can at least give Him thanks and praise for it.

I'd say that's the least we can do for the endless things He's done for us.

5

CONFIDENCE: *PARRĒSIA* (παρρησία)

---

*Let us then with **confidence** draw near to the throne of grace, that we may receive mercy and find grace to help in time of need.* (Hebrews 4:16)

προσερχώμεθα οὖν μετὰ παρρησίας τῷ θρόνῳ τῆς χάριτος, ἵνα λάβωμεν ἔλεος καὶ χάριν εὕρωμεν εἰς εὔκαιρον βοήθειαν. (ΠΡΟΣ ΕΒΡΑΙΟΥΣ 4:16)

The First Amendment of the U.S. Constitution is one that we in the United States have been blessed to live under and enjoy. It states:

Congress shall make no law respecting an establishment of religion, or prohibiting the free exercise thereof; or abridging the freedom of speech, or of the press; or the right of the people peaceably to assemble, and to petition the government for a redress of grievances.

Under the First Amendment, we have the right to *freedom of speech*, which allows American citizens to freely express their ideas, opinions, and values without having to fear consequences from the government, such as censorship, fines, or imprisonment.

> The ancient Greeks deliberated between two concepts of free speech: *isēgoria* and *parrēsia*. *Isēgoria* is the right of citizens to participate in public, democratic debate. *Parrēsia* is the right of citizens to say whatever they want, whenever they want, to whomever they want.

Even if the opinion or idea is preposterous, it is protected by the First Amendment.[7] You have the right to wear a shirt that proclaims your approval or disapproval of the president, stand on the street corner with a sign that says an alien invasion is coming in 2097, or appear on television to openly defend your religious views. Those who have emigrated from countries without this basic human right truly understand what a blessing it is.

Take, for instance, a gentleman from my church. He's an immigrant from a Middle Eastern country that was under an oppressive dictatorship in the 1970s. He's often told me what life was like for him as a teenager under that regime. He vividly recalls riding on a city bus and complaining to a friend that he didn't like the conditions of the country, which he blamed on the government. An eavesdropper reported him to the police. He was arrested and taken before the authorities, who threatened to kill him and throw his body into the sewer.

Fortunately, he had another friend who was a government official and was able to get him out of that mess. Before leaving, they warned him that if he ever spoke against the government again, there would be no mercy. As you can imagine, this made him nervous about speaking openly until he came to the United States. Now, he can say what he wants, wherever he wants. What a blessing free speech is.

It makes sense, then, that we find this blessing in God's Word. In Hebrews 4:16, the writer is discussing the superiority of the high priesthood of Jesus Christ and what it has accomplished for us as believers. The work of Christ, under the new covenant, has given us access into the presence of God. The writer of Hebrews affirms that this has had a great effect on our prayers or, as we might say today, our *prayer life.*

Here, we meet the idea of free speech. The writer of Hebrews says, *"Let us then with confidence draw near to the throne of grace…"* The Greek word for "confidence" here is *parrēsias.* It means "frankness," "outspokenness," "fearlessness." In other places of Scripture, it is translated as "boldness." (See Acts 4:13.)

The idea behind this word becomes particularly interesting when we trace its usage in antiquity. *Parrēsia* was used by the ancient Greeks in the political sphere, as it meant "freedom of speech." This free speech was a trademark of their democracy and it was the right of every citizen. Philosophers, lawyers, politicians, and the average person were allowed to say what was on their mind with "frankness," "outspokenness," and without fear of how the government might respond. As a result, the Greek society thrived and flourished. Being a citizen had its benefits.

Over time, the word became identified with the idea of saying whatever needed to be said, even if it was unpopular and in opposition to the norms. For that, it took on the nuance of "shamelessness," as well as "candor." It was a joy for Greeks to be able to speak with an open mind and live unhindered by restrictions that could prevent the disclosure of truth. Hence, with *parrēsia* comes joy.

For this reason, *parrēsia* was an excellent, descriptive word choice to describe the believer's prayer life. You see, the work of Christ has made us citizens of the kingdom of God and members of God's family. This has resulted in our marvelous liberties, one of which is the joy of being able to approach the throne of God with candor, shamelessness, and the frankness to tell God Almighty what is on our hearts and minds without fear that He will punish us or do us any harm. We have the right to stand before God and express ourselves.

A passage in John 18:20 goes further to show us what *parrēsia* means. Here, Jesus tells the high priest, *"I have spoken openly to the world. I have always taught in synagogues and in the temple, where all Jews come together. I have said nothing in secret."* The word "openly" here is also *parrēsia*. It is interesting to note that Jesus contrasts it with "secretly," or the Greek word *kryptō*, which comes from the word *kryptos*, meaning "secret" or "hidden."

Kryptos implies a "secret chamber" and even "a corner." Hence, the opposite of saying something openly and with freedom of speech is to cower in fear and whisper it in the broom closet. Perhaps unhealthy traditions and strict fundamentalism have, in the past, given you a nervous sense about approaching God in prayer. Perhaps you are afraid to say the wrong thing when you pray.

When we approach God, He doesn't want us to act like scared children who timidly stand in the corner and plead with fear. He wants us to approach Him with joy and shamelessness because we belong in His kingdom family.

How have you been praying? Are you timid because you feel that God is a tyrannical dictator and will punish you if you say the wrong thing? Or, are you taking advantage of your right to freedom of speech?

Let God's Word set you free. Take advantage of the work of Christ and ask the Holy Spirit to help you use your freedom of speech. Be the citizen that God has given you the right to be and tell Him what is really on your heart. When you do, you'll notice a tremendous difference in your prayers.

6

SOUND FORTH: *EXĒCHEŌ*
(ἐξηχέω)

For not only has the word of the Lord sounded forth *from you in Macedonia and Achaia, but your faith in God has gone forth everywhere, so that we need not say anything.*

(1 Thessalonians 1:8)

ἀφ᾽ ὑμῶν γὰρ ἐξήχηται ὁ λόγος τοῦ κυρίου οὐ μόνον ἐν τῇ Μακεδονίᾳ καὶ [ἐν τῇ] Ἀχαΐᾳ, ἀλλ᾽ ἐν παντὶ τόπῳ ἡ πίστις ὑμῶν ἡ πρὸς τὸν θεὸν ἐξελήλυθεν, ὥστε μὴ χρείαν ἔχειν ἡμᾶς λαλεῖν τι.

(ΠΡΟΣ ΘΕΣΣΑΛΟΝΙΚΕΙΣ Α 1:8)

What's the loudest sound you've ever heard? If you ask me, I'm taken back to my college dorm in 2002. One of the musicians who lived on my floor owned a high-powered amp and we were determined to see how much noise that baby could put out. However, our floor was made of cinderblocks, creating the perfect echo chamber for the sound to reverberate. By the time we cranked the volume to maximum capacity, I was surprised we hadn't gone deaf. Not sure how to describe it other than to say the sound was blasting us. Sound is a mechanical thing and it has a connection to the physical world. It was coming out of that speaker, going out all over the hallway, and hitting us right in the face. We could literally feel it on our faces.

Yet the sound coming out of our amp was nothing in comparison to some of the other loud sounds in the world. Take the loudest sound in recorded history, for example: the eruption of Mt. Krakatoa in Indonesia on August 27, 1883. Scientists said this explosion, a 6 on the Volcanic Explosivity Index (VEI), was ten times more powerful than the Mount St. Helens blast in 1980, which was a 5 on the VEI.

To understand this sort of power, that's about 200 *megatons* of TNT. The bomb that devastated Hiroshima had only 20 *kilotons*, meaning the eruption of Krakatoa was 10,000 times more powerful than the atom bomb.

The blast sent eleven cubic miles of ash into the air and landed on ships up to 3,775 miles away. The sky became dark up to 275 miles away and remained dark for three days. The powerful explosion also affected the world's atmosphere. Global temperatures were 1.2 degrees cooler for the next five years.

But what might be the most colossal thing about this event was the sound it produced—it is said that it ruptured the eardrums of people forty miles away. The sound traveled around the world *four times* and was heard *clearly* by people 3,000 miles away. That is like being in Chicago, Illinois, and hearing a sound that came from Reykjavik, Iceland. Because sound travels at 767.1 mph, people heard the eruption four hours after it occurred. To this day, the explosion of Krakatoa remains the farthest noise anyone has ever heard. It began in Indonesia and rang out all over the world.

In 1 Thessalonians 1:8, we are told about a different sound that rang out all over the world: the gospel. Here, Paul was writing to the Thessalonians, telling them that they had been an example to other believers, especially those in Macedonia and Achaia. In fact, they had developed a worldwide reputation due to their fierce evangelistic efforts. Numerous individuals from this church had gone out to preach, including Aristarchus and Secundus (Acts 20:4) as well as Jason (Acts 17:6–9). From Thessalonica, the Thessalonians were determined to bring God's message to every part of the world.

To illustrate this, Paul says that the word of the Lord "sounded forth" from them. The Greek word here for "sounded forth" is *exēchētai*, which means "to ring out." It was used in antiquity to describe things like a clap of thunder, the sound of a multitude, a rumor that spreads all over the place, the roaring sea, and even a trumpet blast. Like the power of Krakatoa, there was a colossal gospel blast in Thessalonica. The sound of it rushed forth, reaching people all over the world. It reverberated in every direction. From it, people near and far were touched by the saving message of Christ. As a result, many were saved and the kingdom of God grew. There is tangible power in the sound of the gospel.

But this wasn't something that only the Thessalonians were supposed to do. We are all called to sound forth the gospel into the world. (See Mark 16:15–16; Matthew 28:19–20; Acts 1:8.) This is the Great Commission. All of us should resound the message of Jesus wherever we are. Do you spread the good news into the world? You may not have to go to a foreign country to spread your faith. But do you spread it in the places that you *do* go, like the locker-room at the gym or in the cafeteria at lunch? Even if you are shy and introverted, the Holy Spirit can still use you to boom the sound of the gospel. When He fills you with His boldness and a heart for the kingdom of God, there will be moments when you feel like exploding with the message of Jesus. Don't allow anything to be an excuse. If you aren't already, believe God to make you a Krakatoa for the kingdom.

Rumors spread quickly in ancient Greece, particularly in the marketplace and by women. The Greek goddess, Pheme (Ossa), was the goddess of renown and was notorious for spreading swift rumors as revenge. In Homer's *Odyssey*, Rumor/Pheme/Ossa "went swiftly throughout all the city, telling of the terrible death and fate of the wooers."

How about making a decision, right now, that you will "sound forth" the tangible power of the gospel from here on out? It first begins by asking the Holy Spirit to baptize you into His power. When He does that, He will give you an overwhelming desire to see souls saved and people reconciled to God. This will produce an explosion in your soul that will make you want to go out and express to the world that Jesus is Lord. I've seen tiny, elderly women in their eighties who are so full of the Spirit that they are still erupting with the gospel.

Be encouraged. God can turn you into a volcano for Jesus. Just ask Him for the help of His Spirit. When you do, you'll be erupting with the sound of the gospel in no time. And the world around you will be impacted in a great and glorious way.

7

EARNEST: *EKTENES*
(ἐκτενής)

Above all, keep loving one another **earnestly***, since love covers a multitude of sins.* (1 Peter 4:8)

πρὸ πάντων τὴν εἰς ἑαυτοὺς ἀγάπην ἐκτενῆ ἔχοντες, ὅτι ἀγάπη καλύπτει πλῆθος ἁμαρτιῶν (ΠΕΤΡΟΥ Α 4:8)

What are you usually doing at 5:00 a.m.? Nowadays, I'm in bed enjoying my last couple hours of sleep. Unless I'm catching an early-morning flight, nothing at this point in my life requires me to be up *that* early. However, that hasn't always been the case. There was a time when I thought that sculpting my body at the gym was a nobler task than flipping my pillow to the cool side for the last round of rest.

During that season, I had a workout buddy who was an ex-college football player. At the gym, he acted more like a dictator or martinet rather than a friend. He created the workout routines and made sure we stuck to them. If it had been up to me, we might have mingled with the barbells while telling jokes and watching morning talk shows on the gym TV. Instead, he punished us with a specific number of workouts, repetitions, and weights for each rep. According to him, this was for muscle building. It was more tormenting than a YouTube commercial.

> Athletes trained very hard in antiquity. Platus describes the discipline of athletes in *Bacchides*: "There [in the gym] did they exercise themselves rather with running, wrestling, the quoit, the javelin, boxing, the ball, and leaping, rather than with harlots or with kissing; there did they prolong their lives, and not in secret-lurking holes [brothels]."

I did learn a term used among the gym rat culture: *maxing out*. Basically, it means pushing every atom in your body as far as it can possibly go. Instead of putting the weight down when your muscles tell you that they've had enough, you veto your muscles and keep on going. Your muscles protest; they feel like they are on fire and sweat avalanches off your face. You are usually watching this take place in one of the 16 million mirrors at the gym. If there is any consolation at all, it's that your muscles look pretty good. They are taut and chiseled because they are being stretched to the absolute limit. It's an incredible effort and the results are even more incredible. You don't look this way when you are playing Fortnite, that's for sure.

In 1 Peter 4:8, Peter is telling the Christians in Asia Minor a little something about maxing out, but he's talking about stretching their *love*, not their muscles. This was important because the Christian community Peter was writing to had been experiencing various forms of suffering. To withstand it, they needed to maintain their unity. And loving one another earnestly was the key.

In light of this, Peter says, *"Above all, keep loving one another earnestly, since love covers a multitude of sins."* The Greek word here for "earnestly" is *ektenē*, which means "outstretched" and describes something that is extended, often as far as it can possibly go—like *maxed out* muscles. In ancient Greek culture, this word was used to describe someone who was stretched out while sleeping, with limbs extended to each corner of the bed. It was also used to describe anchors that had been lowered to keep a ship from drifting. (See Acts 27:30.) If you've been on a cruise, you know what this is like. When the ship comes to port and anchors, the ropes become so taut you can hear them groaning. Finally, *ektenēs* was used to describe the muscles of athletes or horses during intense competition, strained to their breaking point. No matter what is *ektenēs,* or "outstretched," serious exertion is involved.

This enhances Peter's expectation of love in 1 Peter 4:8. Love stretches beyond the banal excitement of loving those who love us in return. It is taut resolve to do good to those who have injured us, insulted us, and irritated us. It requires an intense effort and pushes our regard for others' well-being to the brink. This outstretched sort of love is the only way to overcome offense and bury the wrongdoings that divide.

When you were born again and the Spirit of God came to dwell inside you, God's love was poured into your heart. (See Romans 5:5.) It's sitting there, waiting for you to stretch it out. Believe me, it can go a lot further than you might think is possible. It has to: it is meant to be used for your enemies. But it's up to you to take what God has given you and extend it to those who might not deserve it.

I remember a particular day when I was meditating on this. After my time of study, I was putting on my boots, getting ready to leave the house and go out into the sub-zero cold. The garbage truck was roaming the neighborhood and I could hear it near my house. I happened to look outside and I saw the trash collector take the lid off my trash can and purposely throw it at my garage. To top it off, he left my trash cans in the middle of the street. I thought, *Now this jerk is going to get a piece of my mind. I'm going to report him.* (I have a hot temper.) I couldn't wait for him to see my garage door opening and realize he was busted. (Yes, this is petty, but many of the instances in which we become offended are petty.)

Suddenly, the Spirit of God cooled my anger. I decided to stretch the love of God out to the curb until it covered the man who was flinging my trash can lids like Chinese stars. When I emerged from my garage, he looked at me like *he knew I knew* what he'd done. I glanced at him and he paused. "Stay warm," I said. "It's really cold out here. Be careful in this." He looked surprised. He smiled and said, "Thanks so much. I appreciate the concern, man." It may seem small, but it became a pleasant moment. You would have sensed it if you had been there. The offense had been covered by outstretched love. I wasn't going to be angry about it for the next two hours and he got off the hook. A win-win.

How do you handle the people who annoy you, hurt you, or cause you grief? Do you get back at them? Or do you max out your love and stretch it over them? Your love is capable of going further than you might expect. Give it a try today.

8

DEBAUCHERY: *ASŌTIA*
(ἀσωτία)

With respect to this they are surprised when you do not join them in the same flood of debauchery, *and they malign you.*

(1 Peter 4:4)

ἐν ᾧ ξενίζονται μὴ συντρεχόντων ὑμῶν εἰς τὴν αὐτὴν τῆς ἀσωτίας ἀνάχυσιν βλασφημοῦντες   (ΠΕΤΡΟΥ Α 4:4)

Ever thought about winning the lottery? On a weary, Monday-morning drive to work? After a tough day in the grind? I'm sure many of us have imagined the feeling of scratching off those magic numbers and realizing, in an instant, that we never have to work for money again.

Or would we? While some lottery winners have made good use of their money, plenty of stories exist of those who have wasted their winnings and are now broke. How could this happen? How do you go from having millions of dollars in the bank to getting a part-time job to pay the rent? We'd have to ask someone who has done it. Twice.

Evelyn Adams won the New Jersey lottery in 1985 and again in 1986, amassing a total of $5.6 million dollars. That's more money that many of us will ever see in a lifetime. Yet, after all was said and done, Adams was living in a trailer.

When asked about it, she said, "Everybody wanted my money. Everybody had their hand out. I never learned one simple word in the English language: 'No.'"

A simple "no" could have put the brakes on her wild spending habits, which included bad investments, gifts to friends, and even more gambling. How important it is for us to live with discipline and self-restraint, learning when to say, "No."

This doesn't just go for state lottery, Lotto, or Powerball winners. It goes for all of us, whether we have money or not. Think about your own life for a moment. Have there been long wasted stretches because you could have said, "No" and didn't? Can you think of seasons in which you accomplished nothing, except for setting yourself back a little—or a lot? If so, what characterized those seasons? In my experience in counseling and pastoring, these times in life are often characterized by self-gratification to an unhealthy degree.

In 1 Peter 4:4, God's Word teaches us about wasteful living and the importance of avoiding it by saying "no." The apostle Peter was contrasting the believers' behavior before conversion with their behavior afterward. These Christians were no longer living sinfully. They were saying no to their former depravities and they were committed to living in accordance with the standards that pleased the Lord. As a result, unbelievers began to slander them. Peter exhorts the believers to carry on with their disciplined behavior in spite of the persecution, all the while calling the unbelievers' behavior "debauchery."

The Greek word for "debauchery" here is *asōtias*, and it means "reckless abandon," "wild and undisciplined living," "behavior that does not regard consequence," and "the conduct of someone when the mind is absent." It is describing behavior that is free of logical inhibitions and without concern for the results. People involved in debauchery are not using their reasoning or common sense; they are irresponsible and have abandoned their morals.

> In the first century, the Roman city of Baiae, located near Naples, Italy, was the Las Vegas of the Roman Empire. The Roman elite went there to vacation and indulge in gross debauchery and decadence.

Asōtia was used in Plutarch's *Parallel Lives*. Soldiers had become weakened by "debauchery," which included voluptuous banqueting and senseless living. When we consider the totality of the word, we see that "debauchery" is unrestrained and uncontrolled indulgence in pleasing one's passions. It is seeking pleasure at all costs without any will or desire to say "no."

Interestingly enough, the root of *asōtia* comes from the word that means to "save," *sōzō*. Yet it has an alpha-privative in front, which negates it so that it means the opposite of "to save." Therefore, it means "to save nothing" or "to waste totally." A person who lives in debauchery wastes their life, a season of their life, or their resources by saying "yes" to everything they relish.

We are given the story of the Prodigal Son in Luke that illustrates what this looks like. (See Luke 15:11–32.) We are told this young man *"squandered his property in reckless (asōtōs) living"* (verse 13). The Prodigal Son was consumed by immediate gratification and there's no evidence that he considered anything beyond the present moment. His debaucherous lifestyle came to a screeching halt, but not before he had wasted his inheritance. He became filled with regret and remorse as the consequences grew too hard to bear on his own. (See verses 14–19.) Nevertheless, he could have avoided the mess altogether had he exercised self-discipline and said "no" to his immediate desire for gratification.

As those who are in Christ, we have been called to patience and self-control. (See Galatians 5:22–23.) God has called us to walk in these fruits of the Holy Spirit in order to make the best use of our time and resources, so we don't squander them. Our society has become so flesh-driven and "now" oriented that without the help of the Spirit, it's easy to start living to fulfill our most pleasure-centered desires without concern for what trouble they may cause. That certainly isn't the best that God has for your life.

Instead of chasing all that delights your eye, ask the Holy Spirit to give you self-control and the ability to say "no" to carnal appetites that will waste the time and resources that God has given you. Saying "no" is one of the greatest weapons that a Christian has at their disposal to fight the devil. If you use it when you are supposed to, you'll never have to worry about falling into a life of debauchery and the pain that comes later.

Instead, you'll always have plenty and be much happier with the divine richness you have made of your life.

9

MALCONTENT: *MEMPSIMOIROS* (μεμψίμοιρος)

---

*These are grumblers, **malcontents**, following their own sinful desires; they are loud-mouthed boasters, showing favoritism to gain advantage.* (Jude 1:16)

Οὗτοί εἰσιν γογγυσταὶ μεμψίμοιροι κατὰ τὰς ἐπιθυμίας ἑαυτῶν πορευόμενοι, καὶ τὸ στόμα αὐτῶν λαλεῖ ὑπέρογκα, θαυμάζοντες πρόσωπα ὠφελείας χάριν. (ΙΟΥΔΑ 1:16)

We all know a complainer. Perhaps we're one. If we are honest about it, I'm certain that we can recall times when we've complained about our lot in life and thought, *Woe is me*. "The grass is greener on the other side," we whine. Looking at what we *don't* have while ignoring what we *do* have is one of the great struggles of the human experience.

If we don't walk close to the Holy Spirit, we can fall into this trap so frequently that it becomes a habit that moves us further and further away from the presence of the Lord.

The truth is, nobody enjoys being around a chronic complainer. Their negativity becomes a huge challenge. It is often impossible to convince complainers that they are not, in fact, always on the losing end of things. If they have a complainer's mindset, they will refuse to see it any other way. They don't see their complaining as negativity, but rather as the right response to the wrong that has been dealt to them.

> According to Will Bowen, founder of Complaint-Free World, the average person complains between fifteen and thirty times each day. He challenges people to go twenty-one days without complaining, criticizing, or gossiping.

The ancient Greeks had complainers in their culture, too. The philosopher Theophrastus (371 BC–287 BC), a student of Plato and Aristotle, wrote a book called *Characters* in which he created character sketches of different types of people. Some of these include the Ironical Man, the Flatterer, the Chatty Man, the Gossip, the Stupid Man, and, for our study, the Grumbler, a complainer or malcontent. Of him, Theophrastus says:

> The Grumbler is one who…if he finds a purse on the road, 'Ah,' he will say, 'but I have never found a treasure.' … To one who brings him good news, 'A son is born to you,' he will reply, 'If you add that I have lost half my property, you will speak the truth.' … When he has won a lawsuit by unanimous verdict, he will find fault with the composer of his speech for having left out several points.

You get the picture; the Grumbler is one who can find a way to complain about any situation, even if it's good.

This reminds me of an embarrassing moment when I worked overtime to find a reason to complain. When I was first pastoring, we held services on both Sunday morning and Sunday evening. After one evening service, a woman who had been at both services approached me and said, "Pastor Palmer, the sermon this evening just blessed me so much. It was tremendous." She walked away joyfully, with a smile on her face, yet I turned and walked the other way with a scowl, thinking, *She obviously didn't enjoy the morning service. That was her way of saying that my preaching this morning stunk. I must be a horrible preacher. I'm sure not as good as the other pastors in this town.*

I let this eat away at me for two days and found myself trying to figure out ways to improve Sunday morning sermons. That sure does sounds like the Grumbler.

God's Word mentions grumblers in Jude 1:16. Yet these are much more serious complainers because they are complaining against the laws of God. Here, Jude is describing the false teachers he was contending with by listing charges against them. He calls them "malcontents." The Greek word for "malcontents" here is *mempsimoiroi*. It is a two-part Greek word that comes from *memphomai*, which means "to blame" or "to find fault," and *moira*, which means "lot in life" or "fate." Together, it describes someone who is always finding fault with their lot in life. It is "a complainer," "someone constantly fault-finding," and "one who always thinks they are on the losing side of things—the brown side of the grass."

Jude was clever in selecting *mempsimoiros* to describe his opponents who complained about God's laws because it was the same word Theophrastus used for the Grumbler in his book *Characters*. Jude's audience would have likely recognized the allusion and understood the parallel right away.

The false teachers were grumbling about the faith that had been delivered to the saints. (See verse 3.) They were not content with true Christianity. To them, the commands of Jesus had become too much to bear. Peeking over the fence, they thought the unbelievers had it better because they could gratify their flesh however they wanted. And so, they complained and complained about Christianity and its moral demands until it drew them into a lascivious lifestyle, away from the presence of God.

While Jude describes this over 2,000 years ago, we still have "malcontents" or "grumblers" among us today. They are the ones who complain about the moral and ethical requirements of serving Christ and being a Christian. They protest by relaxing biblical standards and twisting Scripture in ways that enable them to say they love Jesus while giving in to their own sinful desires and passions. God sees this as serious sin because it is an indictment and complaint against *His* standards. They are murmuring against *His* truth.

Have you seen examples of this today? Are you familiar with ways that God's laws have been changed by those seeking to live ungodly lifestyles while maintaining a form of supposed "godliness"? At its core, this sort of behavior is grumbling and complaining against God despite every good thing that Jesus Christ has done for us—and it turns God off.

Instead of finding reasons to whine, we need to find reasons to be thankful. The key to being a powerful Christian is to give God thanks for the things the Holy Spirit has empowered us to do and not be focused on the things He has forbidden. There are good reasons for His restrictions.

Let's be happy with our lot as Christians. The grass isn't greener anywhere else.

10

FAN INTO FLAME: *ANAZŌPYREŌ* (ἀναζωπυρέω)

---

*For this reason I remind you to **fan into flame** the gift of God, which is in you through the laying on of my hands.*

(2 Timothy 1:6)

δι᾽ ἣν αἰτίαν ἀναμιμνήσκω σε ἀναζωπυρεῖν τὸ χάρισμα τοῦ θεοῦ, ὅ ἐστιν ἐν σοὶ διὰ τῆς ἐπιθέσεως τῶν χειρῶν μου. (ΠΡΟΣ ΤΙΜΟΘΕΟΝ Β 1:6)

No blazing inferno begins that way. Someone or something produced a small spark—just enough to ignite debris, which then burst into a raging firestorm. FOX13 News in Sarasota, Florida, reminded its residents of this in an April 2017 report entitled, "Officer Shows How Small Spark Can Become Wildfire." Conditions were dry in Florida and wildfires had begun to spread all around Sarasota, even near highways. The blazes caused traffic delays and people were becoming increasingly concerned.

The Myakka River District Rangers, who worked around the clock to put out the fires, noted they may have started when a lawnmower kicked up a tiny spark. Those sparks can set dry brush on fire and it can quickly get out of control, especially if the wind is right.

Other common, accidental fire starters include metal dragging from a vehicle (like a loose, low-hanging exhaust system), trains, electric fences, cigarettes, hay that spontaneously combusts, grass growing near powerlines, and even broken glass magnifying sunlight and causing brush to burst into flame.

I've seen a few of these blazes myself. In one instance, I was in South Africa and the whole side of the road was on fire and billowing black smoke. My driver informed me that those fires were common, the result of people throwing cigarettes out the window.

On July 19, AD 64, a single fire in a Roman shop near the Circus Maximus turned into a massive blaze that burned down ten of Rome's fourteen districts. History has blamed Emperor Nero for starting the inferno.

People may not realize that a flame the size of a cigarette tip can cause a citywide firestorm. Yet, in 2 Timothy 1:6, God's Word reminds us how powerful a small spark can be if it is fanned into flame.

Here, the apostle Paul was writing to young, green Timothy. Paul had put Timothy in charge of the important church of Ephesus. This was a heavy responsibility, to say the least. Timothy needed encouragement, so Paul began his letter by reminding Timothy about the call of God that was upon his life. (See verses 5–7.) To shepherd the flock in Ephesus, God had given Timothy a special grace: those supernatural abilities known as the gifts of the Spirit. (See 1 Corinthians 12:8–10). This endowment occurred when Paul laid hands on Timothy and commissioned him for the task at hand. The point was, Timothy already had the gift of God in him; despite how he may have felt, he didn't need a new gift. Rather, Paul charged him to "*fan into flame*" the gift that God had already placed in him.

The Greek word for "fan into flame" here is *anazōpyrein*, a two-part word made up of: *ana* ("up," "again") and *zopyron* ("ember," "spark," "hot coal"). Together the two words mean something like "to stir up the ember" and "rekindle the hot coal." The idea is reigniting a tiny fire until it bursts into larger flames. Given the right wind, it can be stirred up into a wildfire or a raging inferno.

In the midst of his difficulty, it's possible that Timothy wasn't cognizant of the tiny ember and spark within him—the gifts and graces of God. He didn't need to question his call or beg God for something more. Rather, Timothy already had what it took to get the job done. All he needed was to rekindle the embers and fan them into an all-consuming fire.

Whether you realize it or not, if God has called you to do something, you have what it takes to do it. The gifts of God are in you now. Don't be discouraged if God's grace isn't as evident as a forest fire. In many instances, God's gifts don't show up that way. They come as little coals or tiny sparks that God expects us to feed and fan into flame until the fire grows. It's not that you are inadequate for the task. A tiny spark is more than adequate to become a massive blaze. It's just a matter of what that spark can ignite.

Are you putting those coals around things that will quickly set fire? Are you fanning into flame the gifts and graces God has placed in you?

You can do this by praying in the Spirit, meditating on the Word of God, acting on the leading of the Holy Spirit, and even stepping out in faith when God gives you an assignment. You'll discover the more you allow yourself to be near the things of God, the sooner your fire will start to blaze. Instead of questioning whether or not you are called, do what you need to do to start kicking up the sparks.

When you do, it won't be long before the gifts God has given to you are brightly lit. And you can be certain, that is one blaze that nobody can put out.

11

RESCUE: *RHYOMAI*
(ῥύομαι)

But the Lord stood by me and strengthened me, so that through me the message might be fully proclaimed and all the Gentiles might hear it. So I was rescued *from the lion's mouth. The Lord will* rescue *me from every evil deed and bring me safely into his heavenly kingdom. To him be the glory forever and ever. Amen.* (2 Timothy 4:17–18)

ὁ δὲ κύριός μοι παρέστη καὶ ἐνεδυνάμωσέν με, ἵνα δι' ἐμοῦ τὸ κήρυγμα πληροφορηθῇ καὶ ἀκούσωσιν πάντα τὰ ἔθνη, καὶ ἐρρύσθην ἐκ στόματος λέοντος. ῥύσεταί με ὁ κύριος ἀπὸ παντὸς ἔργου πονηροῦ καὶ σώσει εἰς τὴν βασιλείαν αὐτοῦ τὴν ἐπουράνιον· ᾧ ἡ δόξα εἰς τοὺς αἰῶνας τῶν αἰώνων, ἀμην. (ΠΡΟΣ ΤΙΜΟΘΕΟΝ Β 4:17–18)

Can you remember a moment in your life when harm crept upon you unexpectedly? Perhaps it even threatened your life. While I certainly pray you haven't had many instances like this, the fact is that there are times in our lives when we will come face to face with grave danger and be challenged by imminent threat. Even David admits this in Psalm 3:1–2, in which he says, *"O LORD, how many are my foes! Many are rising against me; many are saying of my soul, 'There is no salvation for him in God.'"*

These threats are often so large that we are unable to defend ourselves from them. If we want any chance of survival, we need to be shielded and rescued by a power greater than our own. David understood this, which is why he goes on to say, *"But you, O LORD, are a shield about me"* (verse 3). In times of danger, we can trust in the protection of the Lord, whose strength is greater than our threats.

An interesting incident occurred in Atherton, Australia, in 2007 that marvelously illustrates this. A family adopted a Doberman Pinscher named Khan from an animal shelter. He had been starved and suffered broken ribs; it was clear his previous owner had beaten and abused him. In fact, Khan's condition was so bad it's a wonder that the animal shelter hadn't euthanized him.

Khan was in his new family's backyard garden with seventeen-month-old Charlotte and her mother. Suddenly, the dog began to act strangely, nudging Charlotte aggressively away from where they were playing. Unknown to Charlotte or her mother, slithering toward them was a king brown snake—the third most venomous snake in the world. Little Charlotte was in peril. Although Khan was nudging her, she wasn't moving.

The snake was just about to strike Charlotte when Khan did the only thing he knew to do: he yanked Charlotte's diaper and threw her over his shoulder—more than a meter away from the snake and out of harm's way. The snake struck Khan in his paw. The dog ran into the house and collapsed; he was taken to the vet and recovered after receiving antivenom.

It's very likely Charlotte would have died had the snake bitten her. Thankfully, the heroic Khan rescued her from attack.

Have you ever faced a foe out to do you as much harm as a deadly snake? The apostle Paul writes of such an experience in 2 Timothy 4:17–18. Paul was serving his second Roman imprisonment shortly before his death. While writing to Timothy, he recounts the many times the Lord had "rescued" him from the "lion's mouth" and assured Timothy that the Lord would do so again. The Greek words here for "rescued/rescue" (*errysthēn/rhysetai*) come from the Greek word *rhyomai*. It means "to snatch from," "to ward off," and "to show defensive power." Whenever this word was used, it implied that an attack was imminent, so a nuance of urgency and jumping into action attaches to the word.

> The Servian Wall was one of the most important defensive barriers ever built by the Romans. Named after the Roman king, Servius Tullius, its construction dates back to the sixth century BC. Remains of the wall are still visible around Rome today. It was originally seven miles long, twelve feet thick, and up to ten feet high—enough to deter Carthaginian general Hannibal's forces during the Second Punic War.

Because it was associated with defense, its cognate words were used to describe things like "a castle," "walls of protection," "helmets," and "armor." In Homer's *Iliad*, the word was used to describe the guards' defensive protection against an enemy's sneak attack. Hence, the overall idea behind this word describes an urgent defensive display that protects, shields, and fortifies one from an impending threat—like Khan's efforts to save Charlotte from the king brown snake.

Paul was telling Timothy that, throughout the course of his ministry, he had faced extreme danger. He likened it to "a lion's mouth,"[8] comparing his difficulties to Daniel's in the lion's den. (See Daniel 6.) Despite the oncoming "lion," God snatched him from its jaws and preserved his life. Though the trials were too great for Paul to protect himself, the Lord was faithful and always intervened to shield him.

Finally, Paul was writing 2 Timothy in his last hour as he faced his final foe, martyrdom. Though Paul knew he would die, he was convinced that God would give him boldness and deliver him from any cowardice or fear that would make him anything other than a powerful witness for Jesus. God would snatch him from all that would undermine his courage and bring him safely to heaven, where he could rest in the Lord.

Fear, lions, snakes, persecution—life is so full of things that could destroy us. While we can't escape the world in which these things exist, God wants us to know He is our deliverer. He is faithful to snatch us from their jaws. When threats arise unexpectedly, you can depend on God to rise up swiftly and show forth His defensive might to preserve you from harm.

Walk closely to the Spirit today and listen for His voice. Obey Him when He nudges you and do what He leads you to do. It could be that He is moving you out of harm's way and rescuing you from impending danger. He's a faithful protector and a shield of defense.

12

IMMEASURABLE:
HYPERBALLŌ (ὑπερβάλλω)

And what is the immeasurable *greatness of his power toward us who believe, according to the working of his great might.*
(Ephesians 1:19)

καὶ τί τὸ ὑπερβάλλον μέγεθος τῆς δυνάμεως αὐτοῦ εἰς ἡμᾶς τοὺς πιστεύοντας κατὰ τὴν ἐνέργειαν τοῦ κράτους τῆς ἰσχύος αὐτοῦ. (ΠΡΟΣ ΕΦΕΣΙΟΥΣ 1:19)

Over the years, I've been privileged to travel to many lands and countries to preach the gospel. One of the best parts about this is experiencing the different cultures, particularly their food and cuisines. Meals are times of joy and jubilee, when the hosts go *all out* to make me feel at home.

This is especially true in Sicily. I've often joked with my Sicilian friends that eating is a full-time job there. Sicilians take pride in making sure you are well fed, and you'll often hear them say, "Mangia" (eat) or "Mangia qualcosa" (eat something), even right after you've *just* eaten. Food is of the utmost importance there and the answer to many of life's problems. I understand this because my grandparents were of Sicilian descent.

There's a joke in Sicily about a young man with a guilty conscience who tells his mother, "Mama, I've robbed a bank." She says, "Well, that's not good." Then, he says, "And I've stolen a car." His mama says, "I see. That's not good either." Then he says, "And I haven't eaten today." And she jumps up from her seat and screams, "What! You haven't eaten? What's wrong with you!?"

I once invented a joke of my own that the Sicilians found funny. I said, "After studying God's Word, I've discovered the disciples of Jesus were Sicilian." They looked perplexed. While they were still scratching their heads, I had them turn to John 4:31, which says, *"Meanwhile the disciples were urging him* [Jesus], *saying, 'Rabbi,* **eat.**'" I think that joke has been making its way around Italy ever since.

Needless to say, there's never been a time when I've been disappointed with mealtimes. I've been to Sicily twelve times and I can't think of one instance when I didn't have *more than enough* food placed before my eyes. I will never forget the first meal I had in Sicily. It was on a Sunday afternoon after church. I was told we were going to have "a little something" before dinner that evening. They brought out course after course after course. I was stuffed to the gills before the main course even arrived—and this wasn't even dinner.

My translator told me later, "Chris, the Sicilians go all out for every meal. You are never going to survive if you try eating everything." If I've learned anything about the wonderful Sicilian people over the years, it's that they don't mess around when it comes to food: it's always going to be over and above, more than enough, and plenty left afterwards.

An anonymous buyer went all out to buy the bronze sculpture *Artemis and the Stag*, created by an unknown artist between 1 BC and AD 1. The work sold for $28.6 million at a Sotheby's auction in New York City in 2007. At the time, it was the highest price anyone had ever bid for a sculpture.

The apostle Paul talks about God's power this way in Ephesians 1:19. Here, Paul was sharing with his church in Ephesus what he prays for them. He tells them that he prays they will know the hope that God has called them to and the riches of God's *"glorious inheritance in the saints"* (verse 18).

The hope that God called us to represents the beginning of the Christian life. While we did call upon God to be saved (see Romans 10:13), He first called us. He called us to belong to Christ and have a new life free from sin, to be holy and separate from the world, and be part of God's celestial family.

The riches of His glorious inheritance in the saints alludes to the end of the Christian life. It is our total inheritance, which we will receive when the fullness of time comes. Until then, we are waiting for it with patience. In short, verse 18 speaks about the beginning and end of the Christian life.

At present, we find ourselves in the middle. Our Christian life has taken off, but we have yet to receive the totality of God's promises. As we make our way toward receiving this final inheritance, we find our path strewn with all sorts of challenges, difficulties, and suffering. To push us past these and over the goal line, God has given us His power—*"what is the **immeasurable** greatness of his power toward us who believe."*

The Greek word for "immeasurable" is *hyperballō*. It is a two-part Greek word that comes from: *hyper* (above, over, beyond, more than) and *ballō* (to throw or cast). It literally meant to "throw beyond" or "surpass." Over time, it came to express other means of excessiveness such as outbidding someone at an auction, extreme heat from a fire, unbearable pain, and the intense brightness of stars. Hence, it was a word used for something that stood out, excelled the norms, and went beyond the standard amount.

The idea in this Scripture is that God supplies an over-and-above ration of His power to help us overcome the obstacles and challenges we face so we can receive the full inheritance promised to us. Not just a little, just enough, or even more than enough, but an over-and-above, highly excessive amount, like a meal in Sicily. We can stuff ourselves with God's power and never come close to exhausting it. It's all around us and is ours for the taking. And we aren't to be stingy with it because there is enough to go around and plenty to take home.

Perhaps you are wondering how you can tap into this smorgasbord of power. The way Paul tapped into it: through prayer. When you come into prayer, you stand before a banquet table that is heaped with everything you could possibly need to overcome your troubles. And you are free to take.

You may be walking through difficulties and trials today; it's possible you are asking yourself, "Where is God?" The presence of difficulties doesn't mean that God has left you. Jesus told us, *"In the world you will have tribulation"* (John 16:33). But God has given you the immense abundance of His power so you can go from the beginning of your Christian life all the way to the end. Pray. Mangia. Fill yourself up with God's power.

13

TEMPTATION: *PEIRASMOS*
(πειρασμός)

And forgive us our sins, for we ourselves forgive everyone who is indebted to us. And lead us not into temptation.

(Luke 11:4)

καὶ ἄφες ἡμῖν τὰς ἁμαρτίας ἡμῶν, καὶ γὰρ αὐτοὶ ἀφίομεν παντὶ ὀφείλοντι ἡμῖν καὶ μὴ εἰσενέγκῃς ἡμᾶς εἰς πειρασμόν.　　　　　　(ΚΑΤΑ ΛΟΥΚΑΝ 11:4)

In 1971, Philip Zimbardo, now professor emeritus of psychology at Stanford University, wanted to put human nature to the test by studying *good* people in *evil* situations. In an experiment now considered unethical and methodologically questionable, the professor placed healthy college men into a mock prison situation. The project was funded by the U.S. Office of

Naval Research to gain insights on relations between guards and prisoners in the Navy and Marines.

After answering a newspaper ad seeking subjects for the study, twenty-four men were assigned either the role of prisoner or guard by way of a coin flip. Those in the role of prisoner were later arrested by police, put in a squad car, and driven to the jail for processing. The warden informed them of the severity of their offense. They were now prisoners.

They were stripped naked, searched, and doused with spray to make sure they weren't bringing any germs into the prison quarters. After this, the prisoners were given a smock with their prison ID number on it, rubber sandals, and a stocking cap to cover their hair. A heavy chain was then bolted onto their right ankle. It was worn at all times and reminded prisoners that they could not escape.

The guards were given no instructions for their role. They were free to act however they wanted to maintain order at the prison. They wasted no time in exercising their authority.

The inmates didn't put up with it. On the second day of the experiment, they revolted. They taunted the guards, then barricaded themselves in their cells. The guards began to hassle and blame one another for the revolt. Nevertheless, they tried to gain control by shooting fire extinguisher foam at the inmates. This was the beginning of the mess that ensued.

It became more than an experiment. The guards stepped up their control by using psychological tactics on the inmates. The inmates muttered about an escape plot. Less than three days into the experiment, one prisoner became emotionally disturbed. By the end of the sixth day, the inmates were all behaving in pathological ways and the guards began acting sadistically.

The study was shut down. The researchers could no longer allow it to continue.

Lots of things can be derived from this macabre study, one being the tendency of people to act unsuitably when put to the test, like the researchers who thought it up in the first place.

What's the hardest test in the world? It just might be the Master Sommelier Diploma exam. This by-invitation-only wine examination has a pass rate of around 8 percent.

God's Word tells us that we will be tested at some point. While not a psychological prison experiment, our tests will give us the opportunity to show who we are as people of God. We need to understand what these tests are so we can pass them.

This brings us to Luke 11, where one of Jesus's disciples asks him how to pray. (See verse 1.) Jesus answers this question by giving a prayer model, including the petition *"and lead us not into temptation"* (verse 4).

Here, the Greek word for "temptation" is *peirasmon*. It refers to "an extensive test that tries the nature or character of someone or something." It was used in antiquity to describe a "medical experiment." Through such testing, the nature of the subject would come to light. Hence, what Jesus is referring to here is "a test or examination that tries us and reveals what's inside of us." Because this word is most often used in a negative sense, we can assume that these temptations are seductions, persecutions, and tribulations that characterize this age. James is clear that these do not come from God. (See James 1:13.) They can come from the devil, the fallen social order that we live in, or even from our own fleshly desires.

They can bring out the best or worst in us—and that's why Jesus tells us to ask God for His help in the midst of them.

While you may wonder why anyone would sign up for a prison experiment and put themselves through something so horrific, the truth is that you and I face character-testing examinations every single day. Maybe you'll never be locked in a cell and face sadistic prison guards, but perhaps you'll find yourself at work, facing an assistant or boss who is tempting you to have an affair. Or you'll face a secularist family member who wants to drive you mad with criticisms of Jesus. Or an ex-girlfriend or ex-boyfriend who has hurt you so deeply that you want to take revenge, even if it's in a passive way.

Will you let this situation prove that you are a flesh-driven, compulsive person? Or will you let the divine nature of Jesus Christ living inside of you handle the matter?

In the midst of whatever temptation or test you are facing, take time and ask the Lord for His help before you do anything in response. Express to Him your desire to behave like Jesus.

Ask His Spirit for help so that you pass the test with flying colors and prove to the examiner that, unlike those in the Stanford Prison Experiment, only the best comes out of you when you are put to the test.

14

ESTABLISH: *STĒRIZŌ*
(στηρίζω)

But the Lord is faithful. He will establish *you and guard you against the evil one.* (2 Thessalonians 3:3)

πιστὸς δέ ἐστιν ὁ κύριος, ὃς στηρίξει ὑμᾶς καὶ φυλάξει ἀπὸ τοῦ πονηροῦ. (ΠΡΟΣ ΘΕΣΣΑΛΟΝΙΚΕΙΣ Β 3:3)

Can you think of anything more constant than a tree? It stands tall in winter, spring, summer, or fall. It was there when your dad and mom first brought you home from the hospital. You played under it and perhaps it held a swing or a treehouse. It was where you and your first sweetheart carved your initials. It watched you pack up your stuff and move away to college.

It's easy to take a tree for granted because it doesn't seek attention, complain, take a break, or change. It's just there, same as it's always been.

A bristlecone pine tree known as Prometheus is considered by *Guinness Book of World Records* to be the oldest tree ever recorded. Cut down in 1963, it stood on Mt. Wheeler in Nevada. Growing in a harsh environment, Prometheus had 4,867 rings and was believed to be 5,200 years old.

If you're a tree lover, I imagine you admire the giant redwoods along the West Coast of the United States. (Some grow in China, too.) Coast redwoods can grow up to 300 feet tall. In fact, a coast redwood named Hyperion is the world's tallest known living tree, standing at 380.3 feet. It's believed to be between 600 and 800 years old.

Let's say Hyperion began growing 700 years ago, in the 1300s. That means it has been around since the Black Plague (1347–1351), the Ming Dynasty (1368), and the establishment of the Aztec city of Tenochtitlán in Mexico. Think how much world history has taken place between then and now. Yet, Hyperion has just gone about its business, standing tall in its usual display of strength and consistency.

A compelling thing about these behemoth trees is that they stand in areas where there is ample *seismic activity.* The ground is shifting beneath them, but they have a way to counter it. If they begin to lean, they are able to accelerate the growth of that side to strengthen themselves against the lean. This keeps them standing tall and firm, despite their environs, for years and decades to come.

In 2 Thessalonians 3:3, God's Word tells us about how, like the redwood, God strengthens us against our reverberating surroundings so that we can consistently stand tall for Jesus throughout our Christian lives. The apostle Paul and the Thessalonians were engaged in spiritual warfare and attacks from Satan. Rumblings were going on around them. But Paul reminds the Thessalonians about the faithfulness of God, which was a main theme of the Old Testament. (See, for example, Deuteronomy 7:9.) Just as God had been faithful to the Old Testament saints in all their various trials, He would be faithful to Paul and the church saints in Thessalonica by helping them overcome the assaults of Satan.

Paul explicitly notes how God would do this: He would "establish" them. The Greek word "establish" here is *stērixei*, which means "to fix firmly in place," "to strengthen," and "to support." It was actually a word that was used to describe a vine being supported by a stake, so it would grow straight. You understand this if you do any gardening. It also described an aging man supporting himself upright with a cane. (It makes me think of my grandpa who used to walk around with a fancy cane with a duck's head handle.)

The notion behind the word is a supply of added strength so the thing being supported can stand upright and tall. The idea further develops when we learn that *stērizō* was used in Euripides's play, *The Bacchae*, to describe a pine tree that stood firmly and grew uprightly into the sky. Here, the word implies the fixed secureness of a healthy tree that has grown despite its fragile surroundings.

The Thessalonians would have been encouraged that Paul used *stērizō* to describe how God was going to help them. They would have understood it to mean that God was going to give them a firm resolve to stay unswerving and strong in the face of the wiles and temptations of Satan. As you know, the devil comes to sift us and shake our faith. (See Luke 22:31.)

But in those times of shaking, the Thessalonians were told, they could expect the Lord to buttress them so they could remain strong, outlast the shaking, and continue to grow tall. God was going to brace them, just as a cane braces an old man who is having trouble walking, or a stake braces a vine that can't grow straight on its own. They would outlast their troubles and temptations.

You may be experiencing some sort of seismic activity that is causing your world to tremble and shake. Perhaps your job is in jeopardy, or a new financial need has arisen. Maybe you are having troubles with your spouse or children.

While this can be enough to make us want to collapse, God is not going to let it happen if you will stand on His promise and His sustenance. He will keep you standing by supporting you exactly the way you need during this time of your life. He can provide emotional support, spiritual support, financial support, and whatever other support you need so that you can consistently stand tall for Jesus, day after day, in the midst of the tremors.

If you get discouraged today, simply remember your favorite tree. Perhaps God has placed it here to evoke His faithfulness. If He can keep a tree unswerving and standing tall, there's no doubt He can do so with you.

15

FRAGRANCE: *OSMĒ* (ὀσμή)

But thanks be to God, who in Christ always leads us in triumphal procession, and through us spreads the fragrance of the knowledge of him everywhere. (2 Corinthians 2:14)

Τῷ δὲ θεῷ χάρις τῷ πάντοτε θριαμβεύοντι ἡμᾶς ἐν τῷ Χριστῷ καὶ τὴν ὀσμὴν τῆς γνώσεως αὐτοῦ φανεροῦντι δι' ἡμῶν ἐν παντὶ τόπῳ. (ΠΡΟΣ ΚΟΡΙΝΘΙΟΥΣ Β 2:14)

I have been to Disney World eighteen times and counting. It's safe to say I love it. I can't take all the credit, however, since my family has gone to Disney World for vacation nearly every year. There's hardly anything I haven't seen 1,000 times there. I often say if ministry doesn't work out, I could be a tour guide in any of the Disney parks, or drive the Disney Ferry on the Seven Seas Lagoon. I wouldn't complain. Seems like a dream job to me. I'd get to be at Disney every day.

But *why* would I want to be there every day? How come when adults—even the elderly—walk into the Magic Kingdom, they experience reverse aging, come alive, and start acting like kids again? What's invigorating them?

Think about it: these people stand in long lines all day in the blistering heat, pay three to four times the normal price of things, and walk all day long, meaning aching legs and blisters. Yet everyone is so happy. Why? I've contemplated it and I've talked it over with other Disney buffs like myself. While there's no way to prove our hypothesis, we believe it makes sense.

It's the smells. That's right. Disney has all of these different aromas that put the life right into you. When you get a whiff, they take you away from the stress of the job back home, make you forget about problems in school, and for those few moments, you are in Fantasyland, living the dream.

When I learned other people notice the smells at the entertainment complex and love them as much as I do, I went on a travel blog to see what the bloggers had to say. Sure enough, they listed some of the same smells I had grown to love—the water in the Pirates of the Caribbean ride, the smell of the resorts (Wilderness Lodge, Animal Kingdom Lodge, and Polynesian Resort), the smell of hamburgers and fries in Tomorrowland, the smoky smell in Frontierland, and the great smells of ice cream, corn nuggets, candy, and other goodies on Main Street USA. Do you have a favorite smell at Disney that makes you happy inside?

Our sense of smell is closely linked to memory and emotion. When we return to Disney World and inhale our favorite aromas, we return to happy memories of yesteryear and feel *alive* inside.

Chanel No. 5 may be the best-selling fragrance of all time. It made its debut in 1921 and yet a bottle is still sold every thirty seconds today. Its aroma is described as a floral bouquet of rose and jasmine with a touch of vanilla.

In 2 Corinthians 2:14, the apostle Paul uses olfactory imagery to convey the life-giving power of the gospel. He had just finished telling the Corinthian church about his difficulties and suffering. Despite them, God had caused Paul to emerge victorious. Paul illustrates this victory by calling it a *"triumphal procession"* in which *"the fragrance of the knowledge"* of Christ was spread. He was alluding to Rome's military leaders returning from battle, riding chariots through the streets and declaring victory over their enemies. During these processions, fragrances were burned to heighten the sensory experience.

The Greek word for fragrance here is *osmēn*. It means "smell," "odor," "something that stimulates a sense of smell," "perfume," and "scent." In antiquity, it was used to describe lovely smells such as flowers, ointments, acceptance sacrifices, and other aromatic things.[9]

There is a key aspect of *osmē* that we encounter in Job 14:9 in the LXX (Greek Old Testament).[10] It is used to describe the scent of water by which a dying tree can be resuscitated. Here, we see that *osmē* is often connected to the idea that a scent or fragrance can bring life and power to emit energy that strengthens and renews. We also see this in other places in the Old Testament. For instance, we learn that God looked favorably on men when He received sacrifices with a pleasing aroma. (See, for example, Genesis 8:21.) That the ancient Greeks believed this, too, is reflected in their own religious history. Often, Greek gods were depicted as having scents that proceeded from them and gave life.

Hence, *osmē* can be a smell that releases a life-giving force, which is why they were key in a Roman victory procession. Over time, these fragrances became symbolic of victory, triumph, and the glory of Rome. Smelling these fragrances would remind the Romans of their valor and enliven them.

Now, we can better understand 2 Corinthians 2:14. God gave Paul victory throughout his journey of sufferings. Therefore, Paul saw it as a triumphal procession. The *fragrance* emitted and spread along the way was the knowledge of Christ, the life-giving aroma of the gospel. Throughout the journey, Paul spread this scent as he preached Jesus. And it invigorated others with eternal life.

The fragrance of God's Word is a sweet aroma that can strengthen all who catch its scent. Don't let your troubles hold you back. Invigorate your environment with gospel aroma and watch the world around you come alive.

16

PEDDLE: *KAPĒLEUŌ*
(καπηλεύω)

For we are not, like so many, peddlers of God's word, but as men of sincerity, as commissioned by God, in the sight of God we speak in Christ. (2 Corinthians 2:17)

οὐ γάρ ἐσμεν ὡς οἱ πολλοὶ καπηλεύοντες τὸν λόγον τοῦ θεοῦ, ἀλλ᾽ ὡς ἐξ εἰλικρινείας, ἀλλ᾽ ὡς ἐκ θεοῦ κατέναντι θεοῦ ἐν Χριστῷ λαλοῦμεν.

(ΠΡΟΣ ΚΟΡΙΝΘΙΟΥΣ Β 2:17)

It frustrates me when I don't get my money's worth, especially at restaurants. I have worked in three restaurants, so you can't fool me. If the food has been sitting under the heat lamp too long, if it has been mishandled, is not fresh, or has been prepared haphazardly, I'm going to notice. Before I even touch my plate, I'm going to look at my server and say, "I'm not paying for this," in a tone that suggests, "Please take this back to the kitchen and get me some *real* food." I have a zero-tolerance policy when restaurants serve me food that looks like they scraped it off the curb of some alley. It irritates me that they think I am going to pay for something that belongs in the garbage disposal.

There are restaurants that will try to shortchange you by giving you the bottom of the barrel. I used to watch it happen all the time when I worked in the restaurant business. Once, a short order cook was putting pieces of fish and fries on a plate. One of the golden, crispy pieces of fish fell on the floor and slid under the fryer. The cook slid his hand down there, retrieved the missing piece of fish, and put it right on the plate like nothing was wrong with it. To make this terrible situation worse, they laughed at the customer who was eating it. I kid you not. Yes, some restaurants will peddle anything, hoping you don't notice that you are being shortchanged. Don't settle for cold fries and a steak that could be used as a door stop. Get the real deal.

In 2 Corinthians 2:17, God's Word says something along the same lines. Here, we find the apostle Paul writing another letter to his Corinthian church. He is dealing with opponents, false teachers who had made their way to Corinth and had accused Paul. They said he was weak and a poor speaker. (See 2 Corinthians 10:10.) They were also bragging that they were better than Paul because he was undergoing tremendous suffering and they weren't. This was their proof that God was with *them* and *not* Paul. (See 2 Corinthians 11:16–33.) And of course, these false apostles claimed to have more spiritual gifts and more exclusive revelations than the apostle Paul. (See 2 Corinthians 12:1–10.)

You might imagine where all this is going. These false teachers—whom Paul facetiously called *super apostles*—demanded financial support from the Corinthians. No big surprise; this still happens today. There are still preachers who claim to have higher spiritual authority, spiritual gifts, and more revelations than the rest of us lowly pastors who just don't have the re- lationship with Jesus that they have. They flood the social media pipelines with ecstatic revelations, demonstrations of showmanship, and displays of charisma, asking you to send in money so God can bless you, too. *Of course.*

And don't think about giving that money elsewhere, they will insinuate. If you aren't giving it to them, you are missing God. Hey, at least we know this isn't a new trick. It's been around since Paul's time.

The apostle called this brand of preacher a "peddler." Here, the Greek word for "peddlers" is *kapēleuontes*. This word was generally used in a negative sense. It meant "to hawk goods" or "to be a retailer," a *middle man* between the wholesaler and the general public. In antiquity, the middle man was notorious for manipulating prices and selling the general public short to make a few extra dollars. The peddler would dilute a wholesaler's wine with water, cheapening it before selling it. They were ripping off customers like the cheap restaurant where I once worked. Peddlers were seen by society as shady, mendacious, and insincere. Their true love was money and they sought to make it at anyone's expense.

The apostle Paul was saying that peddlers aren't limited to the wine business. They also debase the Word of God. Instead of preaching the whole gospel—including the raw truth that could cause people to unfollow their social platform or not return to their church—they water down Scripture, lessening its value and cheapening its life-changing power. And they do it so they can fill their accounts with cash, gain popularity, sell more books, further their brand, fraternize with the elite—anything that's glam.

> Wine was the most common beverage consumed in the ancient Greek and Roman cultures. It was generally thought of as a safer alternative to water, which was often contaminated. Amidst the abundance of wine, the Greeks and Romans were critical of drunkenness and alcoholism.

This problem *has* always existed and *will* always exist. Therefore, our attitude must be right on this. We shouldn't walk away from the church with an *all they want is my money* attitude. It's true that all *peddlers* want is your money, but peddlers don't represent the majority of pastors and ministers who are doing God's work.

Consider the apostle Paul. In light of all of the suffering and criticism he was facing, he refused to accept money from the Corinthian church.

The Corinthians *should* have been supporting *him* because he was *their* pastor. But Paul would not accept it because he did not want to be a burden to them and he wanted to prove to them that he wasn't in it for the money. (See 2 Corinthians 11:1–15.) His heart shone through. Even when money wasn't involved, Paul still gave his best. This is the heart of a *true* servant of God. *Those* are the pastors and ministers we need to get behind and support, not the ones who claim superiority and demand you pay them for it.

Maybe you've been turned off and hurt by a *peddler* who has conned you in the past. I know it stings and I know it can make you hesitant to trust another pastor or minister. But remember, Jesus told us that the weeds would always grow alongside the wheat. (See Matthew 13:24–30.) The good will always be accompanied by the bad. But the good *does* exist. You don't write off all restaurants because one served terrible food or charged exorbitant prices for itty-bitty entrees. You just never go back to the ones that ripped you off. That's the right way to think.

17

WORKMANSHIP: *POIĒMA* (ποίημα)

---

*For we are his **workmanship**, created in Christ Jesus for good works, which God prepared beforehand, that we should walk in them.* (Ephesians 2:10)

αὐτοῦ γάρ ἐσμεν ποίημα, κτισθέντες ἐν Χριστῷ Ἰησοῦ ἐπὶ ἔργοις ἀγαθοῖς οἷς προητοίμασεν ὁ θεός, ἵνα ἐν αὐτοῖς περιπατήσωμεν. (ΠΡΟΣ ΕΦΕΣΙΟΥΣ 2:10)

Artists are amazing people. There's really nothing they can't do. They help to make the world a beautiful place and enable us to see things in *ways* we've never seen them before.

I'm thinking of one artist in particular: Angela Haseltine Pozzi of Oregon. According to *The Seattle Times*, she lost her husband and went to the coast to heal. She says, "I went to the ocean to heal and found that the ocean needed healing." Pozzi was appalled by the amount of trash she saw washing up on the beach. So she decided to make something beautiful out of the ugly. And just like that, "Washed Ashore: Art to Save the Sea" was born.

Pozzi began to collect the plastic trash and turn it into larger-than-life sculptures of sea creatures. There's a great white shark made from bottle caps, a jellyfish comprised of water bottles, a whale ribcage made of white jugs, and dozens of other works. They make up three exhibits traveling around the United States and displayed in aquariums, zoos, museums, and botanical gardens. It's incredible.

Since 2010, Pozzi has enlisted the help of over 10,000 volunteers who've helped her pull trash out of the ocean and turn it into beautiful art that creates awareness. Well done, Angela. See, an artist can take the ugliest sides of life and make something spectacular. That's no surprise though. Artists are just like *their* Artist: God. Before we had da Vinci, Monet, and Michelangelo, there was Almighty God. He is still the original artist—the epicenter of art, if you will. And He takes the lowliest materials and turns them into the finest creations imaginable. I mean, man was created out of dirt. (See Genesis 2:7.) It doesn't get more amazing than that.

Or does it? In Ephesians 2:10, the apostle Paul talks about the pitiful life of sin that humanity has experienced since the fall of Adam. There were heinous things about life that made it far uglier than the disgusting piles of plastic that taint our seas and choke our aquatic life. (See Ephesians 2:1–3.) Humanity was doomed. But then, an artist came along, saw the potential in humanity, and gave His life in order to make something beautiful out of the ugly.

This is what Paul means when he says, *"For we are his workmanship, created in Christ Jesus."* The Greek word for "workmanship" here is *poiēma*. It means "a creation, invention, or a thing produced by an artisan." It gets even more interesting when we discover that this word is used only one other time in the Bible, when it refers to God creating (or inventing) the cosmos. Notice:

For his invisible attributes, namely, his eternal power and divine nature, have been clearly perceived, ever since the creation of the world, in the things that have been made [poiēmasin]. (Romans 1:20)

By using *poiēma* in his letter to the Ephesians, Paul makes a connection between those who are in Christ and the creation account in Genesis. That connection is profound. Humanity had been created along with the rest of the earth. (See Genesis 1–3.) But when Adam sinned, all of creation became corrupted, including mankind. By using *poiēma*, Paul was hinting that God didn't just leave His creation in this state. He refused to allow garbage to wash up while He sat back and watched. No, the original Artist began inventing again. And through the work of Jesus Christ, God began a *new creation*.

> The English word "poem" comes from *poiēma*. The oldest known poem ever written is believed to be the risqué *Epic of Gilgamesh*, written in 2000 BC in ancient Mesopotamia.

When we accept the grace of God that was given to us in Jesus, we are reinvented. The old, corrupt, sinful nature goes and the Holy Spirit comes to dwell inside us. Our nature is changed and we become loving, peaceful, joyful, and free. (See Galatians 5:22–23.) This new nature tells us that the Inventor has been busy conceiving and we are the proof that He is in the process of *"making all things new"* (Revelation 21:5). How amazing it is to think that *you* are the evidence that the Almighty is at work, making beautiful things out of the ugly.

While it's true we live in a world that is entrenched in severe problems and grotesque crises, we need to understand that God hasn't left His creation this way. He didn't forget about us. He's been busy in His shop since day one, welding together a new world that's far better than the first.

I have an idea how wonderful this world is going to be. When I hang out with other Christians and witness their genuine love and get a first-hand look at their kindness, I think of a world in which *everything* is going to be made from this sort of virtue. It's going to be fantastic and it's going to be a testament that the universe has been in the hands of a master artist the whole time.

Wherever you find yourself today, be encouraged. The world around you isn't the finished product. Although the process might seem slow to you, rest assured that God *is* still reinventing. When you see the ugly, just remember, God knows exactly what to do with it. And He's doing it now, even as you read this.

18

DIFFICULT: *CHALEPOS*
(χαλεπός)

But understand this, that in the last days there will come times of **difficulty**. (2 Timothy 3:1)

Τοῦτο δὲ γίνωσκε, ὅτι ἐν ἐσχάταις ἡμέραις ἐνστήσονται καιροὶ χαλεποί. (ΠΡΟΣ ΤΙΜΟΘΕΟΝ Β 3:1)

When you turn on the news, you might cringe at what the world has become. Times change—and there's always something new that makes the yesteryears seem better than today. My grandfather would often say that the 1930s were better than the 1960s, noting, "When *I* was a kid, we *never* had to lock our doors before we went to bed at night." My dad says the 1950s were better than the 1990s, explaining, "When *I* was a kid, we *never* saw this much rebellion on TV."

And I, of course, can say that the 1990s were better than the 2010s because when *I* was a kid, we *never* had to take off our shoes to go through airport security. I can only imagine what *my* children will tell *their* children one day.

In 2 Timothy 3:1–8, the Bible tells us to expect more evil the closer we get to the second coming of Jesus Christ. The apostle Paul gives us a rapid-fire list of depravities that will become part of the normal fabric of our culture: *"lovers of self, lovers of money, proud, arrogant, abusive, disobedient to their parents, ungrateful, unholy…"* The list goes on and on, naming twenty-two immoralities before giving us a chance to catch our breath. It seems overwhelming.

Yet, the pace attests to how the times really are. Has there ever been a day in history when we've been given a chance to catch our breath from sin and its effects? Can we take a pause from corruption, even for just one day? The fact is, the madness is never going to stop. It's going to keep coming at us, full force.

I call 2 Timothy 3:1–7 "the Billy Joel verses" because they often remind me of his rapid-fire song, "We Didn't Start the Fire,"[11] which alludes to an inferno of trouble that has been burning since the beginning of time. Joel's examples refer to more than a hundred headline events between 1949, the year of his birth, and 1989, when the song was released.

In an interview at Oxford University in 1994, Joel said he got the idea for the song after meeting a guy who had just turned twenty-one and said it was a terrible time to be that age.[12] Joel empathized with him, saying when he himself was twenty-one, there were drug problems, the fight for civil rights, and the Vietnam War. But the guy told him, "Yeah, but it was different for you. You were a kid in the fifties and everybody knows nothing happened in the fifties."

Joel realized this young man had never heard of the Korean War (1950–1953) or the Suez Crisis (1956–1957), so he started to jot down things that have happened in his lifetime, many of which are tragic, and turned them into a song.

By the time the song is over, you're left with a lot to think about. Imagine if Joel redid the song with headlines from the *last* thirty years.

One thing is clear: every generation sees its fair share of horrific things, although things are becoming more troublesome with time, despite our modern advances. Second Timothy 3:1 tells us to come to grips with this instead of being surprised and taken aback: *"But understand this, that in the last days there will come times of difficulty."*

"Understand this" is an imperative command in the Greek. It's not an option or a suggestion. By putting it this way, Paul is saying, "Get this into your brains and don't forget it, lest you be surprised." He then says the "last days"—the time between the first coming of Christ and His second coming—will be times of "difficulty." The Greek word for "difficulty" here is *chalepoi*. It means "fierce," "violent," "dangerous," and "troublesome."

The hippopotamus is considered to be the most dangerous mammal in the world. Although they are vegetarian, hippos are temperamental and territorial. They are responsible for the deaths of almost 3,000 people every year. That's more than lions, elephants, leopards, buffaloes, and rhinoceroses combined.

The only other time this word is used in Scripture is to describe the actions of a man possessed by a demon. (See Matthew 8:28.) In fact, this word described wild animals of prey. With this in mind, we could say that the times we are currently living in have been and will continue to be ferocious, savage, and merciless, like the fire Billy Joel described.

The fact is, for as long as you live and for as long as your great-grandchildren live, wild flames can be expected. These are flames that no one of any political persuasion, economic ideology, philosophy, or belief system will ever be able to put out. Though "they try to fight it," as Billy Joel would say, the only one who can extinguish them is King Jesus. And the Lord has promised to come soon and do it. Until then, we'll have to lock our doors at night, change the channel on the TV, and take our shoes off when we go through airport security.

Billy Joel could keep adding new headlines to his song if he desired. But not forever. Tamer times are coming and the fire will be quenched. If not today, let's pray it's tomorrow.

19

COWARDLY: *DEILOS* (δειλός)

But as for the cowardly, the faithless, the detestable, as for murderers, the sexually immoral, sorcerers, idolaters, and all liars, their portion will be in the lake that burns with fire and sulfur, which is the second death." (Revelation 21:8)

τοῖς δὲ δειλοῖς καὶ ἀπίστοις καὶ ἐβδελυγμένοις καὶ φονεῦσιν καὶ πόρνοις καὶ φαρμάκοις καὶ εἰδωλολάτραις καὶ πᾶσιν τοῖς ψευδέσιν τὸ μέρος αὐτῶν ἐν τῇ λίμνῃ τῇ καιομένῃ πυρὶ καὶ θείῳ, ὅ ἐστιν ὁ θάνατος ὁ δεύτερος.
(ΑΠΟΚΑΛΥΨΙΣ ΙΩΑΝΝΟΥ 21:8)

The Wizard of Oz is easily one of the greatest movies ever made. For over eighty years, it has been winning the hearts of its viewers and ranks among the most-watched movies of all time. It's safe to say it has become an icon of American culture. Think about it. If we daydream, we conceive of life *somewhere over the rainbow*. We might boorishly refer to a female nemesis as *a wicked witch*. Ominous weather still stirs up vivid recollections of the twister that carried Dorothy to Oz. And, in an uncommon situation, we often say, "We're not in Kansas anymore." *The Wizard of Oz* is here to stay.

One of the things that makes the film great are the lovable characters L. Frank Baum brought to life for us: Dorothy, Toto, Glinda, and that famous trio—the Tin Man, Scarecrow, and Cowardly Lion. This unique band makes us do a little reflecting. Are we searching for intellect, like Scarecrow? Do we need to be more compassionate, like Tin Man? Or are we fearful and in need of courage, like Cowardly Lion?

Which of the three is our hands-down favorite? While completely subjective and only a matter of opinion, a leisurely surf of blog sites seems to point to Cowardly Lion as the winner.[13] Or loser.... His wimpiness is so pathetic, it's funny and unforgettable—the way he cries after being slapped by Dorothy, shakes in fear as he pulls his own tail, or jumps out of the window in the Emerald City. These embellished portrayals of cowardice put us in touch with our own feelings of trepidation. Cowardly Lion reminds us how pitiful cowardice is and, in the end, he challenges us to rise in the face of fear.

Cowardly Lion actually demonstrates something that God's Word tells us in Revelation 21:8. The Lord was encouraging His people to persevere through their challenges so they could inherit the fullness of God's blessing in the eschaton, the end times. The trials were not frivolous: political idolatry, persecution, isolation from society, and the temptation to assimilate into a wicked culture. In order to be faithful to Christ and endure these trials, they needed to be bold and courageous. They'd have to stand up against the beast (see Revelation 13) and refuse to give worship to Caesar.

In fact, this was so serious that the Lord says, *"The cowardly...their portion will be in the lake that burns with fire and sulfur, which is the second death."* The Greek word for "cowardly" here is *deilois*. It means "timid," "afraid," "one who always runs away," and even, "one who runs away at nothing"—kind of like our friend, Cowardly Lion. It was used to describe skittish and nervous animals that fled at the slightest hint of the unknown. Here, it refers to those who have empty faith and no courage, who can't be counted on to stay faithful to Christ when their personal comforts and safety are at risk. They'd rather run in terror and jump out the window than stand and face any opposition the Christian life brings.

> We need to pray that our fellow Christians around the world may be bold and courageous in the face of suffering. According to Open Doors USA, over 245 million Christians worldwide currently experience high levels of persecution. This is one out of every nine Christians.

This is displeasing to God. Revelation tells us that these people will be excluded from His presence for all eternity. It's that real. Therefore, we must be courageous and stand with Christ no matter what the world says or does next. Nevertheless, God's Word tells us that there are those within our church communities who won't. They will end up cowering when given the chance. This might mean they are modifying their practices to suit secularism, dismissing or explaining away biblical truths in order to seem more tolerant, or even compromising the exclusivity of Christ and the cross so as not to come off as bigoted.

You might shake your head now, but one thing is certain, you can expect there will come a time when you'll have to be bold for Jesus. Push comes to shove for all of us, especially as the current culture continues to chuck lasciviousness our way. Christianity will require more than an *amen* from the pew or a *like* on Instagram. In that moment, we will find out if we have what it takes to stand with the Lion of Judah, or if we will run away like Cowardly Lion.

If you quiver at the thought of what it costs to serve Christ, you can seek the Master for courage. Through His Word and Spirit and the fellowship we share with one another as His church, He will strengthen your heart and establish your resolve. Making the weak strong is the Lord's specialty. He knows your heart. He can transform it as soon as you surrender it to Him.

So be cheerful and courageous, just as Cowardly Lion finally was.

20

GRIEVE: *LYPEŌ* (λυπέω)

And do not grieve the Holy Spirit of God, by whom you were sealed for the day of redemption. (Ephesians 4:30)

καὶ μὴ λυπεῖτε τὸ πνεῦμα τὸ ἅγιον τοῦ θεοῦ, ἐν ᾧ ἐσφραγίσθητε εἰς ἡμέραν ἀπολυτρώσεως.
(ΠΡΟΣ ΕΦΕΣΙΟΥΣ 4:30)

What annoys you? I'm sure there are a few things that get under your skin so obnoxiously that they make you want to hit the fan. Kids screaming in public. Bad customer service. Cold, soggy french fries!

These come to mind first for me. My mood changes fast. With displeasure, I quickly move away from the kids and their parents. If a cashier ignores me, I leave the products someplace and walk out. I send the fries back and have the waiter remove them from my bill. It's annoying to be annoyed.

In 2019, *BestLife* published an article entitled "50 Things You Do Everyday That Annoy Other People." See if some of these hit home with you:

+ Humblebragging—hinting around at your success by pretending to denigrate it

+ Sniffing loudly instead of blowing your nose, as if there's a tissue shortage

+ Making every conversation about you and wondering why your friends keep disappearing

+ Not returning your shopping cart to the corral, allowing it to take off and ding others' cars

+ Talking about how busy you are—because, hey, no one else has a life

+ Starting an order with, "Can I get a…?" Gee, can you?

+ Singing along to a song like you are trying to win a Grammy when you're *not* in the shower

+ Taking a phone call at the gym so you can exercise those eardrums

+ Listening to music on your headphones so loudly that everyone around you knows your playlist

These are among the behaviors that quickly turn you into the most unpleasant person in your social circles.

Whether you realize it or not, God gets annoyed, too. We find this in Ephesians 4:30, where Paul is telling the Ephesian church how they should behave toward one another, as people who have new life in Christ. He cautions the Ephesians that misbehaving can actually "grieve" the Holy Spirit. The Greek word for "grieve" here is *lypeite*. In ancient times, it was used a number of different ways, including "to cause pain," "to cause mental and/or emotional distress," "to make sad," "to hurt someone's feelings," "to harass," and yes, "to annoy." In fact, *lypeō* was once used to describe an army that had become "annoyed" because of constant attacks. The idea is to irritate to the point of distress, whatever form of distress that might be, including sorrow, anger, frustration, or pain.

What "annoys" the Holy Spirit, though, are things far more substantial than texting with your keyboard sound on, or not being ready to order when it's your turn in line. In fact, a list of *"corrupting talk"* that annoys

Him can be found in Ephesians 4:29–31: bitterness, wrath, anger, clamor, slander, and malice.

A survey by 9Round Kickbox Fitness found that Americans who admit to swearing say their first cuss word of the day by 10:54 a.m. These aren't old-timey words like muckspout either.

God wants us to do all things in love, speaking well *of* each other and *to* one another; being encouraging, kind, and gracious; and using gentleness of speech. This keeps the church body united as one and gives it a powerful presence in the world.

Harsh or hostile words, gossiping, cursing, and the like are all ill-mannered ways of speaking that divide the body of Christ. These annoy the Holy Spirit because He is the one who created the bond of unity between us to begin with. (See Ephesians 4:3.) When we speak cruelly of and to each other, we are pulling apart what He has worked to create. How would you feel if you worked on something with great effort and care and someone came along and began to tear it into shreds? I'd certainly be annoyed and "grieved," wouldn't you? That's exactly what we are doing, though, when we malign our brothers and sisters in the Lord. And the Holy Spirit doesn't like it. It is unloving and goes against the Holy Spirit's nature. It causes distress.

The presence of the Holy Spirit in our lives is something that we should honor and respect. We should have love and consideration for Him. Don't be insensitive like the guy who brings last night's fish dinner to the office and heats it up in the microwave. Do what pleases the Spirit instead. Speak the best about others. Talk about them kindly when they aren't around. Be gentle, without harshness. When you do this, you can expect to enjoy the Holy Spirit's company.

If you've been wondering why you haven't felt the presence of God lately, consider whether you have been annoying Him. Has He been grieved by the way you speak about others? If so, take a moment and repent for this. He is loving and kind and will gladly forgive you.

Now, ask for His help. When you do, He will turn you into the kind of person that He likes to be around.

21

PRESS ON: *DIŌKŌ* (διώκω)

---

*I **press on** toward the goal for the prize of the upward call of God in Christ Jesus.*   (Philippians 3:14)

κατὰ σκοπὸν διώκω εἰς τὸ βραβεῖον τῆς ἄνω κλήσεως τοῦ θεοῦ ἐν Χριστῷ Ἰησοῦ. (ΠΡΟΣ ΦΙΛΙΠΠΗΣΙΟΥΣ 3:14)

There's something about watching a high-speed police chase that gets your blood pumping. That's why the best action movies have chase scenes that push the limits—Ferraris careening, Hummers hurtling, stunt men and women jumping from vehicle to vehicle, cop cars getting hammered, and, of course, lots of explosions. Car chases sell.

On YouTube, videos of real-life police chases have hundreds of thousands or even millions of views. Audiences watch with bated breath to see what's going to happen. Will the driver lose control? Are the police going to bump him off the road or shoot out his tires? Watch out for the pedestrians! Usually, before too long, the driver makes a mistake and the chase ends abruptly.

But not in Michael Massie's case. He was the driver in one of the longest police chases of all time—720 kilometers (about 450 miles). The chase took place on South Island in New Zealand on October 14, 2016. Massie, age twenty, was going 10 kilometers per hour (km/h) over the speed limit when New Zealand Police warned him to stop. For whatever reason, he sped off and the chase ensued. It began near the city of Nelson at 1:00 a.m. and didn't end until 5:00 p.m. the next day in the city of Waikouaiti. A sixteen-hour pursuit!

Witnesses say Massie, driving a souped-up Subaru, was doing 180 km/h to 200 km/h in a 50 km/h zone. On three occasions, the police eased up because the speed was just too dicey. But they never let up.

Police officers followed Massie until he finally decided to dump his car and make a run for it. That's when a police dog and his handler ran him down and arrested him. You have to give the police credit for staying on Massie's tail. Although he had the faster car, they were relentless and determined not to let him get away, even if that meant following him for sixteen hours.

Although there are no high-speed police chases in God's Word, Scripture does tell us a little something about hot pursuit. We find this in Philippians 3:13–14. Here, the apostle Paul is reflecting back on his life. Like anyone else's past, it contained failures, defeats, and miserable downfalls. Would Paul allow these to define his identity? Would they keep him from fulfilling what God had called him to do? Certainly not.

Paul resolved not to look back on his past. Rather, he determined to look at what God had put in front of him and to *press on toward the goal…*" The Greek word for "press on" here is *diōkō*. It means "to pursue," "to chase, like in war or in hunting," "to follow something in haste," "to move quickly and definitively toward something," "to march," and "to set in swift motion."

> Despite what people may commonly think about lions, they aren't good runners, nor are they prone to long chases. They usually give up on pursuing their prey after fifty or 110 yards.

It was once used in an old tale to describe a lion who pursued a man into the desert. The idea is a gritty chase, a solid, hot pursuit wherein the pursuer refuses to give up. In fact, the word also meant "to harass," to be so insistent and adamant that it becomes harassment. Like the New Zealand police who stayed on Michael Massie's tail, a person who is "pressing on" refuses to give up and let what they are pursuing get away. They overcome all obstacles until they win what they're after.

By using the word *diōkō*, Paul was saying that he was staying on the tail of the reward and eternal glories that Christ had placed in front of him. He wasn't going to waste his time or energy trying to fix bygones. The past is the past. There is no way we can change what happened yesterday. Instead, Paul was resolute about putting his energy into knowing Jesus more deeply and hunting down the rewards God has in store for those who are faithful to Him. He was in hot pursuit, like a cop chasing a speeding car.

How about you? Are you chasing the things that God has placed in front of you? Or are you driving in reverse and looking at what you might have missed along the way? We can't be successful in God unless we have our eyes and heart fixed ahead. While it might be tempting to try to do something about the past, the fact is that we won't find God in the past. He puts our gifts *before* us, not behind.

Why not commit to God that you will be in hot pursuit of what He has in store for you? How about becoming intense about knowing Jesus more deeply, walking in His will for your life, and obeying the things He has called you to do? That will create a lot more joy and a greater sense of purpose than agonizing over regrets that you cannot fix.

There's too much in front of you to let it get away. You'll need all the energy you have to chase what God has for your life. There's an amazing and exciting pursuit ahead, even more amazing than the police chases on YouTube.

So what are you waiting for? Press on. Pursue.

22

UNCLEAN: *AKATHARTOS*
(ἀκάθαρτος)

And in the synagogue there was a man who had the spirit of an
unclean demon, and he cried out with a loud voice.

(Luke 4:33)

καὶ ἐν τῇ συναγωγῇ ἦν ἄνθρωπος ἔχων πνεῦμα δαιμονίου
ἀκαθάρτου καὶ ἀνέκραξεν φωνῇ μεγάλῃ.

(ΚΑΤΑ ΛΟΥΚΑΝ 4:33)

Headfirst in a septic system is not the best way to spend Christmas
Eve. We've all had holiday plans go afoul, but few have had it as bad
as Robert Schoff of Des Moines, Iowa, on Christmas Eve 2007. *The Desert
News* reported his upside-down fiasco in an article entitled "Septic Tank
Mishap Ruins Christmas Eve."

If you're an apartment dweller or your home is connected to a municipal system, you may not be familiar with septic tanks. These are underground containers holding 750 to 1,250 gallons of excrement and other household wastes. Eventually, liquid and solid waste separate; the waste water is distributed into a drain field and the solid waste decomposes. The tank must be pumped out once in a while. It's a good way to manage waste in a rural area, but it's no place to hang out.

Schoff's tank had a clog. He went outside to investigate, lost his balance, and became wedged, headfirst, in the tank opening. He began to yell and scream for help, but no one heard him. After a whole hour passed, his wife walked by the window and saw his feet sticking out of the ground. She immediately called 911. Sheriff's deputies rushed to the scene to pull Schoff out. Unsurprisingly, he was steeped in raw sewage. The poor guy must have needed a long shower after that.

In Luke 4:33, we are faced with the reality of defilement. But unlike Robert Schoff's, this was spiritual defilement. On one Sabbath, Jesus had gone into the Capernaum synagogue in Galilee, where he was teaching. Something peculiar happened. Jesus was met by a man with an "unclean" demon.

The Greek word "unclean" here is *akathartos*, and it is an adjective that describes the demon. In more than twenty places in the New Testament, we find *akathartos* in relation to an evil spirit. This tells us something about demons and spiritual warfare.

Akathartos comes from the Greek word *katharos*, which means "clean," "innocent," and "morally pure." However, *akathartos* begins with an alpha, the "alpha privative" in Koine Greek, which negates the word that follows it. Hence, *akathartos* is "unclean," the exact opposite of clean.

It also meant "containing impurities," "foul," and "infected." It was used to describe a defiling agent that clung to a host and could be transferred to another. Everything carrying a defiling agent was considered to be contaminated—such as unclean reptiles, corpses, dead animals, excrement, or lepers—and was something to be avoided.

Furthermore, in ancient Jewish thinking, being "unclean" often went beyond a lack of cleanliness. It often meant being contaminated by a demonic spirit. These polluting powers were averse to God. The Law was given to protect God's people from becoming sullied by these spirits and playing host to their contaminating influences. If a person was under the influence of one, their behavior was considered "unclean" and their association in the community of God's people was restricted. (See Leviticus 5; 13; 15.)

There are three common theological views about where demons came from: 1) they are spirits from a pre-Adamic race; 2) they are spirits from the offspring of the union between fallen angels and women; or 3) they are simply fallen angels.

With this in mind, we can better understand what an "unclean" demon is, like the one in Luke 4:33. It is a spiritual entity, opposed to God, that clings to a person and compels them to behave foully and against God's laws. This makes the person unclean and unfit to participate in the worship of God or in the religious functions of the community. Those with unclean demons in the New Testament would have been morally profane, defiant toward the Law, and despised by the religious community. They may have been sexually perverse, violent, rebellious, idol worshippers, or occult practitioners.

Unclean demons drive this sort of behavior because they are leading a spiritual rebellion against God, desiring to make a mockery of His ways. They wish to separate us from the Lord and prevent us from being part of His holy, end-times people. Jesus has defeated these powers, but they still try to defile us and draw us away from God. This will go on until Jesus comes again.

In our world today, there are still those who are contaminated by unclean demons and the proof is in their lewd behavior. Of course, we are called to show love to others, but we must have balance. Buddying up with defiled people could mean getting close to the unclean demons that influence them. Therefore, one of the greatest lessons in spiritual warfare is to be prayerful about your associates, lest the wrong influences get too close and you end up face-first in the septic tank. (See 1 Corinthians 15:33.)

Be careful. Be picky about your close friendships. A life apart from God and His holy people is nasty—like sewage.

23

CONTEND: *EPAGŌNIZOMAI*
(ἐπαγωνίζομαι)

Beloved, although I was very eager to write to you about our common salvation, I found it necessary to write appealing to you to contend *for the faith that was once for all delivered to the saints.* (Jude 1:3)

Ἀγαπητοί, πᾶσαν σπουδὴν ποιούμενος γράφειν ὑμῖν περὶ τῆς κοινῆς ἡμῶν σωτηρίας ἀνάγκην ἔσχον γράψαι ὑμῖν παρακαλῶν ἐπαγωνίζεσθαι τῇ ἅπαξ παραδοθείσῃ τοῖς ἁγίοις πίστει. (ΙΟΥΔΑ 1:3)

My cousin Jenny is one impressive woman—she's an Ironman. As of this writing, she's competed in the Ironman Competition fourteen times. This grueling sporting event, organized by the World Triathlon

Corporation (WTC), is considered to be one of the most difficult athletic competitions in the world. Competitors usually have sixteen or seventeen hours to complete a 2.4-mile swim, a 112-mile bicycle ride, and a 26.22-mile run—without a break. I get dog-tired just thinking about it. And to think, Jenny has done it fourteen times. I'm not sure I've walked around my block fourteen times.

John Newsom, a triathlon coach from New Zealand and founder of the NZ Multisport and Triathlon Centre in Christchurch, provides aspiring Ironmen with a six-month training plan to prepare. Yes, that's right: you must begin preparing for race day at least six months in advance just for a chance to complete it. Here's what Newsom suggests:

Six months before the race: an hour of swim on Monday, and hour of cycle on Tuesday, an hour run on Thursday, an hour swim on Friday, an hour run on Saturday, two to three hours of cycling on Sunday.

Four months before the race: an hour-and-a-half cycle and an hour run on Tuesday, an hour swim on Wednesday, an hour-and-a-half cycle and an hour run on Thursday, an hour swim on Friday, three-to-four-hour cycle on Saturday, and a 40-minute ocean swim and an hour-and-a-half run on Sunday.

Three months before the race: an hour-and-a-half cycle and 70-minute run on Tuesday, one-hour swim on Wednesday, two-hour cycle on Thursday, one-hour swim on Friday, five-hour cycle and 20-minute run on Saturday, a 45-minute ocean swim and 1.45 mile run on Sunday.

Two months before the race: two-hour cycle and one hour run on Tuesday, 4km swim on Wednesday, hour-and-a-half cycle and hour-and-a-half run on Thursday, hour swim on Friday, six-to-seven-hour cycle on Saturday, 45-minute ocean swim/hour cycle/two-hour run on Sunday.

One month before the race: hour-and-a-half cycle and hour run on Tuesday, 4km swim on Wednesday, hour cycle and hour-and-a-half run on Thursday, hour swim on Friday, four-hour cycle on

Saturday, 30-minute ocean swim/an hour cycle/hour-and-a-half run on Sunday.

A single triathlon calls for at least 180 days of training, and the above list doesn't even include diet and other necessary preparations. It's not just about the race day itself; it's about the earnest struggle that goes on beforehand. It's the time, commitment, consistency, and denial of distractions for half a year, sometimes even more. To be an Ironman, you have to be skilled at contending.

As a sport, the triathlon is relatively new, but its roots date to 1901, when a suburban community in Paris, France, held a contest called "les trois sports" (three sports). Contestants went for a run, a bike ride, and a canoe race. Eventually, the latter was replaced with a swim.

While there are no Ironmen competitions in God's Word, there is plenty about contending. In the Epistle of Jude, the disciple wrote to what was likely a group of Jewish Christians in Asia Minor. He felt it particularly necessary to confront false teachers who had found their way into the churches. These evil workers were denying the truth of Jesus Christ and Jude was pressed to confront them and challenge their teaching with what Christ had actually taught. Jude called this "contending" for the faith.

The Greek verb for "contend" here is *epagōnizesthai*. It is related to the noun *agōn*, which means "a competition," "a contest," and "a deadly struggle." Hence, the verb *epagōnizomai* means "to carry on a competition, contest, or a struggle." It was used in ancient times to describe an individual who was fighting with every last ounce of might within them, many times to the death. The force behind the word implies a passionate struggle that is powered by intense focus and the utmost seriousness. Someone who was "contending" was not distracted with other things but was fixed on the one thing they were wrestling with, like those training for an Ironman competition. It took guts, resilience, and determination.

Jude was ready to get in the dirt with the false teachers. He would do whatever he had to do, for as long as it took, using all of his might to knock out the heresy that these evil workers were perpetuating.

The Christian life is not a walk in the park. It is full of all sorts of battles—in Jude's case, false teachers—that will engage us in the struggle of our lives. Being a Christian means fighting like an Ironman against those struggles until you overcome them with the power of God.

What battles are going on in your life right now? Perhaps there is a prayer you can't seem to get answered. Maybe there is an atheist professor at your university who likes to take jabs at your faith. It could be a spiritual battle that's filling you with heaviness, sadness, or gloom. Whatever the case may be, you are called to contend with it like an Ironman, with a fierce passion to overcome it whether it takes months or years. As long as you stay with it, God will keep supplying you with what you need to win.

Make a decision to be fierce, dogged, and resolute in the face of challenges. You are a Christian—an Ironman—and contending is what you were built to do.

24

REVELATION: *APOKALYPSIS* (ἀποκάλυψις)

That the God of our Lord Jesus Christ, the Father of glory, may give you the Spirit of wisdom and of **revelation** in the knowledge of him. (Ephesians 1:17)

ἵνα ὁ θεὸς τοῦ κυρίου ἡμῶν Ἰησοῦ Χριστοῦ, ὁ πατὴρ τῆς δόξης, δώῃ ὑμῖν πνεῦμα σοφίας καὶ ἀποκαλύψεως ἐν ἐπιγνώσει αὐτοῦ. (ΠΡΟΣ ΕΦΕΣΙΟΥΣ 1:17)

Have you ever discovered something so wonderful that you said, "Where has this been all my life?" The whimsical complaint is actually a compliment. It suggests that the find has enriched your quality of life. This may have been how Chole Gustafson and her team from Columbia University's Lamont-Doherty Earth Observatory felt when they discovered a huge reservoir of what *Newsweek* magazine calls "potentially fresh water" under the ocean floor. This reservoir is suspected to be massive. It is fifty miles off the East Coast of the United States and stretches from Massachusetts to New Jersey.

At this point, scientists estimate that there are 670 cubic miles of water in the reservoir. Just to give you an estimate of how much water that is, Lake Ontario contains 393 cubic miles of water and Lake Erie contains 116 cubic miles of water. If scientists are correct, this underground reservoir contains more fresh water than these two Great Lakes combined. This is an important discovery because it suggests that there could be other reservoirs of fresh water existing under the ocean floor elsewhere, which could help us combat the fresh water scarcity that has become a crisis in many parts of the world.

According to the World Health Organization, 785 million people do not have access to fresh water; by 2025, half the world population will be living in areas considered to be "water-stressed." Fresh water reservoirs under the ocean floor could bring these areas the water they desperately need to improve their standard of living. We can pray for technological advances that will enable us to locate and access these reservoirs. It's amazing how a new discovery can change the quality of our lives, forever.

In God's Word, we learn of the discovery of living water that leads to eternal life. (See John 4:13–15).

In Ephesians 1:17, the apostle Paul was writing to the Ephesian church about all the blessings that have come as a result of being in Christ. Paul tells them that he prays for them with these blessings in mind. One of these blessings is *"the Spirit of wisdom and of revelation,"* or the Holy Spirit. For the sake of our study, it's important to note that the Holy Spirit is associated with "revelation."

The Greek word for "revelation" here is *apoklypseōs*. In antiquity it meant an "uncovering," or "disclosure." The verbal use of the word meant "to uncover," "to take out of hiding," "to make fully known," and "to disclose something that was formerly unknown." In everyday life, it was used to describe the discovery of hidden things, like the hidden springs in Plutarch's *The Parallel Lives*.

General Aemilius Paullus and his men were facing a water shortage near Mt. Olympus. The troops had become frustrated and angry. Surveying the land, Aemilius noticed there were green trees growing near the mountain and realized there must be an underground water supply there. So he dug a number of vents and wells for his men along the foot of Mt. Olympus so they could drink. Plutarch uses *apokalypsis* to describe the hidden water that came to light.

> Plutarch's *Parallel Lives*, written at the beginning of the second century AD, compares the lives of notable Greek and Roman men. By so doing, Plutarch hoped to encourage joint respect between the two cultures. Perhaps his most significant comparison was Alexander the Great and Julius Caesar.

With this in mind, we could say that the Columbia University researchers had a "revelation" when they uncovered the underwater reservoir.

In Ephesians 1:17, God's Word is telling us that the Holy Spirit has the ministry of "uncovering" and "revealing" to us the hidden reservoir of *living water*: Jesus Christ. The Spirit of revelation discloses to us everything we need to know about Christ so that we can drink from Him and live eternally. When this happens, it is truly a startling discovery that vastly improves the quality of our well-being in every way. If you have drunk from this well, then you know what I mean.

Can you recall when the Holy Spirit revealed Jesus to you? Was it an epiphany-like experience? Did it occur to you that you needed Him to save you from your sin? Did you realize that He loves you and is the true meaning and purpose of life? This is the work of the Spirit of revelation.

Over the years, I have heard the personal testimonies of men and women, young and old, from countries near and far, who have talked about what it was like to have a revelation of Jesus. One of my friends, now a pastor, who had lived a profane life of drugs and self-gratification, gave his life to Jesus while he was hunting in the woods, alone. According to his testimony, he was sitting in his tree stand, waiting for deer to come by. Suddenly, his heart grew conscious of his own sin and his need for Jesus to save him. He'd heard about Jesus in church, but Jesus hadn't become a reality until this instant. Tears began to flow down his face. He lifted his hand and asked the Lord to forgive him of his sins. In that moment, he chose to follow Christ.

Now, a couple of decades later, he has led many others to Christ and has been all over the world, proclaiming Christ's goodness. The Holy Spirit had led him to Jesus, a hidden spring of pure water, and he has been drinking from it ever since.

The Spirit of revelation's job is to reveal spiritual truths about Jesus that we can't uncover on our own. These "revelations" will help us grow and mature in our walk with the Lord.

As you read God's Word, welcome the Spirit and ask for His guidance. What He reveals will enrich your life in such a tremendous way that you'll wonder, "Where has this been all my life?"

25

REGENERATION: *PALINGENESIA* (παλιγγενεσία)

He saved us, not because of works done by us in righteousness,
but according to his own mercy, by the washing of regeneration
and renewal of the Holy Spirit. (Titus 3:5)

οὐκ ἐξ ἔργων τῶν ἐν δικαιοσύνῃ ἃ ἐποιήσαμεν ἡμεῖς
ἀλλὰ κατὰ τὸ αὐτοῦ ἔλεος ἔσωσεν ἡμᾶς διὰ λουτροῦ
παλιγγενεσίας καὶ ἀνακαινώσεως πνεύματος ἁγίου.
(ΠΡΟΣ ΤΙΤΟΝ 3:5)

Have you ever wished for *a clean slate*? We all have. This popular idiom came about in the mid-1800s and referred to chalkboards that hung in schools and taverns. It was easy to wipe off the chalk and write something new. In elementary school, I used to beg my teacher to let me clean the chalkboard after class. There is nothing quite like using a warm, soapy sponge to wash away the chalk dust. It kind of reminded me of a Zamboni cleaning the ice during intermission at a hockey game. The grubby, dusty surface was scrubbed and came out looking brand-new. Ahh…clean slate!

Sometimes, I would clean the chalkboard and wish I could wipe away my mistakes just as easily. *If only I could start over, I wouldn't have talked back to Mom in the car…. I would have done my homework on time…. I wouldn't have punched my brother in the arm…. Gosh, I never would have traded that basketball card away!*

As life became more complicated and mistakes became more consequential, the illustration of the chalkboard still served to make me wish for a clean slate. Cell phone users who wish for a life do-over might say they'd like a *hard reset* instead.

The good news is that we don't have to settle for just *wishing* for a "clean slate." God's Word tells us that we can have one. That's right: you can become so squeaky clean it's as if you had never made those mistakes.

This is what God's Word tells us in Titus 3:5. The apostle Paul is writing to Titus, who was pastoring the church on the island of Crete. The Cretans were notorious for poor character, even according to one of their own, Epimenides, a sixth century BC philosopher from Crete. Paul quotes him in Titus 1:12: "*One of the Cretans, a prophet of their own, said, 'Cretans are always liars, evil beasts, lazy gluttons.'*" And it was Titus's job to pastor these people. Yikes.

Epimenides's statement, "All Cretans are liars," is known as *the Epimenides paradox* and is still used today as an exercise in logic. Since Epimenides himself is a Cretan, is he lying when he says all Cretans are liars? Logically, as Mr. Spock would point out, since he did not say Cretans lie *all* of the time, he could be telling the truth.

Nevertheless, Paul didn't want Titus to become disheartened by the Cretans' behavior. To encourage him, Paul reminded Titus about their own pasts: *"We ourselves were once foolish, disobedient, led astray, slaves to various passions and pleasures, passing our days in malice and envy, hated by others and hating one another"* (Titus 3:3). But the saving work of Christ changed all of that.

Paul calls this change of life "regeneration." The Greek word for "regeneration" here is *palingenesias*, a two-part Greek word made up of *palin* ("again") and *ginomai* ("to be," "become," "take place," "be born"). Together, they mean "to become again," "to be born again," "to have life again like being born a second time," and even "a new genesis."[14] In the ancient world, it was used to describe restoration of health, or preventing the regrowth of something such as a tumor. It is even the word that is used in Matthew 19:28 to describe the renovation of the world under the Messiah. The idea is new life, a second existence, another chance, and, for the sake of our discussion, a clean slate.

When we trust Jesus Christ as our Lord and Savior, we aren't signing up for a list of do's and don'ts. It is much deeper than that. We experience a cleansing of the soul. Just like a soapy sponge on a chalkboard, the blood of Jesus washes away what we've done in the past and gives us a new life to go forward. Paul's point to Titus was that if God could give *them* new slates, he was certainly capable enough to do it for the Cretans. And that goes for us as well. Everyone who puts their hope and trust in the finished work of Jesus Christ receives a clean slate from God.

No matter what you have done, even if it is the worst thing imaginable, you will be a brand-new person as soon as Christ enters your life and makes you clean. Racism, anger, unforgiveness, addiction, mistreatment, neglect of others, abuse—it's all wiped away when the blood of Christ is applied. As the old hymn by Robert Lowry goes:

What can wash away my sin?
Nothing but the blood of Jesus.
What can make me whole again?
Nothing but the blood of Jesus.

If you haven't done so yet, let Jesus clean your slate with His blood today.

26

CREEP IN UNNOTICED: *PAREISDYŌ* (παρεισδύω)

For certain people have crept in unnoticed who long ago were designated for this condemnation, ungodly people, who pervert the grace of our God into sensuality and deny our only Master and Lord, Jesus Christ. (Jude 1:4)

παρεισέδυσαν γάρ τινες ἄνθρωποι, οἱ πάλαι προγεγραμμένοι εἰς τοῦτο τὸ κρίμα, ἀσεβεῖς, τὴν τοῦ θεοῦ ἡμῶν χάριτα μετατιθέντες εἰς ἀσέλγειαν καὶ τὸν μόνον δεσπότην καὶ κύριον ἡμῶν Ἰησοῦν Χριστὸν ἀρνούμενοι.

(ΙΟΥΔΑ 1:4)

Leeches are nasty critters. Fishermen like myself understand this and when we wade in the water, we're always conscious that there could be some lurking nearby. And good luck to you if there are because you won't feel one attach itself to you. At some point, you'll just notice it's drinking your blood. The thought *will* cross your mind, *How long has this sucker been feasting on me?!*

I've had the unfortunate experience of being a leech's meal a time or two. It never dawned on me to check for them until I was actually done fishing and on my way home. (Sorry if I'm grossing you out.) The first time it happened, I was sitting in the passenger seat, glanced down, and saw a leech snacking on my foot. I quickly ripped it off and threw it out the window with disgust. I was frustrated with myself. I had been warned that leeches were lurking. *How could I let this happen? Why wasn't I paying attention? Why was I so careless?*

Yet, there is a fascinating reason why you can't feel a leech when it attaches itself to you and begins to suck your blood. According to Mehdi Jaffari, a leech therapist, these worms release an anesthetic while they are latching on. This makes you insensitive to pain and lets the leech carry on unnoticed. This buys the leech all the time it needs to enjoy your blood until it is sated. Then it just falls off and moves on—with your blood. Certainly gives you the heebie-jeebies, doesn't it?

In Jude 1:4, we are confronted with a different kind of leech: false teachers and workers of evil. They lurk around Christians, trying to attach themselves to congregations and well-intentioned believers in order to rob them of the truth and carry away their innocence. They had found their way into the churches of Asia Minor in the first century. Jude says they *"have crept in unnoticed."*

Here the Greek word that encompasses this whole phrase is *paredotheisē*. It means "to slip in covertly," "to secretly penetrate," "to worm one's way into." In *The Extant Works of Aretaeus of Cappadocia*, *pareisdyō* was used to describe a leech bite. Aretaeus was a first-century physician who lived in Asia Minor and wrote about disease treatments. In a chapter entitled, "Cure of the Acute Affections About the Liver," Aretaeus says the leech's deep bite caused a steady flow of blood.

Aretaues was a highly-acclaimed, first-century physician. He was an acquaintance of Emperor Nero's personal physician, Andromachos, who formulated a medical compound that was widely adopted in the ancient world.

Jude considered this a fitting description for those who had joined themselves to the churches, yet were propagating a false faith. Like a leech, they encroached undetected. Their initial behavior probably didn't alarm anyone. But as soon as they were close enough and had the chance to bite down deep, they began steadily sucking the life out of the churches with their false doctrines and relaxed versions of morality. It's likely that they had been feeding on the churches for a while and Jude was writing to expose them so they could be ripped away.

We serve a God who is serious about upholding the truth that is in His Word. He expects us to defend it from leeches that try to creep in and pervert it. This happens all the time today. In our churches and Christian communities, we find influencers with *progressive* ideas and doctrines that reduce morality to simply being *nice* and *accepting*, rather than behaving within the ethical boundaries that God gave for society's greatest good. Using a call to love and unity, they anesthetize the sting of their bite. Oblivious, Christians sometimes don't notice and go on participating in their schemes instead of breaking away from them, as God's Word instructs. And if this doesn't seem very loving, if this is upsetting to you, it's possible you've allowed them to creep into your own life...and bite.

Yes, *"God is love"* (1 John 4:8). However, loving the Lord means obeying His commands. (See John 14:15.) Twisting these commands so people can do whatever they want and not feel *judged* is not a scriptural idea. It troubles our commitment to God and negates our love toward His ways. There is no place in our lives for any influence that would try to creep in and carry off the values and doctrines that make our lives pleasing to the Lord.

Be alert like a fisherman standing in a creek. Recognize that there are *leeches* lurking nearby that will attach themselves to you if you aren't careful. They could come through a YouTube channel that intrigues you, a friend with a *new* take on things, or a *woke* spiritual leader who has left traditional approaches behind. While it all may seem harmless at first, it is going to suck the life out of your walk with God. If these influences have already latched on to you, it's time to get them out. You don't have to be mean or abrasive about it. Simply stop giving them time and redirect your attention toward God's Word and influences that are teaching the truth.

27

DISARM: *APEKDYOMAI* (ἀπεκδύομαι)

---

*He **disarmed** the rulers and authorities and put them to open shame, by triumphing over them in him.*   (Colossians 2:15)

ἀπεκδυσάμενος τὰς ἀρχὰς καὶ τὰς ἐξουσίας ἐδειγμάτισεν ἐν παρρησίᾳ, θριαμβεύσας αὐτοὺς ἐν αὐτῷ.
(ΠΡΟΣ ΚΟΛΟΣΣΑΕΙΣ 2:15)

P*antsing* is a savage prank in which you walk up behind an unsuspecting target and pull their pants down to their ankles. I don't recommend it. You risk losing friends if you aren't sure about their sense of humor. Yet it was a source of hilarity among my high school friends. The prank, of course, caused humiliation. Even better, the person being pantsed couldn't chase you—at least not immediately.

Perhaps the greatest pantsing incident in the history of my high school was when I got my brother. We were on the basketball team together; being the younger brother and a grade behind, I was the constant butt of his jokes. For some time, I had been seeking a little payback. I finally saw my chance.

He was the varsity captain and had been asked to instruct the junior varsity in some drills before their practice. There he stood at half-court, back turned, trying the impress the younger team with his know-how. The opportunity seemed too good to be true, but I seized it. I ran up behind him undetected and jerked his shorts down to his ankles. The JV squad laughed and laughed as he stood there in his boxers, shocked. His red face was proof that I had gotten him good. It was a while before he thought of messing with me again.

(Disclaimer: We only pulled this prank among guys who were friends and never did it to bully. We never ever did it in front of women. It was just horseplay that was acceptable under the right circumstances during my era. It's not something that could or should be done today.)

During the first century, Roman citizens were allowed to wear a toga, a long piece of white cloth draped over the shoulders and around the body. However, most citizens did not wear one because it was an expensive garment that was heavy and uncomfortable. As a Roman citizen, the apostle Paul could have worn a toga but it's not believed he did so. (See Acts 16:35–39.) A more common piece of clothing for men and woman was the cloak or *himation* in the Greek.

Losing your clothes is an embarrassing thing; it belittles your importance, diminishes whatever authority you may have, and hurts your dignity.

In Colossians 2:15, Paul describes a kind of pantsing, believe it or not. Here, the apostle is discussing our new position in Christ and how God made it possible for us to break free from the powers of darkness to be part of God's new family. As he concludes, Paul mentions that God through Christ *"disarmed the rulers and authorities and put them to open shame."* To understand what this means, it's first important for us to know who Paul meant by rulers and authorities. Scholars vary on whether this refers to earthly or spiritual rulers. I believe it can be both, especially since we see elsewhere in Scripture that earthly governments are influenced and directed by spiritual powers. (See Daniel 10.)

With that being understood, we can look at the Greek word for "disarmed," which here is *apekdysamenos*. It literally means "to strip clothes off," "to undress," and "to disrobe." The Colossians would think of God stripping off the clothes of the powers and authorities that were against Him. Why would Paul put it this way?

We must consider Christ's crucifixion. The ruling authorities undercut Jesus as the King of kings and Lord of lords by stripping Him naked before nailing Him to the cross. This was *meant* to display His powerlessness and lack of authority, to humiliate Him. It was intended to be a celebratory event for the powers of darkness because it ridiculed the Lord. Paradoxically, Paul points out that the opposite happened. The cross of Christ was how God broke the hold these powers had on mankind. Jesus was actually stripping *them* of *their* clothes: He was overturning *their* power and divesting *them* of *their* authority and whatever hold they had on people. No longer would mankind have to be bullied by the ways of the world. The powers of darkness were depantsed, stripped down, and shriveled by the power of God, even as Jesus hung without clothes on the cross.

While the illustration may seem a little crude, nothing has ever been truer. Jesus has totally and completely overcome the wicked systems of the world and the demonic powers that stand behind them. Part of having a successful Christian life is realizing that we are no longer under the power of its evil ways, behavior, and manner of thinking. We belong to Jesus *because* of His victorious work on the cross.

Are you living like Jesus, embarrassing the wickedness that's in the world? Or are you under the specious impression that sin is the master over you? Listen, Jesus depantsed drugs, anger, and addictions. He disrobed wicked and depraved mindsets such racism, misogyny, and bigotry. All authority and power now belong to Him and He has freed you with it. Instead of thinking you are the servant of sin, today it is time to begin functioning like sin has lost its pants.

Why not begin identifying with the work of Christ by asking the Holy Spirit to give you a revelation of the authority that we have been given in Jesus? Ask Him to help you see how this power compares to the thing that has been defeating you. You'll see that you've been running from an enemy that has its pants around its ankles. Because we are in Christ, wickedness cannot bully us or push us around.

28

WARFARE: *STRATEIA*
(στρατεία)

For the weapons of our warfare are not of the flesh but have divine power to destroy strongholds. (2 Corinthians 10:4)

τὰ γὰρ ὅπλα τῆς στρατείας ἡμῶν οὐ σαρκικὰ ἀλλὰ δυνατὰ τῷ θεῷ πρὸς καθαίρεσιν ὀχυρωμάτων, λογισμοὺς καθαιροῦντες. (ΠΡΟΣ ΚΟΡΙΝΘΙΟΥΣ Β 10:4)

Men and women who serve in war together form an unbreakable bond. Warfare is one of the most tragic things in the human experience, yet stories of courage shine in the midst of darkness. One such story is about four chaplains who served in World War II. George Fox, Alexander Goode, John Washington, and Clark Poling met at the Harvard chaplaincy school in 1942 and quickly became friends.

On January 23, 1943, the chaplains and hundreds of young soldiers boarded the United States Army Transport *Dorchester*, an aging coastal liner, headed toward an Army base in Greenland. There were 902 people aboard. Soldiers were terrified because German submarines had been torpedoing Allied ships at a rate of a hundred per month—and the *Dorchester* would be sailing right into their path. The chaplains had to encourage and comfort the troops. They relied on one another for strength.

On February 2, just 150 miles from Greenland, the *Dorchester* received word that an enemy submarine was lurking nearby. Most of the men were asleep when the first torpedo hit at 1 a.m. A hundred men in the hull were killed and the ship's power went out as it tilted and began to sink. When the men screamed in terror, the four chaplains rose to the occasion. They spoke words of comfort to the panic-stricken and prayed with the dying men so they could make their peace with God before they reached eternity.

In the midst of all the chaos, the chaplains steered many of the men to the deck and passed out life jackets. When those ran out, the four chaplains took off their own and gave them to others. Together, as a band of brothers, they sacrificed their own hopes of survival. As the soldiers in the lifeboats watched the *Dorchester* sink, they saw the four chaplains brace against the railing, link arms, and sing to God a final declaration of faith. The chaplains disappeared into the dark, icy waters, along with the ship, but the legend of their brotherhood lives into the light of today. Warfare and brotherhood: the two have always gone arm-in-arm.

This is something that God's Word conveys to us in 2 Corinthians 10:4. The apostle Paul was under attack from the enemy. False apostles had come into the Corinthian church to torpedo him by undermining his doctrine and credentials. Writing in his own defense, Paul talks about his mission to preach and defend the gospel, describing this mission as "warfare."

In 216 BC, Hannibal and his Carthaginian forces killed 70,000 Roman soldiers in the Battle of Cannae during the Second Punic War. The Romans rebuilt their army and eventually defeated Hannibal's troops at the Battle of Zama in 202 BC.

The Greek word for "warfare" here is *strateias*. It means "a military engagement or campaign," "the expedition of an army," and "military service." More than that, one of its cognate words meant "comrade in arms." In antiquity, "comrade in arms" was a special title that was used between soldiers. Only those who had been together through the treacheries of war greeted each other using this term. It was a designation that encompassed the brotherhood of battle and was used to greet those who shared this common bond, just as the four chaplains had.

By using *strateia*, Paul is telling us that our mission to preach the gospel is like a military engagement and an operation in the army of God. As in any military effort, there will be times of great difficulty, with challenges and attacks from our enemies, such as what Paul was facing from the false apostles. In order to fulfill our duty in this raging warfare, we need a band of brothers, "comrades in arms" to bond with in battle. The mission is too perilous for us to make do without linking arms and finding strength from others. Paul had the Corinthians and the four chaplains had each other.

What about you? Are you linked with someone?

When I was first starting in ministry, I used to believe that I could fulfill my ministry alone. I suppose it was my youth that made me reason that I was some kind of super-soldier. *Sure, others might need me, but I don't need them,* I'd think. Wow, was I ever wrong. I can't begin to count the times that I have had to draw strength from others, I was in such need of their prayers. These spiritual soldiers would have gone down in the ship with me. Having been through skirmishes and battles together, they are now my best of friends and those for whom I would fight at any moment. It was the battlefield of the common duty to the gospel that brought us together and forged the brotherhood.

If you have people you are linked with, give God thanks for them. It is one of the greatest blessings of the Christian life to have people you can go to spiritual war with. For no other reason, they will help you fulfill the mission God has given you.

If you aren't yet linked with anyone, begin praying about it. God knows the struggle ahead. He wants to give you fellow Christians to link arms with so you can overcome when a torpedo heads your way.

29

DEMON-POSSESSED:
DAIMONIZOMAI
(δαιμονίζομαι)

---

*And those who had seen it told them how the **demon-possessed**
man had been healed.* (Luke 8:36)

ἀπήγγειλαν δὲ αὐτοῖς οἱ ἰδόντες πῶς ἐσώθη ὁ
δαιμονισθείς. (ΚΑΤΑ ΛΟΥΚΑΝ 8:36)

Demon possession is a topic that I've talked about since I first began
to preach, although it is controversial. It has been through a lot of
mishandling because people fall into a ditch on either side of it. Either they
run with it and turn every little issue into a demon problem, or they avoid
talking about it altogether. I believe truth is usually found in the middle.

I've noticed that many people seem to have gotten their information about demon possession from movies rather than the Word of God. This probably explains why, when I finish teaching about it, I am frequently asked if people who are possessed by demons speak and act like Regan did in *The Exorcist*. While I've never watched that movie—and I don't plan to either—I know it has influenced how culture understands the demonic. This is one reason pastors and church leaders need to teach on demons from their pulpits. The church should be teaching culture what God's Word has to say about the subject, rather than vice versa.

If you aren't familiar with *The Exorcist*, it's a 1973 film about a twelve-year-old girl named Regan who begins to exhibit strange behavior after playing with an Ouija board. (Note: you should never play with Ouija boards, tarot cards, or anything of that sort.) Regan becomes hyperactive, starts swearing and lying, and begins exhibiting a lack of concentration. It's first thought that these symptoms are stress-related, but then the girl becomes incredibly strong and violent. It's obvious to those around Regan that she is possessed by an invisible force. The movie is dark, graphic, and heavy; it horrified audiences when it first came out. Some people were fainting and throwing up in the theaters.

But more bizarre things transpired. For starters, the movie set for Regan's house burned to the ground during production—yet, for some inexplicable reason, her room was completely untouched. The cast and crew began to believe the set was inhabited by real demons. A priest was regularly brought to the set to bless the actors while filming. Nevertheless, nine people associated with the movie died during or shortly after it was made, including two cast members whose characters died in the movie: Jack McGowran who played Burke Dennings and Vasiliki Maliaros who played Mary Karras.[15] Then, in 1987, years later, Mercedes McCambridge, who was the voice behind the demon in the movie, experienced a horrific tragedy: her own son murdered his wife, then took his own life. These peculiarities made the public wonder about the reality of demon possession. Is it *just* in the movies? Because it seemed that those demons had come to life.

Thankfully, God's Word tells us all we need to know.[16] One particular place where we learn about demon possession is in Luke 8:26–39. Here,

Jesus meets a man who had been exhibiting some bizarre qualities of his own. He didn't wear clothes. He lived in a cemetery. Like Regan, he had superhuman strength and often broke the chains and shackles of his guards. Luke says these symptoms were the result of his being "demon-possessed."

The Greek word for "demon-possessed" here is *daimonistheis*. It means "to be taken over by a hostile spirit" or "to be indwelt by a demon." To capture this meaning, we must first look at one of its cognate words, "demon" or *daimōn*, which was associated with "disruption" and "tearing apart."

According to *The Tablet*, a weekly Catholic review published in London, the Catholic Church receives more than 500,000 requests for exorcism every year. The number is growing and priests attribute it to people dabbling in the occult.

In Greek tragedies, *daimon* was used to describe something, often a supernatural force, that overtook a man and disturbed his life. With this in mind, it is easy to see how *daimon* came to mean a supernatural force that assailed people and caused them calamity. This force later became identified with a personal and intelligent sort of entity, less than a god but more than a man. It was an unpredictable entity, present in unusual places at peculiar times, and at work to negate good and propagate evil. Its presence brought dread and resulted in violence such as fires, famine and pestilence, revenge, mishap, and strange behavior. God's Word forbids any dealings with these entities through any means, including witchcraft, idolatry, and the occult.

If there is anything we can construe from this brief understanding of demons, it is that the cultures of antiquity *and* God's Word recognize that they are real and they can overcome people—in some cases, possessing them.

Hence, possession is when one or more of these entities seizes an individual and takes residence inside of them, as in the case of the man possessed in Luke 8 and in the case of *The Exorcist*. That is what makes the movie so disturbing—there have been people since the beginning of time who were plagued like Regan and it still happens today. The Bible is clear on this.

The good news, and the uplifting part, is that Jesus always cast out the demons and sets people free. This tells us that the highest power of all is the supremacy of the Almighty God. It is His power that has come to dwell in our lives through the Holy Spirit. As members of Christ's family, we have power and authority over these influences. (See Luke 10:19–20.) We never need to fear demons. Demons cannot possess a Christian or harm those who walk in their God-given authority.

Demons are afraid of you because Jesus lives in you. Don't be like those who got spooked watching *The Exorcist*. That behavior is displeasing to the Lord because He has told us not to fear the enemy. Instead, you should shout and rejoice that you are born of God and have overcome the world and everything in it, including demonic power and its desire to possess and destroy. You are divinely protected. That should be a relief.

30

FLEE: *PHEUGŌ* (φεύγω)

Flee from sexual immorality. Every other sin a person commits is outside the body, but the sexually immoral person sins against his own body. (1 Corinthians 6:18)

φεύγετε τὴν πορνείαν. πᾶν ἁμάρτημα ὃ ἐὰν ποιήσῃ ἄνθρωπος ἐκτὸς τοῦ σώματός ἐστιν ὁ δὲ πορνεύων εἰς τὸ ἴδιον σῶμα ἁμαρτάνει. (ΠΡΟΣ ΚΟΡΙΝΘΙΟΥΣ Α 6:18)

In 2000, I had the opportunity to tour a great piece of American history: Alcatraz Federal Penitentiary. For over three hours, my family and I perused what has been the most well-known prison in the United States. Alcatraz, an island in the middle of the chilling waters of San Francisco Bay, served as a federal prison from 1934 to 1963. Some of America's most notorious criminals did time there, men like Al Capone, Robert Franklin Stroud ("the Birdman of Alcatraz"), and George "Machine Gun" Kelly.

It was the prison of prisons. Villains weren't sentenced to Alcatraz; they earned sentencing there when they couldn't follow the rules elsewhere. This was particularly true for inmates who had tried to escape from other institutions. The super-maximum security at Alcatraz made that impossible. Or did it?

In June 1962, "the Great Escape from Alcatraz" was attempted by Frank Lee Morris and the Anglin brothers, John and Clarence. In December 1961, six months beforehand, these three desperados began using makeshift tools to dig through six-by-nine-inch vent holes, working each evening from 5:30 to 9:00 p.m. This would be where they'd make their exit. While one dug, the other played lookout.

Meanwhile, they collected various contraband. Raincoats were used to make a raft and life vests to get them across the bay. Using a mixture of toilet paper, soap, and human hair from the barbershop, they crafted dummy heads to place on their pillows to fool the guards into thinking they were in their cells.

At 9:30 p.m. on June 11 after lights out, the escapees set up the dummies on their beds, climbed up the ventilators, crossed the roof, climbed down fifty feet of plumbing to the ground, and used their raft to get across the chilly bay. Whatever happened to them after that remains a mystery. They were never captured, their bodies were never found…and there have been reported sightings of them up and down the East Coast as well as in South America. They may have made the greatest escape on record.

In 1 Corinthians 6:18, God's Word talks about the great escape that believers must make to get away from sexual sin. Here, Paul was instructing his Corinthian church on how they should behave now that they were holy people of God. This was needful because sexual temptation was prevalent in Corinth. Prostitutes were always available and illicit sexual relations were the norm. It would have been easy for the Corinthians to become captive to the sexual vices surrounding them. Instead, Paul urges them to "flee" from these.

The Greek word "flee" here is *pheugete*. It means "to escape," "to take flight," and "to get away." In Homer's *Iliad*, it was used to describe an escape into the darkness while fleeing guards. In the LXX, the Greek Old

Testament, it was used to describe getting away from snakes, enemies, and other dire threats.

> *The Iliad* is the oldest European poem known to us today. Consisting of 15,693 lines, it recounts some of the significant events during the final weeks of the Trojan War and the Greek siege of the city of Troy.

The main idea behind *pheugō* is slipping away from something and escaping unharmed, sort of like Morris and the Anglins. For the Corinthians, fleeing from the prevalent sexual sin surrounding them was like breaking out of a maximum-security prison. Paul was telling them that they had to make an effort to get away from sexual sin.

Successful escapes don't happen by chance. You need to yearn for them and make a plan. The Corinthians couldn't sit passively and hope they could get through the day without being sexually impure. Rather, they needed to be as determined as Morris and the Anglin brothers. They had to realize that sexual sin was not God's highest and best for their life, and they had to do whatever was needed to escape it.

In today's culture, we find ourselves walled in by sexual temptations of all kinds. We find sex floating around social media, on YouTube, and even on the annoying ads that pop up every four seconds when we are using lite apps. Hence, it's easy to succumb to temptation under the guise that, "Everyone is doing it," or "Well, it's culturally acceptable, so it must be okay." Instead, God's Word is instructing us to make a great escape.

Are you determined to escape this sex-crazed culture and remain pure before God? Do you have a plan? It may be a good idea for your spouse to have the passwords to all of your social media accounts. I'm not joking. Many affairs begin when people start private messaging each other. Sharing passwords will keep you pure. It doesn't mean you don't trust one another, but it *does* mean you know the devil is out there, looking to tempt and divide. Married couples are supposed to help each other stay accountable. If you don't want to do this, ask yourself, *What am I trying to hide?*

You might have a friend serve as an accountability partner, someone to talk to when you go out with the opposite sex. Allow them to ask you everything you did. There's also software that will let someone else know what Internet sites you have visited and your Google searches, to help you stay on the straight and narrow path that avoids sin.

Stop and consider how you *"flee from sexual immorality."* It's an escape we all must make.

31

INTERCEDE:
HYPERENTYNCHANŌ
(ὑπερεντυγχάνω)

Likewise the Spirit helps us in our weakness. For we do not know what to pray for as we ought, but the Spirit himself inter-cedes for us with groanings too deep for words.

(Romans 8:26)

Ὡσαύτως δὲ καὶ τὸ πνεῦμα συναντιλαμβάνεται τῇ ἀσθενείᾳ ἡμῶν· τὸ γὰρ τί προσευξώμεθα καθὸ δεῖ οὐκ οἴδαμεν, ἀλλ' αὐτὸ τὸ πνεῦμα ὑπερεντυγχάνει στεναγμοῖς ἀλαλήτοις. (ΠΡΟΣ ΡΩΜΑΙΟΥΣ 8:26)

I'm not much of a marksman. I've been to the gun range a few times and it's never pretty. Usually, my target ends up with scattered holes all over the place, a clear indication that I'm randomly firing into the wind. Hitting a target takes accuracy and skill, two things I don't have when it comes to using a firearm.

There are notable marksmen out there who can hit targets from astounding distances. One is an anonymous Joint Task Force 2 Canadian sniper who, at the time of this writing, holds the world record for the longest kill shot of all time. In May 2017, this soldier used a McMillan Tac-50 to kill an ISIS militant from 3,781 yards away. That is about the distance of thirty-eight football fields, or 2.14 miles—about as long as the National Mall, from the steps of the Capitol Building to the Lincoln Memorial.

In order for the sniper to make this shot, he had to painstakingly dial in the scope while considering all of the external variables, such as wind speed, distance, terrain, and anything else that could cause the round to veer off course. The distance was so great, he even had to take into account the curvature of the earth. On top of that, this expert marksman had to calm his breathing and ready his mind. Incredibly, the MacMillan Tac-50's manufacturer said its effective firing range was half the distance that the Canadian sniper managed. He really outdid himself.

In Romans 8:26, we encounter marksmanship of a different sort. Here, the apostle Paul tells the Romans that they need prayer that hits a bullseye to deal with their weaknesses. Precision is required to pray the right prayer.

Often, we don't know what to say to God. If a family member has been deathly ill for a long time, you may not be certain what's the appropriate prayer for them now. Or perhaps you are praying for a person who has long persisted in rebellion and is destroying their life, but you are unsure if you should keep praying the way you have. Or maybe you've come face-to-face with something ugly in your soul and you don't know how to be free of it. Praying precisely for these needs might feel like shooting at a faraway target. Instead of taking a random shot in the dark, hoping to strike the bullseye, God has given to us an expert marksman—the Holy Spirit—to help us dial in and line up our prayer. He helps us so that we can pray with accuracy and always hit the mark, no matter the circumstances.

To communicate this to the Romans, Paul tells them that the Holy Spirit "intercedes" for us when we pray. This is a heartening insight about the work of the Spirit. The Greek word for "intercedes" here is *hyperentynchanei*, a two-part word that is made of *hyper* ("over" or "above") and *entynchanō* ("to hit" or "to strike").

Entynchanō described the contact between two things. For example, Herodotus used it to describe the sound a crocodile makes when whacking its prey. Xenophon used it to describe lightning striking a human. The idea is two things meeting and coming together to form a connection.

> Herodotus was a Greek historian born in 484 BC. First-century BC Roman orator Cicero called him "the Father of History" because Herodotus was the first writer who systematically collected his materials and arranged them into a historical narrative.

Later on, *entynchanō* became used to describe "complaining" and "raising an objection." If you think about it, when this occurs, two individuals *are* making contact with one another.

Ultimately, the word became used in a religious sense and meant "intercession," or making contact with God for a request. The point is, when a person intercedes, contact is made with God— like a gun round hitting a bullseye.

We have a tendency to come up short in prayer on our own. Yet God's Word tells us He has that covered. The Holy Spirit does the interceding for us. He prays through us. When He does this, He aims the request perfectly and makes sure that our prayer always gets before the throne of God and hits the mark.

In fact, the Spirit prays so accurately through us and hits the mark so perfectly that Paul adds *hyper* to *entynchanō* and we get the word *hyperentynchanō*. This means "to hit the mark over and above." Like the Canadian sniper, the Holy Spirit really outdoes Himself. He can hit the target under any conditions, in any situation, and from any distance. He is a skilled and perfect marksman when it comes to prayer. He always knows how to pray through us exactly so that the request is heard by God and answered. That's why, when we are going into prayer, we should allow the Holy Spirit to do it for us instead of trying to do it on our own.

You aren't alone in prayer, firing into the wind at random. You have a skilled marksman working for you. As you go into prayer, ask the Holy Spirit to line up your requests and petitions. Wait on Him and allow Him to take over your petition-making.

When you do, the skilled marksman will step up and I am certain you'll be impressed with the results.

32

CUT: *KATANYSSOMAI*
(κατανύσσομαι)

*Now when they heard this they were **cut** to the heart, and said to Peter and the rest of the apostles, "Brothers, what shall we do?"* (Acts 2:37)

Ἀκούσαντες δὲ κατενύγησαν τὴν καρδίαν εἶπόν τε πρὸς τὸν Πέτρον καὶ τοὺς λοιποὺς ἀποστόλους, Τί ποιήσωμεν, ἄνδρες ἀδελφοί. (ΠΡΑΞΕΙΣ ΑΠΟΣΤΟΛΩΝ 2:37)

What's the worst cut you've ever had? Does one come to mind? The fact is, most of us have suffered some kind of gash that made us scream in anguish and bellow in pain. It's one of those crisis moments that puts you into shock because your skin has been torn wide open and now your blood is pouring out. Whether you've driven a knife into your flesh while cutting up veggies, slid your finger across a paper edge too fast, or tangled with a power tool, you probably know the bitter sting of a fresh laceration.

If there is an all-time winner for the world's most horrific gash, it has to be psychology's favorite experiment, Phineas Gage, who survived a severe laceration to his face and brain.

A railroad construction foreman in Vermont, Gage was using a thirteen-pound rod to pack explosive powder into rock so it could be blasted on September 13, 1848. The rod created a spark and ignited the explosives; the blast caused it to shoot through Gage's skull. The rod entered at the cheekbone, went behind his left eye, and exited through the top of his head. It was later found *thirty yards* away with blood and brain matter on it.

Somehow, Gage survived. In fact, he was conscious minutes after the accident, walking around and talking about what had just taken place. If you Google the case, you will discover that this wound far surpassed any sort of injury the vast majority of us have ever had. While we may poke ourselves with a sharp object and scream, this man had a massive metal bar shoot through his skull. It was going so fast that witnesses said they heard it whistle through the air before it landed. Some good did come from poor Gage's terrible injury, however: it helped to advance the study of neuroscience.

In Acts 2:37, we see a major cut of the spiritual kind. Here, the apostle Peter is preaching on the day of Pentecost, right after the outpouring of the Holy Spirit. He is explaining the significance of what has taken place and points to how it testifies that Jesus is Lord and Messiah. Peter's sermon had a tremendous impact on his listeners. After he finished, they wanted to know how to be saved. The sermon had convicted them.

To describe this conviction, Luke, who wrote the Acts, says those present "*were cut to the heart.*" The Greek word for "cut" here is *katenygēsan*. It's a two-part Greek word that comes from *kata* ("against" or "through") and *nyssō* ("to nudge" or "to poke").

Before we can understand the full thrust of *katanyssomai*, we should know that *nyssō* by-and-large referred to an ordinary jab. It is used in Acts 12:7 to describe how the angel pokes Peter on the side to wake him up. It was used in antiquity to describe someone nudging another with a dagger to determine if they were alive, or the way a horse's hooves dent the ground when it walks. It's a prod, a prick, or a dent—nothing too intense.

However, with the addition of *kata*, *nyssō* forms *katanyssomai*. This means "to poke totally through," "to stab all the way in," and even "to gouge." It can have the nuance of "a brutal cut" or "making a forceful hole."

Rather than a small poke to the skin, this is more like a thirteen-pound bar shooting through your head, a Phineas Gage cut that God's Word made in the hearts of Peter's listeners. God's Word, under the anointing of the Holy Spirit, penetrated right through the inner being of three thousand individuals. It sliced past every exterior layer, tore past whatever notions they previously held, and struck them deep within their souls. They all came under heavy conviction, desperate to be saved—and they were. God's Word has tremendous cutting power.

> The Nyssanthes is a genus of flowering perennial shrub that grows wild in eastern Australia. The flowers have thorny spikes; the name comes from *nyssō* ("to poke") and *anthos* ("flower").

Often, we get led into thinking that we receive Christ and share Him through our own abilities. But that isn't the case. God's Word contains the gouging power.

When we minister and preach to others, our confidence should be in God's Word. It is enough, on its own, to tear a deep hole into the hearts of those who hear it. Therefore, our focus should be on preaching the Word above *everything* else.

No matter who you are ministering to, remember that God's Word can drive a hole into their hearts. Don't let their philosophies, present sins, or even their opinions of Christianity intimidate you. Instead, you stand firm preaching God's Word, remembering that if it can whistle through the air and penetrate the hearts of three thousand men on the day of Pentecost, surely it can do the same for the person sitting or standing in front of you. Be faithful to deliver what the Holy Spirit tells you to deliver and just sit back and watch the Word of God do all the cutting. You'll be in awe of what it can pierce.

33

MEN WHO PRACTICE HOMOSEXUALITY: *MALAKOS/ARSENOKOITĒS* (μαλακός/ἀρσενοκοίτης)

Or do you not know that the unrighteous will not inherit the kingdom of God? Do not be deceived: neither the sexually immoral, nor idolaters, nor adulterers, nor men who practice homosexuality, nor thieves, nor the greedy, nor drunkards, nor revilers, nor swindlers will inherit the kingdom of God.

(1 Corinthians 6:9–10)

ἢ οὐκ οἴδατε ὅτι ἄδικοι θεοῦ βασιλείαν οὐ κληρονομήσουσιν; μὴ πλανᾶσθε· οὔτε πόρνοι οὔτε εἰδωλολάτραι οὔτε μοιχοὶ οὔτε μαλακοὶ οὔτε ἀρσενοκοῖται οὔτε κλέπται οὔτε πλεονέκται, οὐ μέθυσοι, οὐ λοίδοροι, οὐχ ἅρπαγες βασιλείαν θεοῦ κληρονομήσουσιν.

(ΠΡΟΣ ΚΟΡΙΝΘΙΟΥΣ Α 6:9–10)

'm often asked, "Is homosexuality a sin?" When taking questions on Instagram, it never fails that someone will inquire about this. It's an important question and it's the right question to ask in order to begin a conversation about our approach, as Christians, to the contemporary issues surrounding homosexuality.

In 2013, an article appeared in *USA Today* headlined, "Survey: Big Drop in Those Who Say Being Gay's a Sin." It quoted *LifeWay Research* from 2011, which indicated that 43 percent of people say homosexuality is not a sin. In 2012, that number went up to 45 percent. These statistics pointed toward a shifting acceptance of homosexuality, which eventually led to the 5-4 Supreme Court decision legalizing gay marriage on June 26, 2015.

This shift in societal acceptance of homosexuality was spearheaded by political and corporate forces, celebrities, liberal universities, and even evangelicals (mostly Millennials) who have become more tolerant and accepting of homosexual lifestyles than in previous decades. Today, many schools are teaching that homosexuality and transgender life choices are acceptable. Additionally, there are those sitting next to us in our churches—who lift their hands in worship to God—who support this view.

But what does the Bible say about homosexuality? And what does it say in the original language? Let's put aside all of our notions about homosexuality and examine the text so that *it* can guide us into what we think.

One of the best places to begin inquiring about homosexuality is 1 Corinthians 6:9–10. The apostle Paul, in writing to the Corinthian church, was listing behavior that was displeasing to the Lord. Paul was pointing out that our faith in Christ should cause us to reject the things on this list in order to live a lifestyle that reflected God's created order. The fourth thing on this list of vices is *"men who practice homosexuality."* Two *separate* Greek words are used to construct this concept: *malakoi* and *arsenokoitai*. Translating these words as "men who practice homosexuality" captures the idea; however, a separate examination of each word will enhance the picture of what is being said.

Homer's *Odyssey* inspired other great literary works such as *Inferno* by Dante, *Don Quixote* by Miguel de Cervantes, *The Wonderful Wizard of Oz* by L. Frank Baum, and *Ulysses* by James Joyce.

Malakoi means "soft," "tender," and "delicate." In Homer's *Odyssey*, it is used to describe soft bedding, or a plush, grassy meadow. In other places in antiquity, it was used to describe clothing that was delicate. In using this word to describe a person's sexual behavior, it suggested docility and submissiveness. Hence, it was used to describe the effeminate, *passive partner* who was penetrated in a homosexual relationship. This was considered, even among pagan culture, to be reprehensible. From the classical period of Greek culture and up to the time of Philo, the role of a passive male—often enhanced by cosmetics—was frowned on and considered repugnant. (See Philo *De Specialibus Legibus* 3.37.)

The next word used to describe homosexuality, *arsenokoitai*, is a two-part Greek word that comes from *arsēn* ("male") and *keimai* ("to lie down"). It means "a male who lies down with another male," "sodomite." This word is used specifically to mean the *dominant partner* in a homosexual relationship—the role of the one penetrating. In Paul's day, it was common for heterosexual men, including husbands, to engage in homosexual behavior under the impression that they were still masculine as long as they were not playing the passive role. But Paul was saying that, within God's order, the dominant role, too, was unacceptable.

By mentioning both the passive and dominant roles within homosexual relationships, the apostle was clearly communicating that *all forms* of homosexuality were displeasing to the Lord and forbidden. Paul's position doesn't seem to be based on his own cultural ideas, but rather on the basis of his understanding of creation—that in the beginning, God created humans male and female and it was within God's holy order for sexual expressions to be between man and woman. (See Genesis 1–3; Mark 10:6–8.) This sexual ethic is found within Leviticus 18:22 and 20:13, and Paul sticks with it as the basis for Christian sexual behavior.

Hence, to answer the question at the beginning of this study, a homosexual relationship, whether between two men or two women, is a sin, just as much as adultery, idolatry, greed, and the other vices Paul mentioned.

Our faith in Christ should cause us to reject homosexuality as an acceptable way to practice our sexuality, not to welcome it as adequate.

It's true that countless people who identify as gay, lesbian, or transgender are talented, kind, and loyal people. Long-standing homosexual relationships can even seem like heterosexual relationships. Yet this doesn't change the fact that homosexual behavior is a distortion of God's created order and it remains a sin.

Our response as Christians should *not* be to demonize or mistreat those involved in homosexuality. God loves all people, so we should treat homosexuals with love and respect. At the same time, we must stand firm that it is an unacceptable behavior and cannot become a part of our values, practices, traditions, and education. We must be firm and not compromise the truth just for the sake of being nice and *tolerant*.

If you know someone who practices homosexuality, pray for them and treat them with love. But on the other hand, make sure you keep in mind how God feels about homosexuality when you are determining your stances on the issues that surround it. What God says is far more important than what the culture says. After all, no matter how the culture spins it, God says it's wrong. And so should we.

Finally, if you are someone who has been or is currently practicing homosexuality, God loves you and He wants to help deliver you. It's encouraging to note that in the next verse (1 Corinthians 9:11), the apostle Paul notes that some of the Christians in Corinth had, in the past, practiced homosexuality. Yet, God forgave them and set them free because they had acknowledged it was wrong and repented. If you recognize that homosexuality is wrong and repent of it, God will forgive you and give you a better life.

34

ANXIOUS: *MERIMNAŌ* (μεριμνάω)

Do not be anxious about anything, but in everything by prayer and supplication with thanksgiving let your requests be made known to God. (Philippians 4:6)

μηδὲν μεριμνᾶτε, ἀλλ᾽ ἐν παντὶ τῇ προσευχῇ καὶ τῇ δεήσει μετὰ εὐχαριστίας τὰ αἰτήματα ὑμῶν γνωριζέσθω πρὸς τὸν θεόν. (ΠΡΟΣ ΦΙΛΙΠΠΗΣΙΟΥΣ 4:6)

Bloodhounds have often been called "a nose with a dog attached." Gentle and affectionate, bloodhounds are known for endless zeal to follow their snout. This lovable breed is preoccupied by smells, going in this direction or that, wherever its nose leads it.

They belong to family of dogs known as the *Sagaces*. This is a Latin word with the same root as the word *sagacious*, which means "acute discernment" and "sharp judgment." This is a reference to the bloodhound's inherent ability to discover things by sniffing around. If you have ever been on a trail with a bloodhound or taken a walk with one, you understand.

Police officers have long made good use of the bloodhound's olfactory persistence in criminal investigations. The breed's natural abilities often lead to important evidence and help police arrest dangerous criminals.

Perhaps the most famous dog detective was a Kentucky bloodhound named Nick Carter. He was so good at following trails and man-hunting that crowds came to watch as he tracked for police in the early 1900s. He once pursued a scent for fifty-five miles. In one famous case, Nick followed a mile-long trail to help police catch an arsonist more than four days after the crime. During his tenure, Nick found over 650 pieces of evidence and helped to send 126 criminals to jail. He serves as a prime example of the bloodhound's tenacity.

In Philippians 4:6, Paul speaks of bloodhound-like behavior, but not in a positive way. Here, the apostle is instructing the church in Philippi about their spiritual formation. The believers there had become intensely concerned with the troubles of life. For one, they were anxious for Paul because he was in prison. (See Philippians 1:7.) Epaphroditus, from the church in Philippi, had gone to care for Paul, but fell ill, and the Philippians were worried about him, too. (See Philippians 2:26.) Finally, the Philippians had heard rumors of persecution and this added to their intense stress. (See Philippians 1:29–30.)

Paul was writing to encourage them and give them useful instruction to pray through their issues. He tells them, *"Do not be anxious about anything."*

The Greek word here for "anxious" is *merimnate*. It means "to be occupied" and "to be enormously concerned." In essence, it means "to be engaged in something with extreme care." It implies a fixed concentration on something to the point of stalking it.

Aeschylus was among the first Greek tragedians, who wrote serious drama involving disastrous events. He is said to have introduced more elaborate costumes for his productions. Legend has it that Aeschylus died when a flying eagle dropped a tortoise on his head.

With this in mind, it makes sense that Aeschylus, in *The Eumenides*, a fifth century BC play, uses it to describe the dog who follows its prey with focus and intent, never giving up the trail—like Nick Carter. When used in relation to the troubles of life, *merimnaō* gives us the idea of hounding after worries and endlessly sniffing out our anxieties. Can you relate? When you are worried about something, do you jump on it like a bloodhound after a fresh scent?

The Philippians were doing just that. Their imaginations kept leading them along trails of anxiety and dread. They were worried that Paul would never get out of prison. They probably thought Epaphroditus was going to die. And they likely imagined losing their own heads or, at least, winding up in jail. It distracted them so much that they could not pray effectively and approach the Lord with confidence. Paul was telling them to get off the dirt path of worry and get onto the thoroughfare of faith in God.

What trail are you hounding after today? Are you so concerned about a financial need that it's making you sick? Is there a relationship that has led you off course with all sorts of *what ifs*? Perhaps you doubt yourself and can't seem to stop stewing about it. The fact is, pursuing these worries will get you nowhere but lost.

Instead, God wants us to place our attention and focus onto Him. Doing this will lead us away from the trails that waste our time and put us on the path to productive, fruitful places. There's no better way to do this than through prayer.

When you approach the Lord and tell Him your concerns, you are surrendering the temptation to track down your own troubles. You are inviting Him to do that for you. This approach will fix your focus on the right things—and keep you in peace.

Next time you are tempted to worry, remind yourself that you are not a bloodhound. There's no need to track the trail of your anxieties. You have a better route to follow—the trail God has set before you. (See Psalm 23:3.)

35

IT IS FINISHED: *TETELESTAI* (τετέλεσται)

When Jesus had received the sour wine, he said, "It is finished,"
and he bowed his head and gave up his spirit. (John 19:30)

ὅτε οὖν ἔλαβεν τὸ ὄξος [ὁ] Ἰησοῦς εἶπεν, Τετέλεσται, καὶ
κλίνας τὴν κεφαλὴν παρέδωκεν τὸ πνεῦμα.
(ΚΑΤΑ ΙΩΑΝΝΗΝ 19:30)

When I was a young boy, I'd race to the mailbox just to see if something with my name on it had arrived. And every now and then, something did. Oh, how neat it was to think that someone had mailed something to me! It gave me a taste of identity and individuality. But one afternoon, my mother gave me a dose of reality, "When you get older and start having to pay bills, you won't enjoy going to the mailbox as much."

Decades later, I can attest to the fact that Mom was right. Now, when I open the mailbox, I cheer when there's nothing there. Who wants to get a bill? Forget identity and individuality—I'd be happier if bill collectors forgot all about me.

Nothing is worse than a bill that's sent late—you know the kind, where some creditor has taken their sweet time to invoice you and a request for payment comes a year later. What a hassle. In my state, a vendor has *six years* to send an invoice. That's more than half a decade. So, if you haven't seen a bill, don't think you are out of the woods. It's likely coming, rest assured.

I've had this happen to me. Once, a vendor that I really liked was doing bookkeeping services for our ministry. We had a great relationship and they always did good work. One day, I got a random call from them. I could tell they were a bit nervous. Apparently, they *just* noticed that they hadn't invoiced me in three years. They had a *discounted* invoice on their desk for nearly $14,000. To me, that's a lot of money. Do you know what else I could do with 14 grand?

I knew I had to fork over the money. It was the right thing to do. But I let the bill sit on my desk for as long as I could, hoping it would go away. It never did. That bill stared me in the face every single day. And those days turned into weeks and those weeks grew into months. And I became more and more distraught about it. I began dreading working at my desk and often put other paperwork on top of the bill to hide it from my view.

Finally, I admitted to myself that I couldn't live like that anymore. I had to act. One random day, near their deadline, I mustered up some courage. I grabbed my checkbook out of the drawer, wrote the payment as fast as I could, and drove it down to their office before I could talk myself out of it. When I handed it to the clerk, something happened that I didn't expect: peace.

Peace filled my soul as a weight lifted off my chest. I could breathe again. Then, she handed me another invoice stamped *paid in full* in giant, red block letters. It was my receipt. It served as proof that this debt had been paid. I'd never owe it again. When I got home, I placed the receipt exactly where that bill had been and left it there for a few days. It felt good seeing that *paid in full*. It reminded me that I was free.

One Texas couple was freed from a $236,026 bill for unpaid tolls, parking tickets, and fines when a legal team at a TV station came to their rescue. The pair sold a 1993 Honda Civic, but forgot to remove the license plate. The state kept billing the only owners they had on file.

In John 19:30, we find a very interesting Greek word that refers to paying off debt: *tetelestai*. Translated here, *"It is finished."* According to John, this was Jesus's last word before He died while hanging on the cross. He recorded this as Christ's last word to highlight its tremendous significance.[17] *Tetelestai* means "it is completed, it is accomplished, it is fulfilled, it is brought to an end." It carries the idea that a final step has been taken. Therefore, *tetelestai* was often used on receipts in times of antiquity. It would literally mean "this is paid," "the final payment was given," or "the billing has ended."

Tetelestai is in a tense[18] that describes a completed event, the results of which carry on into the future. A debtor would be relieved to see the word *tetelestai*. It was no different than seeing *paid in full* stamped in big, red block letters. It was proof that the payment process was complete and from here on out, they would never receive that bill again. Their liberty, from that point forward, was guaranteed. They would have felt as I did when I paid off my bookkeeping bill.

The use of *tetelestai* in John 19:30 is telling us that when Jesus hung upon the cross and died, He was paying off the largest debt the world has ever known: the debt caused by sin. God's Word tells us that the only way the debt of sin could be paid off is through the shedding of blood. (See Leviticus 17:11; Hebrews 9:22.) Up until Christ, God's people used sacrificial offerings to account for their sins. (See Hebrews 10:4.) But no amount of sacrificial offering could ever pay off the debt because it required a willing, perfectly sinless being. Christ was just that: 100 percent God, 100 percent man, perfect in all of His ways—and willing to pay off the debt.

When Jesus cried, "*Tetelestai*," He was announcing that the price for mankind to be reconciled to God had been *paid in full.* It was a receipt saying that the last installment needed for mankind to have peace with God had been made. Now, the world is free from ever having to pay the debt again. We can move forward and enjoy the ongoing benefits of being reconciled to our Creator, without feeling enslaved.

It's important for us to remember this word *tetelestai*, especially when the enemy comes to us and brings up our past. We've all sinned (see Romans 3:23) and we've all done things that we are ashamed of that hurt ourselves or others. We sense that we should do something to make up for what we've done and this makes us feel hopeless.

The good news is, God never asked us to pay the price or assume the debt. All He has asked us to do is to believe on Christ and trust that He took our sins upon Himself when He died on the cross. The next time you are feeling low, remember that the debt is paid in full and thank the Lord for that.

36

SOBER-MINDED: *NĒPHŌ*
(νήφω)

The end of all things is at hand; therefore be self-controlled and sober-minded for the sake of your prayers.   (1 Peter 4:7)

Πάντων δὲ τὸ τέλος ἤγγικεν. σωφρονήσατε οὖν καὶ νήψατε εἰς προσευχάς.   (ΠΕΤΡΟΥ Α 4:7)

I t seems like the world can't get enough when it comes to essential oils. It was a $6.63 *billion* industry globally in 2016 and sales keep booming. Connoisseurs will tell you that essential oils do everything from boosting your immune system and improving your blood flow to making you feel more cheerful and many other effects. Around the world, the greatest demand is for orange essential oil, but mint, jasmine, rose, lavender, spearmint, and basil are also popular. I don't really have an essential oil collection, but I have been given a bottle from time to time and I must say, they aren't bad.

The important thing to remember when dealing with essential oils is that they are, essentially, oils. Oils are concentrates. If we think back to science class, we remember that a concentrate is anything that has had its base component removed, like water. That means they are highly potent. A drop of a concentrate goes a *long* way. I learned this the *hard* way.

I'm an extremist. This means I'm probably not a good candidate to possess essential oils. My default thinking always tells me *the more, the merrier. Less is never more. More is more.* Nevertheless, a sweet lady at my church gave me a bottle of spearmint essential oil one day as a gift. I looked at it and said, "Gee, thanks. What am I to do with this?" She laughed and said, "Oh, pastor. You are so funny. Just put a single drop in a glass of water. It will taste great." She took the glass of water from my pulpit and showed me. She was right. Top-notch stuff right there.

Later on, I put the bottle in my car and forgot about it. One day while I was driving, I heard it rolling around in my console and pulled it out. I wanted to taste again it. I didn't have any water to put it in, but I thought, *Well, I know it's safe. I guess I'll just pour some on my tongue. Should be fine.*

Bad move. I can still taste it, four years later. I quickly pulled into the first place selling beverages that I could find to buy a drink to stop the spearmint oil from holding the rest of my life hostage. I couldn't process a thought or think straight until I had hosed out my mouth. Highly potent stuff right there, folks.

God's Word warns us about the dangers of highly potent things. Not essential oils, of course, but rather the things in our society and culture that have the potential to contaminate the way we think and behave. You know—like news, politics, opinions about presidential candidates, or current events, especially sensitive ones that stay in the headlines for weeks. While we need to be informed, we can't let these things make us mad or irrational or send us off the deep end. We see this in 1 Peter 4:7: *"The end of all things is at hand; therefore be self-controlled and sober-minded for the sake of your prayers."*

Peter is telling us that the return of Jesus is approaching. Christ can come and set up his millennial kingdom *at any time*. Until it happens, it's essential for us to continue praying for it in the face of events that are disquieting and cause our emotions to stir. That's why Peter commands us to be "sober-minded." Here the Greek word for "sober-minded" is *nēpsate* and comes from the word *nēphō*, which meant "well-balanced" and "self-controlled."

> In the U.S., anyone who has a blood alcohol content (BAC) level of 0.08 percent or higher is considered legally intoxicated. However, drivers who've been drinking can still be convicted of driving under the influence (DUI) if their BAC is below 0.08 percent.

In ancient Greco-Roman culture, *nēphō* was a word often used to describe diluted wine that was less potent and intoxicating, like essential oils reduced of their potency when mixed with water. When used in connection with people, *nēphō* referred to those who were not intoxicated with wine's seductive power. They were wary, sharp thinkers who reasoned things through fairly. Their conclusions weren't wobbly or off-base. When Peter spoke of being sober-minded, he was describing someone whose thinking was not drunk with the madness of culture. This is because they have God's Word in their life to dilute potent opinions and inebriating emotions.

It's interesting that Peter connects being sober-minded to prayer. He was saying that if we want our prayers for the kingdom to be effective, we need to see events the way God sees them. We should come to reasonable conclusions about them instead of going crazy, starting an argument at a family picnic, or pushing a conspiracy theory. Getting all worked up about something to the point where we lose our peace of mind and composure doesn't impress God or move Him to act on our behalf. It's certainly not the way to approach God's throne and pray.

In order to be sober-minded, we need to make sure that God's Word is consistently being added to what we see and hear. Don't allow any news into your life that doesn't first get diluted by the Word of God. You don't want to be like one of those people who has their favorite network on all day long but never stops to read the Bible. Individuals like that often end up so radical and off-center, that nobody will listens to them—and that's the least of their problems.

So, mix your media intake with the Word. When you do this, you will be sure to find the proper balance in your thinking. You'll be sober-minded, have a much greater outlook on where the world is in God's plan, find your prayers have a greater impact, and be a source of wisdom for those who are seeking answers in light of the times.

37

PHILIP: *PHILIPPOS*
(Φίλιππος)

Now among those who went up to worship at the feast were
some Greeks. So these came to Philip, who was from Bethsaida
in Galilee, and asked him, "Sir, we wish to see Jesus."

(John 12:20–21)

Ἦσαν δὲ Ἕλληνές τινες ἐκ τῶν ἀναβαινόντων ἵνα
προσκυνήσωσιν ἐν τῇ ἑορτῇ οὗτοι οὖν προσῆλθον
Φιλίππῳ τῷ ἀπὸ Βηθσαϊδὰ τῆς Γαλιλαίας καὶ ἠρώτων
αὐτὸν λέγοντες, Κύριε, θέλομεν τὸν Ἰησοῦν ἰδεῖν.

(ΚΑΤΑ ΙΩΑΝΝΗΝ 12:20–21)

What does your name mean? Have you ever taken the time to look
it up? Names carry meaning and, in biblical times, picking out a

name was extremely important. Destiny was often behind a child's name. Therefore, God's Word portrays parents being very careful to choose a name to suit the purpose of their child's life. (See Exodus 2:10; 1 Samuel 1:20; Matthew 1:21; Luke 1:13.) Believe it or not, God uses our names.

Take my name, *Christopher*, which my parents chose for me on June 2, 1984. It just so happens to have a Greek origin. It comes from two Greek words: *Christos* meaning "Christ" and *pherō* meaning "I carry." Together, it means "I carry Christ," and describes someone who represents Jesus Christ everywhere they go. At first, it was a simple designation for someone who proclaimed the gospel—a title like *athlete* or *lawyer*. Eventually, it became a proper name. It's funny how my parents had no idea I would be an international missionary, pastor, and teacher of God's Word, including biblical Greek, and yet they chose this name for me. One thing is certain: God has used my name for what it represents. God is into names and He takes advantage of them when He sees the chance.

Perhaps there is no greater example of this than in John 12. By this time, Jesus had already raised Lazarus from the dead and was making His triumphal entry into Jerusalem on a donkey. As He rode, Jesus was accompanied by those who had witnessed Lazarus's resurrection. (See John 12:17.) These witnesses spread the word of this mighty miracle all over town and, soon, a massive crowd surrounded the Lord. The number of people continued to swell. It was a diverse crowd, not just Jews. The Pharisees had noted that "the world" had begun to follow Him. (See John 12:19.) People of many different ethnic backgrounds had come to meet Jesus.

The crowd included some Greeks and John makes it a specific point to mention them (verse 20). Why? Because the Greeks represented the great harvest of Gentiles who would receive eternal life after Christ's death. The church would include both Jews and Gentiles. (See John 12:23–26.)

If you were one of the Greeks trying to meet Jesus at this time, you might have felt a bit intimidated. After all, you'd be at a Jewish religious celebration in Jerusalem, the largest Jewish city, surrounded by Jewish pilgrims and religious leaders, all trying to meet the most popular Jewish rabbi of the time. Have you ever been the minority at another culture's celebration? It's easy to feel out of place, like you don't belong.

In a situation like this, it's good to know someone who can make you feel comfortable and welcome. Since the Greeks wanted to meet Jesus, they needed a connection, someone to help them pull a string, to get a meeting with Him. And God's Word tells us that person was Philip.

> *Philippos* is made up of two Greek words: *philos* meaning "love" and *hippos* meaning "horse." It means "someone who loves or is fond of horses."

Although Philip was a Jew, his name happened to be Greek: *Philippos*. There were several Macedonian kings named *Philippos*, including Philip II, the father of Alexander the Great. Philip II expanded the Greek Empire and spread Hellenic culture all over the world, even before his son came on the scene. As a result, *Philippos* was a well-respected Greek name that embodied their culture.

Because of this, the Greeks would have felt very comfortable approaching Philip. After all, they had something in common that they could bond over. They probably imagined that Philip would be warm toward them and possibly show them favor, giving them special access to the Lord. And that's exactly what Philip did. He ran and told Andrew, the only other disciple with a Greek name (*Andreas*). Together, they told Jesus that the Greeks would like to meet with Him.

This was a prophetic moment that pointed to the coming together of Jew and Gentile under the lordship of Christ. What a singular moment and sign to those who were watching! And God used Philip's name. Don't think the Lord didn't know what He was doing when He selected His disciples. God stacked the deck with everything needed, down to every last detail. This means everything in your life is important, even *your* name.

Don't take any detail of your life for granted. Stop and consider what seemingly insignificant thing God may use in your life to cause His will to come to pass. Often, we think we need God to give us *more* in order for Him to accomplish His purpose for our lives, but we may be overlooking something we already have that He plans to use. I certainly don't think Philip had any idea that God would use something as simple as his name to bring about this great prophetic event. And I certainly never expected my name to be the blueprint to my life's work and call. Who knows—there may be something behind your name that God will use for His kingdom. And if that isn't quite the case, I'm certain there is something else in your life that God plans to use.

38

SNARE: *PAGIS* (παγίς)

Moreover, he must be well thought of by outsiders, so that he may not fall into disgrace, into a snare of the devil.

(1 Timothy 3:7)

δεῖ δὲ καὶ μαρτυρίαν καλὴν ἔχειν ἀπὸ τῶν ἔξωθεν, ἵνα μὴ εἰς ὀνειδισμὸν ἐμπέσῃ καὶ παγίδα τοῦ διαβόλου.

(ΠΡΟΣ ΤΙΜΟΘΕΟΝ Α 3:7)

The first time I saw an orchid mantis, I had no idea I was looking at an insect. It looks like a flower. Go ahead—stop reading for a second and Google one. You'll see what I'm talking about. It makes sense why it's often called "the walking flower mantis."

As beautiful as the orchid mantis is, it's a deadly predator. And smart. Somehow, it knows it looks like a flower and takes advantage of this to fool its prey. Entomologists have discovered that the orchid mantis examines different plants until it finds one with flowers. Then it sets up camp and uses a swaying motion to draw the curiosity of smaller bugs, such as flies. When the mantis is pleased with its prey, it seizes it without mercy and devours it.

This swaying motion is extremely effective because it's actually mimicking the flower itself. The orchid mantis has a really good gig going on. In fact, it attracts more insects than the flower it's pretending to be. Needless to say, flies don't stand a chance if they fall into the snare of an intelligent, beautiful, bloodthirsty orchid mantis.

While we're too big to worry about falling into this lovely insect's trap, we do have a nasty foe smacking his lips as he tries to trick us. First Timothy 3:7 tells us that the devil is out there, setting his own traps. Here, Paul is writing to his young understudy, Timothy, and is explaining that the devil has a particular interest in hunting pastors. That's right. Satan's favorite prey are those who are in the ministry, representing the gospel of Jesus Christ. When Satan takes out a pastor or church leader, it causes a ripple effect of problems: churches split, people walk away from God, and the world accuses Christians of being hypocrites. Sometimes, one pastor who sins makes other pastors think they can get away with it, too.

Have you ever been part of a church or ministry when the leader fails? It's always a shock. Here they are, powerful men and women of God, laying hands on the sick, casting out devils, doing outreaches for the poor, building up the community, and bringing restoration to families…and suddenly, a scandal. Your first thought is, *How did this happen?* It was the devil acting like a ravenous orchid mantis, laying his snares to catch another prey.

The Greek word for "snare" here is *pagida*. In antiquity, it described the nets, traps, and pits that were used to trap innocent animals. Because of this, the word took on a sinister sense and became associated with ruin and destruction. In fact, *pagis* was used in ancient Hellenistic literature to describe the Trojan Horse. You remember the story: the Greeks built a massive wooden horse and the Trojans thought it made quite a trophy, so they brought it into their city. Later, the Greek soldiers hiding inside the horse crept out and opened the city gates for the invading Greek army. Paul was telling Timothy that Satan has a tricky, deceitful Trojan Horse up his sleeve for everyone preaching the gospel.

> The Trojan Horse is first mentioned in Homer's *Odyssey* and is discussed at length in Virgil's *Aeneid*. Virgil coined a phrase that we still use today: "Be wary of Greeks bearing gifts."

Pagis has another interesting connection to antiquity. Among the Babylonians, Persians, Sumerians, and Greeks, it was thought that demons carried around traps and nets for the purpose of catching their victims. The devil described in the New Testament is no exception. He and his minions are equipped with all sorts of devious devices that seek to capture and impede. We cannot take the devil for granted. When everything is going well and we are living on cloud nine, Satan will do what he can to snag you in a ruse. Be careful.

The appropriate response, of course, is not to be fearful or go around looking for Satan under every rock. Instead, we must live our lives humbly and full of the power of the Holy Spirit. Each day, we must decide not to be self-centered and live with our own selves in mind, or be dependent upon our own strength and wisdom. If we do, we are bound to be caught. Rather, our strength and wisdom must come from the Spirit of God, the one who will give us discernment that keeps us from being caught. With the Holy Spirit's eyes, we will notice the masquerading of Satan and see what's behind what he is pretending to be.

Has someone entered your life who is tempting you? Is there a situation that looks too good to be true? Perhaps you are being led by pride into making a decision that won't be good in the long run. Stop what you are doing right now. Pause. Hit the brakes. Let the peace of the Holy Spirit arrest your decision-making. Now ask, "Holy Spirit, show me what is *actually* going on? Is this from you or is this a *trap*?" If you are quiet, I am sure He will show you. And if it's a trap, He will give you a way around it.

39

PUT TO DEATH: *NEKROŌ* (νεκρόω)

Put to death therefore what is earthly in you: sexual immorality, impurity, passion, evil desire, and covetousness, which is idolatry. (Colossians 3:5)

Νεκρώσατε οὖν τὰ μέλη τὰ ἐπὶ τῆς γῆς, πορνείαν ἀκαθαρσίαν πάθος ἐπιθυμίαν κακήν, καὶ τὴν πλεονεξίαν, ἥτις ἐστὶν εἰδωλολατρία. (ΠΡΟΣ ΚΟΛΟΣΣΑΕΙΣ 3:5)

Muscle atrophy occurs when muscles waste away. They literally shrivel up and deteriorate. I experienced muscle atrophy for a brief period of time when I was in my early twenties. I had been struggling with severe, sharp pain in my left shoulder for several weeks. I was taking pain killers to manage the intense discomfort, but it was becoming impossible to lift anything with my left arm. I grew especially concerned one afternoon when I couldn't lift a ten-pound backpack. Something was wrong.

One morning, I looked in the mirror after getting out of the shower and I noticed that my left shoulder had caved in. It was curved inward, like a cereal bowl. It was time to get my stubborn self to the doctor.

A specialist diagnosed my condition. He said, "Chris, you should have come and seen me sooner. Your muscle is deteriorating because you haven't been using it. It's slowly withering away because it is not being exercised at all." We soon found out that this was the result of a pinched nerve caused by my athletic experiences in high school. The specialist performed a surgery, moved the nerve, and sewed me up; my left arm was quickly back up and running. The dent filled out and my shoulder is no longer bowl-shaped. The old saying proved true: *If you don't use it, you lose it.* You can also say: *If you don't use you, you will atrophy into nothing.*

God's Word mentions atrophy in Colossians 3:5. In fact, Paul tells us that undergoing a sort of *atrophy* is one of the keys to successful Christian living. To understand, we need to know a little bit about the Colossian church. They were fairly new Christians living in Asia Minor, still learning what it meant to follow Christ. Before they had converted to Christ, they lived as pagans. Paul mentions their pagan past several times in this letter. (See Colossians 1:12–13; 2:13; 3:7.) As pagans, they followed the practices of Greco-Roman gods and mystery cults. The rites within these practices were highly lascivious and obscene. Now that they had come to Christ, Paul was explaining to them that they could no longer practice these acts and other acts of the flesh. Following Jesus meant adopting a new standard of ethics and morality. The old set of practices, then, would have to be "put to death." Paul states this emphatically in Colossians 3:5: *"Put to death therefore what is earthly in you: sexual immorality, impurity, passion, evil desire, and covetousness, which is idolatry."*

A "necropolis" is another word for a cemetery, particularly a large one in an ancient city. It comes from the Greek words *nekros* ("dead") and *polis* ("city"). Hence, it means "a city for the dead."

The Greek word here for "put to death" is *nekrōsate*. It means, "to deaden," "to mortify," "to kill," or "to cause to cease completely." Interestingly enough, in antiquity, this word was used by doctors when they were describing muscle atrophy. Due to lack of use or neglect, for whatever reason, the patient's muscle would get weaker and weaker until there was nothing left. It would die and the patient would no longer be able to utilize it.

Paul made a comparison to the Christian life. We are all converts from something; we all have past lives of sin. When we come into Christ, we need to forfeit whatever that past life included. For some, like the Colossians, it is various sensual vices. For others, it may be anger, violence, revenge, racism, theft, lying, deception, manipulation, or other issues. Whatever it is, we need to make sure that it atrophies, that it's put to death.

How do you *put to death* a former way of thinking, behaving, or feeling? You *neglect* it until it dies. Whatever you feed will grow and whatever you starve dies. So consider this the next time you are in a situation where you have the risk of repeating something that your former life of sin included.

Let's use a simple situation that happens to *all of us* in everyday life: text messaging. Most of us will admit to lambasting someone through text messages. The offender did something to enrage us and we react by smashing the buttons on our keyboard in a *serves them right* attitude of revenge. But is that really fruitful? Maybe you felt a little better the moment you sent it, but were you better for it in the long run? This would have been a good place to neglect the old practice of anger and revenge. I can guarantee you that if you neglect a vice once, it will be a little easier to do it again… and again…and again. Soon, bombing your enemies with text messages is no longer part of your M.O. That's what growing in Christ looks like.

Are there areas in your life that you need to let die? Do jealousy and competition need to dissolve into nothingness? Get off social media for a while. Are you talking negatively about everyone and everything? Zip it. Maybe you need to remove yourself from the crowd of people who let you talk negatively. Whatever the situation is, you can change it through a little neglect. Think of any behavior that is keeping you from drawing closer to Jesus and decide to neglect it. The more it weakens, the more your relationship with the Lord will strengthen.

40

BLASPHEME: *BLASPHĒMEŌ* (βλασφημέω)

Among whom are Hymenaeus and Alexander, whom I have handed over to Satan that they may learn not to blaspheme.

(1 Timothy 1:20)

ὧν ἐστιν Ὑμέναιος καὶ Ἀλέξανδρος, οὓς παρέδωκα τῷ Σατανᾷ, ἵνα παιδευθῶσιν μὴ βλασφημεῖν.

(ΠΡΟΣ ΤΙΜΟΘΕΟΝ Α 1:20)

Defamation is ugly. You can see what I mean by glancing at a supermarket tabloid or going on Twitter. All kinds of people are slandered—politicians, athletes, celebrities, religious leaders, and even schoolchildren. Defamation is *not* truth-telling, an accurate factual presentation, or a good representation. It is calumny. And it can cause damage beyond reasonable repair. As a result, defamation is treated as a very serious offense within our justice system.

In a precedent-setting case of defamation, Beef Products Inc. (BPI) sued ABC News for a whopping $1.9 billion dollars. That's *billions* with a *B*. ABC News did a series about BPI's lean finely textured beef (LFTB), calling it *pink slime*. As a result, consumers didn't think LFTB was real meat; they believed it was unsafe, unhealthy, and non-nutritious. This caused BPI's sales to drop so dramatically that they had to close three out of their four plants and lay off over 700 workers.

The case lasted almost five years until Disney, which owns ABC News, settled with BPI and paid out over $177 million in damages. Yikes. That is a whole lot of money to anyone. It doesn't pay to defame anyone or anything.

Defamation is mentioned in God's Word, although it is goes by another name: *blaspheme*. We find an example of this in 1 Timothy 1:20. Paul mentions two men within the church, Hymenaeus and Alexander, who were candidates for discipline because they were guilty of blaspheme, among other umbrages. Paul said he handed them over to Satan for their unremorseful offenses. Pretty strong language, eh?

Hymenaeus and Alexander were false teachers in Ephesus. Hymenaeus is mentioned elsewhere in Scripture in 2 Timothy 2:17–18. It is possible that the Alexander in 1 Timothy 1:20 is the same as Alexander the coppersmith found in 2 Timothy 4:14.

In the early church, when congregants went rogue and refused to turn from their sins, they were excommunicated. In many cases, the church would stop praying for them. This would remove the hedge of God's protection and give Satan the opportunity to inflict all kinds of devastation upon the offender, including physical pain and turmoil. The early church's hope was that this suffering would cause the unrepentant sinner to turn back to God for help and find the way back into the fold. (See 1 Corinthians 5:5.)

Paul also hoped that it would teach Hymenaeus and Alexander not to "blaspheme" any more. The Greek word here is *blasphēmein*. It is a two-part Greek word and it is believed to come from *blaptikos* meaning "hurtful" or "injurious" and *phēmi* meaning "to utter" or "to say." Together, it means to utter and say hurtful words about someone or something to the point where you injure their reputation. This is slander—exactly what ABC News had done to BPI.

Hymenaeus and Alexander had blasphemed God. They had become involved in false doctrines and began twisting the Word of God to justify their wrong-doing. This made God look like something He wasn't and made it seem like He had said things He hadn't actually said. It was a gross misrepresentation that defamed God and His holy Word. Because the two men persisted in spreading these false words about God, there was a price to pay. They could have avoided all of this had they been determined to represent the truth that God exemplified, but they had their own lusts in mind when they spoke for the Lord.

As Christians, we need to keep a close guard on our lips and make sure that we are representing the Lord and other people in a way that is accurate and gracious. We must have *their well-being* in mind when we speak, not just our own.

All of us have an audience of people who are going to listen to the things we say, simply because they trust us to tell them the truth. This is a responsibility not to be taken lightly.

In the case of Hymenaeus and Alexander, they twisted the Lord's teachings to fill their own lusts and desires, and thus gave their followers the wrong ideas.

How about you and me? Are we representing people and the Lord the way they deserve? Or is our reporting another way we serve the flesh?

One of the best remedies for this is to be slow to speak. This can be especially hard for those who believe it is their duty to be the first one to *break the news*. These people are the ones most likely to misrepresent what they have heard, adding a spin or a detail they think is harmless. But little details do big harm. It becomes defamation and does untold damage.

The same goes for our understanding of God. If you are not sure what God is saying, seek to find out the truth before you speak for Him. Go to His Word. Ask your pastor. It's better to appear ignorant than to utter a falsehood. Play it safe and admit that you don't know the answer.

Misrepresenting God may cause someone to see God mistakenly and could end up setting that seeker back.

Knowing that blasphemy and defamation have such a high price, why not put a higher premium on the accuracy of your speech instead of the abundance of it? When you do this, you'll find your words will keep you out of trouble instead of getting you into it.

41

DEVOUR: *KATAPINŌ* (καταπίνω)

Be sober-minded; be watchful. Your adversary the devil prowls around like a roaring lion, seeking someone to **devour**.

(1 Peter 5:8)

Νήψατε, γρηγορήσατε. ὁ ἀντίδικος ὑμῶν διάβολος ὡς λέων ὠρυόμενος περιπατεῖ ζητῶν τινα καταπιεῖν.

(ΠΕΤΡΟΥ Α 5:8)

J urassic Park came out in the summer of 1993 and captivated the imaginations of people everywhere. As an elementary-aged child, dinosaurs were fascinating to me. My brother and I begged our parents to see the movie and, finally, we got them to cave. Mom still had reservations about it because critics' reviews indicated it might be a bit too intense for her little boys. But in our innocent minds, we were men—and we insisted we could handle whatever the movie threw at us.

If you've seen this movie, you're familiar with the infamous *T-Rex scene.* Two Jeeps get stuck during an exploration of the island—on a rainy night, of course. The ominous silence hints that something is lurking nearby. Suddenly, a glass of water in one Jeep begins to vibrate. (At this point, my heart was racing and my mouth had become bone dry. I started to wonder if maybe Mom was right and seeing this movie was a bad idea.)

Suddenly, a Tyrannosaurus rex bursts onto the scene. With rage, it starts trying to eat the explorers. One self-centered man leaves the poor little kids behind. Bad idea. T-Rex finds him hiding in a portable toilet and just stares at him. (By now, I was trembling. As much as I disliked that guy, I still didn't want to see what happened next. The twenty-foot carnivore bit down and swallowed him whole. I had never seen anything like it. A man. Swallowed whole. Nothing left. Not a trace. I'm pretty sure all color drained from my face.)

In 1 Peter 5:8, the apostle Peter gives us a clear warning about our worst enemy—and the way he describes him puts him on par with the T-Rex. Peter says our enemy is seeking someone to "devour." The Greek word here for "devour" is *katapiein.* It is made up of two Greek words: *kata,* which means "down," and *pinō,* which means "to drink." Together, it literally means to "drink down." It gives the idea of "swallowing up" and "consuming fully." In antiquity, *katapinō* became an idiom that wasn't always associated with literal drinking. It described a hostile destruction in which nothing remained, not even a trace.

In God's word, *katapinō* describes the aggressive actions of monstrous enemies. It describes the fish that swallowed Jonah (see Jonah 2:1)[19]; being swallowed by excessive despair (see 2 Corinthians 2:7); and the Red Sea that swallowed the Egyptians (see Hebrews 11:29). Hence, the word is associated with great power, often beyond human control.

When Peter's audience heard this, they would have gone on high alert. While Peter describes the enemy's tactics as lion-like, they would understand the predator to be more terrible than a lion. A lion may leave the remains of its prey; the predator Peter is describing won't leave a trace. And the most sobering thing is that Peter is saying that this predator is on the loose—and hungry.

How would you feel if you woke up, checked the news, and discovered a T-Rex was running wild in your city? Would you jog to Starbucks as you usually do? Do you think you'd still go to Target and peruse some items you saw in their weekly ad circular? I'm guessing you'd set those plans aside to protect yourself and your family.

> The T-Rex was fifteen to twenty feet tall and forty feet long, with a jaw four feet long that was perfect for annihilating its prey. This monstrous predator also had about fifty teeth, some of which were eight inches long.

While we aren't supposed to stop living our lives because the devil is on the prowl, we *do* need to be constantly mindful and cautious that he is out there trying to sniff us out. If we forget this, we can make the wrong move and he'll swallow us whole. And if that happens, he is not going to leave anything. The devil will suck down your family, your ministry, your reputation, your business, and everything you have built. That is the warning here: he is vicious and dangerous. He doesn't play fair. He will take every single thing you have and leave you without a morsel. Be careful: he's the deadliest predator on the planet.

I'm writing this to warn you, not scare you. Part of understanding God's Word is understanding the cruelty of our enemy. At times, we need to remember just how deadly he is, so we don't get comfortable and end up getting caught. Maybe the enemy is trying to devour you through a situation, a temptation of the flesh, or through a relationship that has become hurtful. Are you offended by something your pastor said? Are you being tempted to cover up a wrong with a lie? Maybe someone other than your spouse is fulfilling an emotional need and you are spending too much time with them, to the point where you're thinking about having an affair. Our T-Rex, the devil, is hunting you down and preparing to devour you.

The good news is that you have been given the power of the Holy Spirit to defend against and even outrun your foe. With His help, you can get away to safety.

42

HYPOCRITE: *HYPOKRITĒS* (ὑποκριτής)

---

*But woe to you, scribes and Pharisees, **hypocrites**! For you shut the kingdom of heaven in people's faces. For you neither enter yourselves nor allow those who would enter to go in.*

(Matthew 23:13)

Οὐαὶ δὲ ὑμῖν, γραμματεῖς καὶ Φαρισαῖοι ὑποκριταί, ὅτι κλείετε τὴν βασιλείαν τῶν οὐρανῶν ἔμπροσθεν τῶν ἀνθρώπων· ὑμεῖς γὰρ οὐκ εἰσέρχεσθε οὐδὲ τοὺς εἰσερχομένους ἀφίετε εἰσελθεῖν.   (ΚΑΤΑ ΜΑΘΘΑΙΟΝ 23:13)

You may not have heard of Robert Hanssen, although two movies have been made about his life: *Master Spy: The Robert Hansen Story* (2002) and *Breach* (2007). He was a beloved husband, a father of six, a graduate of Knox College and Northwestern University, a churchgoer—and a spy. And not just any spy. He is considered to be one of the most destructive infiltrators in United States history. Imagine a guy sitting next to you in church, singing hymns with you…and selling secrets to the Russian government.

Hanssen joined the FBI in 1976. Three years into his career, he was handing over secrets to the Soviets. As he rose in rank, he was, at the same time, giving the Soviets thousands of documents containing classified information, such as the names of Russians who were spying for the Americans, details about the U.S. nuclear program, specifics about national security—including where top U.S. officials would be hidden during a national emergency—and the location of secret underground tunnels.

Hanssen would show up for work wearing a Department of State badge with his name on it and carry a pocketful of business cards stating he was an FBI special agent and unit chief. Who could guess that Hanssen was living a double life and betraying his country? Makes you wonder who people really are.

Hanssen's treason finally caught up with him. He was arrested in Virginia on February 18, 2001, while smuggling some classified documents to the Soviets. He was indicted on twenty-one counts of spying, pled guilty to fifteen counts of espionage, and was sentenced to life in prison without parole. It could have been worse, considering the government was considering giving him the death penalty. For over two decades, Robert Hanssen wasn't who everyone thought he was. He was playing a role.

God's Word has a lot to say about playing the role of someone we aren't. Jesus accuses the Pharisees of this, calling them "hypocrites" *six* times in Matthew 23, as in Matthew 23:13. Talk about making your point clear. The Greek word for "hypocrites" here is *hypokritai* and it's very interesting word indeed.

Originally, it was used to mean "an interpretation." Later, it came to mean "an actor" because it described an actor's interpretation of a poet's words. The actor would interpret the poetry by bringing it to life, using acting, mime, and gesture. He[20] might put on a mask and focus on how he needed to portray his character.

It was said that a good actor could play any role given to him. Most actors could do this without being personally affected. They could portray an angry person, for instance, but inwardly remain calm. It was a total sham, yet many actors could be compelling and convincing. For this reason, it was frowned upon for actors to be in politics. Perhaps the actor might represent himself to be whatever the people wanted and not his true self or how he would actually govern. He could deceive and feel no inward compunction because he was a trained actor.

> The earliest known actor in the Greek theater was Thespis, who first performed as someone other than himself on November 23, 534 BC. It is from him that we get the word *thespian*.

Up until the time of Jesus, the word "hypocrite" wasn't always seen in a negative light. Pretending can be a good thing at times. Yet it took on its negative nuance after the Gospels influenced culture because the Pharisees were the enemies of Jesus. Jesus called them hypocrites—actors, pretenders, those who acted the part and had no inner attachment to it at all.

Publicly, the Pharisees appeared to care about the things of God. Privately, they couldn't care less. (See Matthew 23:27–28.) Jesus knew the Pharisees just wanted to impress people with their knowledge of Jewish laws. They were playing a role—and Jesus was calling them out. There was no hoodwinking Jesus and the Pharisees hated Him for that.

Following Christ is not playing a role. If we are going to serve God, it starts with a personal experience that melts away our coldhearted rigidity and makes us alive toward the things God cares about, such as serving others, justice, and the coming of the kingdom. Only when our innermost parts are thriving can we serve God with true affection, instead of doing it for a photo-op or a chance to be endeared by our community and the people whose attention we covet.

Consider your personal walk with the Lord. Like John Wesley, was your heart "strangely warmed" by the presence of God, leading you into a decision to trust in Christ and follow Him? Or do you just go through the motions and play the part because that's all you know?

Don't settle. There is an experience in God that is so much greater than trying to appear to be religious. You can have a personal encounter with Jesus, through His Holy Spirit, that will make you authentic. When the Spirit fills your life with His transforming power, you can be a genuine follower of Jesus, a new creation.

43

JOIN: *KOLLAŌ* (κολλάω)

Or do you not know that he who is joined to a prostitute becomes one body with her? For, as it is written, "The two will become one flesh." (1 Corinthians 6:16)

[ἢ] οὐκ οἴδατε ὅτι ὁ κολλώμενος τῇ πόρνῃ ἓν σῶμά ἐστιν; Ἔσονται γάρ, φησίν, οἱ δύο εἰς σάρκα μίαν.
(ΠΡΟΣ ΚΟΡΙΝΘΙΟΥΣ Α 6:16)

Sadly, hookups are prevalent today. Outside the bonds of marriage, or even a committed relationship, people are having casual sex.

In an article entitled "Sexual Hook-Up Culture" (2013), Dr. Justin Garcia from the Kinsey Institute for Research in Sex, Gender, and Reproduction at Indiana University concludes with an attention-getting statement: "By definition, sexual hookups provide the allure of sex without strings attached. Despite their increasing social acceptability, however, developing research suggests that sexual hookups may leave more strings attached than many participants might first assume."

A lot of this developing research was included in his article. One statistic showed that hookups resulted in negative feelings. He points to a study of 169 people in a singles bar. Thirty-two percent of men and 72 percent of women said they would feel guilty having intercourse with someone they'd just met. Another statistic showed that both men and women who engaged in a hookup had lower self-esteem scores than those who hadn't. On top of that, research from 200 undergraduates indicated that 78 percent of women and 72 percent of men who engaged in a hookup regretted it.

Among other statistics that show the ill consequences of hooking up, Garcia says research shows that hookups end negatively, many times in emotional and psychological harm, sexually transmitted diseases, unwanted pregnancy, and even violence. It seems the point is clear: don't hookup unless you want a boatload of suffering.

As helpful as Garcia's research is, he isn't the first to tell us this. God's Word actually warns us against the dangers of casual sex. We find this in 1 Corinthians 6. Here, Paul is talking to the Corinthian church about prostitution. When was the last time your pastor gave a sermon about prostitution? Here in the Western world, our values have been long influenced by Judeo-Christian sexual ethics. But in ancient Greece, new converts weren't familiar with the ways of God. They came from a culture that worshipped idols. Prostitution was very much part of that.

Corinth was one of the most prominent cities in antiquity for prostitution. The Corinthian people viewed sex pretty casually—as common as eating, sleeping, and getting a drink of water. In fact, sex was so casual that it was acceptable for married men to visit brothels. They believed prostitutes could give them what their wives couldn't. And the Corinthians thought this was fine.

Paul told them, *"Do you not know that he who is joined to a prostitute becomes one body with her?"* The Greek word for "joined" here is *kollōmenos*. It means "to bind closely," "glue together," or "cement together." It was a technical term used to describe welding two metals into one. Actually, there are examples of this term also being used to describe a handle that was being glued back onto a piece of pottery and two layers of papyrus being pasted together to form a single sheet. The idea is two things coming together to form one thing through the creation of a rigorous bond. Basically, it is hooking up with no intention of unhooking.

According to the Kinsey Institute, the average male loses his virginity at 16.9 years of age and the average female loses her virginity at 17.4 years of age.

Human beings don't bond together through glue, paste, or welding. There is a much stronger bonding agent than any of these: intercourse. It's the bonding agent that God created to seal a man and a woman together. Through it, the bodies, emotions, feelings, and souls of two people become united. (See Genesis 2:24.) No matter whom you have sex with or for what purpose—even if it is just a consensual *one-night stand* between two *friends with benefits*—you can rest assured that this bond is going to form. Your being will hook to their being. Most people aren't signing up for this when they have casual sex. But that's what they end up getting. God forbid it should ever be ripped apart. But it often is, sometimes as early as the morning after. And, oh, it does damage—like ripping apart two pieces of paper after they have been glued. As they are yanked apart, they take pieces of each other with them, creating an uncomfortable mess.

Now, we see why casual sex becomes so damaging to our self-esteem, as Garcia's research suggests. It cheapens who we are. Would you let a stranger take a sip of your beverage? Most people wouldn't. If you absolutely had to, you'd likely feel odd taking a sip after they did. If we feel that way about a can of soda, how much more should we feel about our sacred organs, our deepest emotions, and the most intimate recesses of our physiology? You can't give that to just anyone and feel good about yourself afterward.

God wants us to place a value on the bonding agent He created. Sex needs to have its rightful, God-intended place. If you're still single, don't cheapen it as a quick amusement. Set it aside as sacred and save it until your wedding night. Then, after you are married, use it to join together with your spouse and enjoy the beautiful, valuable, and highly-prized gift that God meant it to be.

44

THE HOLY ONE OF GOD:
HO HAGIOS TOU THEOU
(ὁ ἅγιος τοῦ θεοῦ)

What have you to do with us, Jesus of Nazareth? Have you come to destroy us? I know who you are—the Holy One of God. (Mark 1:24)

λέγων, Τί ἡμῖν καὶ σοί, Ἰησοῦ Ναζαρηνέ; ἦλθες ἀπολέσαι ἡμᾶς; οἶδά σε τίς εἶ, ὁ ἅγιος τοῦ θεοῦ.
(KATA MAPKON 1:24)

Who is Jesus? Throughout history, we find art and literature filled with different answers to this question. Ever since my early days of street ministry, when I first got saved more than twenty years ago, I've found this is the most controversial question of all. I've heard all kinds of answers. I've met people who say Jesus was just a historical figure, but not the Messiah. Some say Jesus didn't even exist. Some believe Jesus was a beachcombing hippie who was all about tolerance and free love, while others think He was a card-carrying member of the National Rifle Association. And, of course, I've met people who have truly believed that *they* are Jesus. Let me tell you, it can be wild out there.

If we want to know *who* Jesus is, there's only one objective source: the Word of God. The New Testament gives us four separate accounts, written by four different authors, describing the life and ministry of Jesus Christ. The ones by Matthew, Mark, and Luke are known as the *synoptic* Gospels; they are somewhat similar, but written from different angles to present various truths about Jesus as Lord and God. In doing so, they help us come to understand more deeply who Jesus is so that we can place our faith in Him and follow.

Mark's gospel presents Jesus as God's servant, doing the work of the Messiah as He had been sent to do. This is why we see so much emphasis on Jesus's activity within Mark's account. He doesn't even begin with Jesus's birth or family heritage, but instead starts right at the beginning of Jesus's ministry. In the first chapter of Mark, an unclean spirit confronts Jesus as He teaches in the synagogue. (See Mark 1:21–28.) Mark gives us a valuable detail that helps us answer the question, "Who is Jesus?" The demon says to Jesus, "*I know who you are—the Holy One of God.*" What exactly could this title mean? In the Greek, this title is *ho hagios tou theou.*

To understand the titles ascribed to Jesus, we need to look at the Old Testament. During Jesus's day, there was a Greek version of the Old Testament known as the Septuagint, or LXX. It had been around since the second century BC. This title, *ho hagios tou theou*, appears within it in a few places.[21] It describes the first high priest, Aaron (see Psalm 106:16)[22], Samson (see Judges 16:17), and Elisha (see 2 Kings 4:9). These were men upon whom God had placed His hand and anointed to serve and defend His people. They had been sent by God to release God's richest blessing upon His covenant community. They were especially equipped to destroy the works of the devil and deliver the children of Israel from their enemies. In other words, they weren't just average folks.

By using this title, the demon was admitting that Jesus was a greater spiritual power than he. This would have been extremely encouraging to those in the synagogue who understood. Jesus had come to free God's people from the power of Satan. He was the Messiah and He had come from God to bring peace with God. He was the deliverer, the healer, the defender of God's people, and the source of all God's blessings. What an astounding way for Mark to begin to answer the question, "Who is Jesus?" The rest of Mark's gospel shows this to be true through the various miracles, teachings, and sufferings of Christ.

The Da Vinci Code movie was banned in numerous countries, including Jordan, Lebanon, Pakistan, and Samoa because of uproars over its inaccuracies about the life of Jesus Christ.

We are left to answer this question for ourselves. Who do *we* believe Jesus is? Is He *just* a lifeline in times of trouble? Is He someone you only think about on a rainy day? Is He a fictional character from *The Da Vinci Code*? Or is He the Holy One of God in your life, your Deliverer and Defender, your Protector, and the One who has reconciled you back to God? Have you gone to Jesus in repentance so He can forgive your sins and make you part of God's family? Do you know Jesus as the One who has overthrown the power of Satan in your life, baptized you in the Spirit, given you the hope of eternal life, and connected you to all the blessings of God?

Are you dealing with a bad habit that is demonic? Jesus has broken the power of everything evil. Perhaps you are worried that you aren't saved. Many people in church deal with this fear. Jesus has come to ensure that you can have eternal life and be part of the family of God. Maybe you have relationship issues. The Lord came to release His blessing over your life, including the blessing of having healthy, fruitful relationships. Let's remember that the strength of our lives is not in who *we* are, it is in who *He is* and has come to be. Don't sell Jesus short. He wants us to experience Him as the Holy One of God, *ho hagios tou theou.*

45

CORRUPT: *SAPROS*
(σαπρὸς)

---

*Let no **corrupting** talk come out of your mouths, but only such as is good for building up, as fits the occasion, that it may give grace to those who hear.* (Ephesians 4:29)

πᾶς λόγος σαπρὸς ἐκ τοῦ στόματος ὑμῶν μὴ ἐκπορευέσθω, ἀλλ᾽ εἴ τις ἀγαθὸς πρὸς οἰκοδομὴν τῆς χρείας, ἵνα δῷ χάριν τοῖς ἀκούουσιν. (ΠΡΟΣ ΕΦΕΣΙΟΥΣ 4:29)

Nothing ruins the moment more than the stink of something rotten. One minute, you're happy and your thoughts are clear. Suddenly, an odious odor comes wafting through the air, invading your peace and taking your composure hostage. You scramble to get as far away from the stink as possible. We all know how this goes, especially my cousin, Justin, a veteran prankster. He once made my life miserable by harnessing the powerful smell of rotten food.

One evening, our families were at dinner and, as he tells the story, I made a comment that somewhat embarrassed him. He felt he should pay me back. When I got up to use the restroom, Justin located a small, somewhat secret pocket on the inside of my jacket—a pocket that I had never noticed before. He proceeded to fill it up with shredded Parmesan cheese from the dinner table. I had no clue.

Justin couldn't have hoped for a better outcome. I have a habit of leaving my jackets in the car, especially in the springtime when the temperatures are unpredictable and you never know when you'll need it. While driving about a week later, I got a whiff of something so horrible that I became nauseous. I assumed it was something I was driving past. The next day, the same thing happened. Now I knew it was in my car. I looked between the seats, checked the glove box, and tore the whole interior apart trying to determine the source of the stench. Still nothing. The smell went on for a whole month. It got to the point where I dreaded getting into my vehicle. It was torture. I had to have the windows down, even if it was raining. Finally, one day, I went to put the jacket on and I gagged. It was the jacket. I looked inside and found the pocket. When I unzipped it, the nasty, moldy, crumbled cheese fell out. It all made sense. Justin had one-upped me.

Like food, our words can be rotten and produce a foul, devastating stench. This stench is harmful because if it seeps into our communities, it will cause trauma, emotional damage, bitterness, and many other problems. In Ephesians 4:29, Paul tells the Ephesian church, *"Let no corrupting talk come out of your mouths."* Here, the Greek word for "corrupting" is *sapros*. It means "putrid," "decayed," and "rancid." In classical Greek, it described something spoiled and in the process of decay, such as bad cheese, rotting flesh, and withered flowers. It was once used to describe grapes that fell on the ground and were left to rot. It defined reeking fish left out in the market too long without a buyer. Needless to say, anything that was *sapros* was poor quality, worthless, and often harmful.

The U.S. Food and Drug Administration suggests using uncooked, refrigerated fish within two days. After that, it starts to go bad and consuming it could lead to food poisoning.

God's Word is telling us that our words can be foul, nasty, and noxious, like the cheese in my jacket. Think about it for a moment. Have you ever been in an environment where rotten words are frequently used? Perhaps in home, a church, or place of work? The atmosphere can be so thick, you can feel the tension in the air. Folks are sickly and stressed out. This is the effect of toxic and poisonous words. It won't be long before people become physically sick.

I once met a pastor who worked in such a treacherous environment at his church, he ended up in the hospital multiple times. While doing the work of the Lord, God's people had begun using foul words toward one another when they disagreed. These words permeated the church office and hospitalized the pastor. This is the work of Satan.

You see, Satan doesn't show up with horns and pitchfork when he wants to cause trouble. He doesn't have to. Instead, he gets us to harm one another so we won't know he's behind it. He gets us to hurl rotten words while he sits back and watches the stench suffocate the life out of us. It's diabolical.

God's Word tells us that we must protect our communities and make sure they are healthy environments, free of rot. This starts with the way we talk to one another. Think about your environments. Does your family build one another up with fresh, pure, life-giving words? When visitors come over, do they find the atmosphere invigorating?

How about your church? If you are a pastor, do you lead with kindness and encourage your workers? Or would your workers say that you use harsh overtones? Just because it is ministry and the Lord's work doesn't give us the right to treat people heartlessly.

Clean up your speech. Here's a good opportunity to ask the Holy Spirit to reveal to you the truth about the words you add to your environment and community. If He points things out that you need to stop saying, consider it a blessing. Doing what He tells you is only going to make your standard of living better, cleaner, and healthier. Not only will others benefit from it, but chances are, you will benefit the most. Kind, loving words ensure the refreshing, invigorating atmosphere of God's presence.

46

FAINTHEARTED:
OLIGOPSYCHOS
(ὀλιγόψυχος)

And we urge you, brothers, admonish the idle, encourage the *fainthearted*, *help the weak, be patient with them all.*

(1 Thessalonians 5:14)

παρακαλοῦμεν δὲ ὑμᾶς, ἀδελφοί, νουθετεῖτε τοὺς ἀτάκτους, παραμυθεῖσθε τοὺς ὀλιγοψύχους.

(ΠΡΟΣ ΘΕΣΣΑΛΟΝΙΚΕΙΣ Α 5:14)

Perhaps you know the name Derek Redmond. If it doesn't ring a bell, maybe you're familiar with what etched him in athletic history. If not, just look him up on YouTube and you'll see what I'm about to share.

Redmond was one of Great Britain's greatest running athletes in the 1980s and 1990s. He broke the British record for the 400-meter with a time of 44.82 seconds. He was selected for the 1600-meter relay in the 1986 European championship in Germany. Redmond and his team won a silver medal at the World Championships in Athletics in Rome in 1987. They also won a gold medal in Tokyo in 1991, with a time that still ranks among the fastest in history. Next stop: the 1992 Olympics in Barcelona.

But things didn't go as well as they had been.

After the starting pistol fired for the men's 400-meter semi-final, Redmond was among the leaders. About sixteen seconds into the race, around the 250-meter mark, his run came to a screeching halt. Something had exploded in his leg, causing him to hobble in agony. Redmond had torn a hamstring, rendering him incapable of competing. Sadness, frustration, pain, and devastation were written on his face as he knelt on the track. The race was over for him, short of the finish line.

Or was it?

Suddenly, Redmond pulled himself up and with his last ounces of energy, began a limping lope toward the finish line. He was determined to cross it. Yet, it seemed like the pain was growing exponentially worse with every agonizing step. The sportscasters declared that trying to finish was a bad idea; he could do more damage to his muscle. There, Redmond was: all alone on the track, being criticized by the announcers and failed by his own legs. It didn't seem like he could get across that line.

Suddenly, a man wearing blue athletic shorts and a white T-shirt fought past security and ran up alongside Redmond. It was his father. He steadied his son's arm over his shoulder and Redmond leaned against him. And his father used his own strength to help his son finish the race. The crowd burst into loud cheers and applause.

This is what athletics is all about. The other runners won medals, but Redmond and his father won a piece of history and the hearts of anyone who witnessed their courageous finish. You didn't have to be a runner to be inspired. It became a testimony to people all over the world that no matter what we do in life, we need each other when times get tough. When we see someone ready to give up, we need to rush beside them, pick them up, and do whatever it takes to get them across the finish line. In fact, God's Word tells us the same.

> The ancient Greek runner Leonidas of Rhodes is considered one of the greatest Olympians of all time. He competed in four Olympiads (in 164 BC, 160 BC, 156 BC, and 152 BC) and won three races in each, making him a twelve-time Olympic champion. After his death, he was worshipped in Rhodes as a god.

In 1 Thessalonians 5:14, Paul tells his church to *"encourage the fainthearted."* This is a very interesting verse, as it tells us that some of the believers within the Thessalonian congregation were ready to give up. The Greek word for "fainthearted" here is *oligopsychos*. It is made of two Greek words: *oligos*, which means "little," and *psychē*, which means "soul" or "breath of life." Together, they mean to have only a little bit of soul left within. A person who is *oligopsychos* is running low on cheerfulness, hope, and inspiration. They are discouraged. Something has happened to them, usually a circumstance or situation that has caused their breath of life to diminish. In fact, *oligopsychos* was used in Greco-Roman times to describe a runner who was short of breath and couldn't finish the race.

This described the Thessalonians. Like Derek Redmond, circumstances had crippled their ability to press on. They were experiencing persecution, carnal temptations, sloth, and confusion about when Christ was going to return. (See 1 Thessalonians 2:14–16; 4:3–8; 4:11–12; 4:13–5:3.)

But there is no quitting in the kingdom of God. Paul called the church's attention to this and implored them to encourage each other. He wanted the strong believers to get behind the fainthearted ones to push them onward in the Christian life, similar to what Derek Redmond's father had done for him.

Most of us know someone who has become fainthearted and is tempted to throw in the towel. Perhaps a moment of temptation got the better of them and caused them to fall into sin. Maybe they succumbed to an old habit. Feeling guilty, it seems they don't want to try anymore.

Maybe it's not sin, but life has been beating them down lately. Nothing seems to be working out. They've been tithing, serving their church faithfully, and everything else they know to do in order to be faithful. But things just keep going wrong and they're wondering, *What is all this faithfulness getting me, except more trouble than I want to reckon with?*

Now is a good time to come to their side. Help them bear their challenges and encourage them until their soul is filled back up with cheerfulness, hope, and inspiration. Your encouragement will likely be the means they need to get them over the finish line. And if *you* are the discouraged one right now, ask the Lord to send someone by *your* side to help *you* keep on going. God always has a shoulder prepared for us to lean on.

47

MOVED WITH PITY: *SPLANCHNIZOMAI* (σπλαγχνίζομαι)

Moved with pity, he stretched out his hand and touched him and said to him, "I will; be clean."   (Mark 1:41)

καὶ σπλαγχνισθεὶς ἐκτείνας τὴν χεῖρα αὐτοῦ ἥψατο καὶ λέγει αὐτῷ, Θέλω, καθαρίσθητι.

(ΚΑΤΑ ΜΑΡΚΟΝ 1:41)

Anthony L. Koaroff, chief editor of the *Harvard Health Letter,* wrote an interesting article on "The Gut-Brain Connection," published online by *Harvard Health Publishing.* He said:

Have you ever had a "gut-wrenching" experience? Do certain situations make you feel "nauseous"? Have you ever felt "butterflies" in your stomach? We use these expressions for a reason. The gastrointestinal tract is sensitive to emotion. Anger, anxiety, sadness, elation—all of these feelings (and others) can trigger symptoms in the gut. The brain has a direct effect on the stomach and intestines…That's because the brain and the gastrointestinal (GI) system are intimately connected.

You may have noticed this when you got that big letter in the mail from your university of choice. Perhaps this happens every time you speak in public or have to make a presentation at work. Most brides and grooms certainly know something about this on their wedding day.

These *butterflies* are an indication that we are profoundly linked to and care more than impassively about the thing before us. Nobody gets butterflies while doing mundane, ordinary tasks like grabbing a cup of coffee or doing laundry. Butterflies are the evidence of your true feelings. If you get them around a certain member of the opposite sex, maybe it's time to step up to the plate to see if that person has them around you, too.

> When you get "butterflies in your stomach," your body is sending more blood to your arms and legs in preparation for a fight-or-flight response. This means less blood is being sent to your stomach and the nerves there, lacking the normal amount, create a fluttery feeling.

In Mark 1:41, we see a situation where our Lord was affected by the *gut-brain connection.* This instance is rich with theological value, as it affirms Christ's humanity. Jesus had been preaching throughout Galilee when a leprous man suddenly approached him. Leprosy is a hideous disease with terrible physical consequences as well as social repercussions. In the first century, according to Jewish Law, an affected person was declared *unclean* by examining priests. The individual was isolated from the public, wore torn clothes, kept their hair unkempt, covered their upper lip, and cried out, "Unclean, unclean," when around others. (See Leviticus 13:44–46.) Their life was ruined.

In a twenty-first century social context, this would be like having a contagious disease and watching others run to the other side of the street to avoid you, maybe waving hello from there…if you were lucky.

Yet Jesus broke the status quo in Mark 1:41. Instead of a curt nod and cold half-smile, Jesus stretched out His hand and touched the leper. Jesus cared too much about the man to pass by him without healing him. He was "moved with pity."

The word "moved with pity" here is *splanchnistheis* in the Greek.[23] The noun form of this word (*splanchna*) referred to the guts of someone or something. In fact, it referred to Judas's "bowels," which spilled out after he hanged himself. (See Acts 1:18.) It was often used to refer to the entrails of a sacrifice, such as the heart, liver, kidney, spleen, and lungs.

The word ultimately became synonymous with the hidden, emotional parts of a person. It referred to the center where feelings come from and implied attitude, character, and even deep passions. As a verb form, the word could mean "touched in the inward parts." A stronger, more descriptive definition is "affected in the deep inner, emotional places where our personal passions and desires exist." It gives us a picture of someone being hit in the stomach by a gut-wrenching situation, causing "butterflies." It's compassion.

What a beautiful picture this word paints about our Lord Jesus. He cared profoundly about the condition of others. He wasn't an on-the-clock Savior who looked at His ministry as an ordinary job where He punched in and punched out without any sort of personal attachment to what He was doing. Rather, His feelings, emotions, and passions were all very much involved in His mission. He was a part of His mission and His mission was a part of Him. Jesus was deeply connected to the people God had sent Him to save. It mattered to Him that those He ministered to would be healed, delivered, and restored from the effects of the fall. You could say that Jesus took it personally. After all, He *is* our burden bearer. (See Psalm 68:19.)

Let's remember that effective service for the kingdom comes from a heart that is filled with care. Are you truly concerned about the people that God has sent you to serve? Are you deeply affected by their situations?

All too often, it's easy to become preoccupied and lose heart for people as we work to serve the kingdom of God. Nevertheless, if we stay close to the Lord through prayer, He will continually invite us to know His heart which, at the center, is for the lost, the broken, and the marginalized. If we continue to seek Jesus, we can always be deeply affected in our inward parts by others the way He would be. This is the key to serving others effectively and developing a ministry to look like His.

48

RUBBISH: *SKYBALON*
(σκύβαλον)

Indeed, I count everything as loss because of the surpassing worth of knowing Christ Jesus my Lord. For his sake I have suffered the loss of all things and count them as rubbish, *in order that I may gain Christ.* (Philippians 3:8)

ἀλλὰ μενοῦνγε καὶ ἡγοῦμαι πάντα ζημίαν εἶναι διὰ τὸ ὑπερέχον τῆς γνώσεως Χριστοῦ Ἰησοῦ τοῦ κυρίου μου, δι' ὃν τὰ πάντα ἐζημιώθην, καὶ ἡγοῦμαι σκύβαλα, ἵνα Χριστὸν κερδήσω. (ΠΡΟΣ ΦΙΛΙΠΠΗΣΙΟΥΣ 3:8)

Certain words can make us cringe and feel uncomfortable. I considered sharing a few of the words on my list, but I cannot bring myself to type them. How could I ever sleep at night knowing someone is reading them because of me?

In fact, I have often gone to significant lengths to avoid using such words, sifting through a thesaurus for a more appropriate choice, rewriting the sentence, or even leaving an idea left unsaid. It's that bad. I've even asked others not to use these words in front of me. It makes me look odd, but I would rather live with that than to hear words that make me recoil.

The New York Times published an article on word aversion entitled, "We Know You Hate 'Moist.' What Other Words Repel You?" It cites research done by Paul Thibodeau, a professor of psychology at Oberlin College, which suggests that *moist* ranks as the most widely averted word in the English language. Almost a quarter of the 2,500 people he studied couldn't stomach hearing the word, no matter how it appeared.

Interestingly enough, words like *hoist*, *foist*, and *rejoice* did not have any effect on those bothered by *moist*. This suggests that word aversion is not phonetic. The mere word is the issue.[24] Thibodeau's research also found that those troubled by *moist* were also bothered by *vomit*, *puke*, and *phlegm*. The conclusion is that detested words set off a visceral reaction due to their association with bodily fluids or bodily functions. Perhaps that's why *crusty*, *mucous*, and even *meat* make it onto the *most hated words* lists.

English isn't the only language that has nauseating words. I imagine all languages have them—and that goes for biblical Greek, too. You might think that because it's God's Word, the Holy Spirit would have sanctioned the inspired writers to use only flowery words. Think again. Effective communication isn't always pretty. Many times, it calls for something barefaced and glaring.

Perhaps the best example of this in the New Testament is found in Philippians 3:8. Here, the apostle Paul uses one of the most nauseating words in the Greek language: *skybala*. It's a word associated with bodily function— definitely not a word that Mom wants her kids using at the dinner table or in church.

Skybala is translated "rubbish" in *The Holy Bible, English Standard Version*, but that is arguably a kind translation. The word itself means "dung," "excrement," and, yes, even "poop." In a papyrus from the first century near the time Paul wrote Philippians, a father uses *skybalon* to inform his son that the donkey driver had purchased rotten hay, which is no better than eating "dung." It was a rude thing to say, describing the lowest of the low—repulsive, sordid, and stomach-churning. In one instance, it was used to describe the remains of a corpse that had been half-eaten by fish during a deadly voyage.

> Sterculius was the Roman god of manure, specifically to be used as fertilizer. Farmers in particular were devoted to him. His name comes from *stercus*, the Latin word for feces.

Are you sick with disgust yet? In essence, *skybalon* is filth; at best, it is refuse that is thrown to the dogs. It's a gross word. The Philippians would hear it that way and wince with repugnance.

But Paul had good reason to use this word. He was not a potty-mouth. He was assessing his life. In light of the wondrous blessing of having a direct and intimate relationship with Jesus Christ, Paul chose the strongest possible word he knew to convey what everything else in his life seemed compared to it. This includes his educational background, his social status, his piety, and his religious achievements.

By using *skybalon*, Paul was not only diminishing these, he was rejecting them with loathing. Knowing Christ, Paul looked at his personal achievements like feces in the toilet. Pardon my language, but that's exactly what the Philippians would have heard. This speaks to the profoundness of purpose that comes *only* from knowing the Creator of our existence and the Savior of our souls. We should be horrified by anything else in life that tries to take the place of Jesus.

Have you accomplished great accolades and feats throughout your life? By themselves, these things aren't bad. Your achievements should make you excited and happy. Yet you should never trust them to give you meaning, divine purpose, or salvation. That comes only through a personal relationship with Christ.

If you have been trusting in those outer things instead of Jesus, you should immediately dispose of them as a source of salvation. As you draw near to Jesus through the Word of God and the Holy Spirit, you will begin to discover that life is more than vacations, large homes, career goals, and social standing.

True life is having the indwelling presence of God in your heart. When you take hold of that, you won't be bothered when the fleeting things of this world come and go. They are waste, dung, and a pile of garbage compared to the glory that comes from being in the presence of God.

49

OPPORTUNITY: *TOPOS* (τόπος)

And give no *opportunity* *to the devil.*   (Ephesians 4:27)

μηδὲ δίδοτε τόπον τῷ διαβόλῳ.
                                    (ΠΡΟΣ ΕΦΕΣΙΟΥΣ 4:27)

A neighborhood is a special place. Here we live in the closest proximity to others who reside on Earth. There are over seven billion people alive right now and we will never share a single interaction with the vast majority of them. Yet we always have some type of relationship with our neighbors. We know which guy on the block is a grill master and who's jogging to lose weight. We watch as the same kids who used to bike or skateboard down the street are now having their prom photos taken on the front lawn.

My family lived in a number of different neighborhoods over the years and there are some neighbors I'll never forget. In our first house, there was the family across the street who had all *the fast cars*, as my big brother and I would say. We'd beg our parents to take us by so we could gawk at the Corvettes they always had parked in the driveway.

In our family's second house, Liz B lived across the way. Liz was our age and she always had her pretty girlfriends over during the summer. We fellas would play basketball on the driveway in hopes that Liz and her friends would come outside so we could drool over them.

Then, in my third house, where I first lived by myself as an adult, there was the *genius boy* who came down to the pool and outsmarted the grown-ups. The kid was only in the fifth grade, but he knew so many facts and insights about the most trivial things. It was hard to have a conversation with him without feeling like a dunce. We would look forward to watching when he took on his next victim. I think he went on to be a mechanical engineer.

It's a blessing when you have wonderful neighbors who add dimension and variety to your life. A great neighborhood is made up of diverse individuals who respect one another and offer something to make the neighborhood a better community. That's why people can be on edge when a new neighbor moves in. Are they going to disrupt the peace? Are they going to have wild parties and blare their music? Will they allow their pets to run wild and relieve themselves on everyone else's lawn? And God forbid they have criminal associations and become the open door to all the wrong influences.

In Ephesians 4:27, God's Word tells us to guard our community from the wrong neighbor, spiritually speaking. Here, the apostle Paul is talking to the Ephesian church about their new life in Christ, which is to be characterized by righteous living. Paul lists certain behaviors that are part of the former way of life and tells the Ephesian church to cease with them. (See Ephesians 4:22–31.)

One of these is unfounded anger—irrational and unmerited rage that has no basis in just cause. This can come for various reasons. It could be temperamental or the result of substance abuse. It could be hurt pride or the result of envy. Whatever the case, God's Word tells us that this sort of anger gives "opportunity" to the devil.

The Greek word here for "opportunity" is *topon.* Its oldest meaning is "a defined place." Over time, it came to mean things associated with "defined places" such as "territory," "area," and "land." In fact, this is where we get our English term "topographic." A *topographic* map is a map that uses an arrangement of contour lines to indicate the shape of the land's surface. As *topos* evolved in antiquity, it came to mean "room for something" or "place" and, eventually, "opportunity" or "occasion."

"Topography" is the study of the shape and features of land surfaces. It comes from the Greek word *topos* ("land") and *graphē* ("writing"). Hence, it means "a writing or description of the land."

As linguists have examined the use of the word in early Greek, they've noted that it seems to narrow down a general space to a smaller area within the whole. Kind of like saying "a place within the field" or "a town within the state." It's possible that's why *topos* also meant "neighborhood," like "a neighborhood within the city."

Considering this in light of Ephesians 4:27, God's Word is saying, "Don't give your neighborhood over to the devil" or "Don't let the devil into your neighborhood." The fact is, Satan is a bad neighbor and you don't want him anywhere near you or the ones you love. We are warned that outbursts of the flesh, such as anger, lying, stealing, and gossip, serve as invites for the devil to come have a look at the neighborhood. They notify him that there is prime property available and it's fine if he moves in. And he is never going to turn down an invite. He's always looking for a new place. He will haul all of his stuff in—things like hatred, jealousy, offense, and unforgiveness—and use them to disturb the peace.

Instead of making room for the devil, defend your community and your own personal life by allowing the Holy Spirit to direct how you act in situations. When you act the way He wants, instead of finding out the devil has moved in, you'll discover that the Lord is next to you. He is the kind of neighbor everyone wants.

50

GET ENTANGLED IN: *EMPLEKŌ* (ἐμπλέκω)

---

*No soldier **gets entangled in** civilian pursuits, since his aim is to please the one who enlisted him.* (2 Timothy 2:4)

οὐδεὶς στρατευόμενος ἐμπλέκεται ταῖς τοῦ βίου πραγματείαις, ἵνα τῷ στρατολογήσαντι ἀρέσῃ.
(ΠΡΟΣ ΤΙΜΟΘΕΟΝ Β 2:4)

There's nothing more frustrating than trying to free a tangle. Your day comes to a screeching halt as you work painstakingly to liberate the mess. Take your in-ear headphones, for instance. Ever leave them in your pocket when you do the laundry? If so, you know that when you find them, they do look exactly like they've been through the spin cycle. It takes a while to undo them. I'm convinced this is why people invest in AirPods.

But what if *you* are in the tangle? A Tennessee man had the unfortunate experience of knowing what this feels like. In an article dated September 9, 2011, WRCBtv reported this man was discovered after *two days*.

The man had ventured alone in the woods and found his way to a climbing wall on a challenge course. There were signs warning hikers not to climb the wall without supervision. But the man had brought his own rope.

He ignored the signs and climbed despite the warnings. Unfortunately, he got tangled up and fell. Though the rope was strong enough to support him, he hung upside down for two days, waiting for someone to find him. At last, he was rescued by a passing hiker. The weakened climber was taken to the hospital in critical condition. Hanging upside down restricts blood to the lower body, something that put the man at risk for amputation. The man was also cold and wet, putting him in peril for hypothermia. Doctors said it was a miracle that he was alive.

This story makes you appreciate only having to deal with a tangle in your headphones.

God's Word understands about the mess that tangles create and implores us to avoid them at all costs. We find this in 2 Timothy 2:4 where Paul is talking to the young minister, Timothy. He compares serving the kingdom to military service, calling those in the ministry *soldiers of Jesus Christ*. Like any warrior, soldiers of Christ cannot be distracted by civilian life.

This reminds me of a friend who got married shortly before he enlisted. When he was deployed, his commanding officer told him, "You are the U.S. military and you are here to serve your country." Referring to his weapon and combat gear, the officer told my friend, "You have everything you need. If you needed a wife while serving in combat, we would have issued you one."

People in the military can't think about their civilian life back home because it would distract them and perhaps compromise their mission. This is the same sentiment that Paul was sharing with Timothy regarding service in the kingdom of God. Nothing should distract us from the assignment that God has given to us as soldiers in His army.

The term "Gordian knot" refers to a difficult problem that's solved using a forceful method. It comes from a story about Alexander the Great, who entered the city of Gordium in modern-day Turkey in 332 BC and was challenged to untangle an intricate knot. After working with the knot for some time, Alexander reportedly cut it in half with his sword.

Paul reiterates this by telling Timothy, *"No soldier gets entangled in civilian pursuits."* The Greek word here for "gets entangled in" is *empleketai.* It means "to scuffle with," "to intertwine," and "to ensnare." It was a word used to describe a sheep whose wool had gotten caught in thorns. It also described someone binding their hands in another person's garments to hold them back. Perhaps this is best illustrated in a game of football, when a defensive linebacker yanks on a ball carrier's jersey in order to stop a first down.

As soldiers of Christ, we are being told that there are many things in this life that can tangle us up and hold us back from serving the kingdom to the highest ability that God has given us. These aren't necessarily bad or sinful. They are simply "civilian," meaning "ordinary" things. They include stuff like careers, friendships, dating, romantic relationships, outside interests, hobbies, social media, people's opinions, and even family and extended family.

Think about it for a moment. Have any of these things ever kept you from doing what God has called you to do? Have they ever distracted you from pursuing *with all your might* the high calling of God? Has the attachment to your family kept you from relocating where God seems to be placing you? Are you back-and-forth in a dating relationship that has become so exhausting and draining that it has taken your focus and energy away from God's assignment? Maybe God has asked you to do something academically, but you'd rather spend your free time tagging friends on social media and watching Netflix instead of applying yourself to learn. Is there a hobby like golf or going to the gym that reduces the quality time that God has asked you to spend fulfilling your call? Has someone's opinion quenched your confidence in what you believe God is calling you to do?

If the answer is yes, you've become caught in the thorns. Like the Tennessee man, you are dangling instead of moving forward the way that God desires. The good news is that the Holy Spirit wants to rescue you and free you from the tangle so you can get back on track and fulfill what God has for you to do.

51

SHUDDER: *PHRISSŌ* (φρίσσω)

You believe that God is one; you do well. Even the demons believe—and shudder! (James 2:19)

σὺ πιστεύεις ὅτι εἷς ἐστιν ὁ θεός, καλῶς ποιεῖς· καὶ τὰ δαιμόνια πιστεύουσιν καὶ φρίσσουσιν. (ΙΑΚΩΒΟΥ 2:19)

It's likely you've had *goosebumps* at some point. These tiny bumps can pop up on our skin when we're scared, happy, sad, cold, or hot. They're called goosebumps because they resemble the skin of poultry after it's been plucked. Each Thanksgiving, as I'm preparing my annual deep-fried turkey, I often think, *This poor bird sure looks scared.* I suppose I would, too, if I were being dropped in a vat of hot peanut oil.

Goosebumps are caused by the contraction of muscles that are attached to our hairs. This is why we get them and our hair *stands on end*. This idiom is a popular way to describe fear of the highest kind. In fact, one of my pastor friends, describing the first time he had to preach to a crowd of people, says, "It made the hairs on the back of my neck stand on end."

It's said that Shakespeare first used this idiom in his tragedy, *Hamlet*, during a conversation between Hamlet and his father's ghost:

> I could a tale unfold, whose lightest word would harrow up thy soul, freeze they young blood, make thy two eyes, like stars, start from their spheres, thy knotted and combined locks to part and each particular hair to stand on end, like quills upon the fretful porcupine.

Have you ever been *so* scared that your thin hairs become stout like porcupine quills? Maybe from sitting around a campfire and telling eerie stories? Or perhaps looking at all the creepy conspiracy stuff that finds its way around YouTube? There must be something out there that gives you goosebumps.

There are three Latin medical terms for goosebumps: *horripilation*, from the Latin *horrere* ("to stand on end") and *pilus* ("hair"); *cutis anserine*, from *cutis* ("skin") and *anser* ("goose"); and *piloerection* , "hair" again plus the Latin word for "to set up."

Believe it or not, humans aren't the only ones who get so frightened they feel goosebumps. Demons do, too. Yes, demons are disembodied spirits without skin or muscle, but God's Word uses the image of them shuddering to convey the kind of fear that demons experience when they consider standing before God and being judged. This is very important for us to know because humanity has had a history of fearing demons. God's Word, however, helps us overcome that fear by showing us that demons fear God. And, of course, God is on *our* side.

We see this in James 2:19. Here, James was writing about the importance of having faith beyond simply believing in God. Genuine faith goes beyond belief and produces godly actions. James uses demons as his example of empty faith. Although they believe in God, they are ungodly. Belief is not enough to save them from judgment; they *will* face it. In light of this judgment, James says demons "shudder." The Greek word here is *phrissousin*. It means "to quiver," "to tremble," and "to be extremely fearful."

Another connotation of the word is "to bristle" or "rise up on end." (Think of the bristles on a brush.) In antiquity, it was used to describe a rough or uneven surface such as the plume of feathers on a helmet, a crowd holding up their hands to vote, and hair on a mane that bristles up. Easy to see how it became associated with being extremely afraid. When a person is terrified, their hair bristles up and their *goosebumps* make their skin look as uneven as a crowd full of voters, holding up their hands.

Every time I see reports of horrific and senseless violence—such as school shootings, rapes, kidnappings, terrorist activity—I think about how demons have instigated this activity. Evil like this is evidence of invisible, malignant beings fostering the rupture and destruction of humanity.

But demons know they aren't going to get away with it. They are ever-conscious that they will face a just God who will respond to every evil action. God is not only keeping record of mankind's actions; He keeps track of demons' actions, too. He is counting up all the times they have prompted hate crimes, depression, war, false religion, violence, perversion, and racism. He is going to make sure they are punished for mocking His ways and opposing His kingdom.

We now have a better picture of the fear that demons experience when they think about standing before God and facing their judgment. James was telling us that such a thought literally gives them the goosebumps. It's the fear demons feel when they think about answering to God for the suffering they have caused throughout world history. Our God is the Almighty and demons shudder at His justice. In His presence, they are as helpless as a plucked turkey.

While demons cause terror and wreak havoc, there's no need for *you* to be afraid of *them*. Instead, rejoice that the same God who is going to show them harsh punishment has shown you love, grace, and mercy, because He cares about you deeply.

If you do happen to get goosebumps, they should come from considering the goodness and faithfulness that God has shown to us.

52

SHOW: *SYNISTĒMI*
(συνίστημι)

But God shows his love for us in that while we were still sinners, Christ died for us. (Romans 5:8)

συνίστησιν δὲ τὴν ἑαυτοῦ ἀγάπην εἰς ἡμᾶς ὁ θεός, ὅτι ἔτι ἁμαρτωλῶν ὄντων ἡμῶν Χριστὸς ὑπὲρ ἡμῶν ἀπέθανεν. (ΠΡΟΣ ΡΩΜΑΙΟΥΣ 5:8)

I am a man who adores desserts. All things chocolate: that's my kryptonite. If you happen to be out for an evening stroll and see someone gawking into the glow of a restaurant window, admiring delicious, chocolatey cakes and pies, chances are it's me, the author of this book.

When it comes to sweets, it's hard to beat what they have going on in Europe. If you haven't been there, let me just say, their dessert game is A-1.

The best part of the meal comes almost immediately after the server clears your plate. They take out this little shiny scraper and rasp away every pesky crumb until your table looks like you are just getting started. Excitement swells in your tummy because you sense that the server is making room for something special.

Suddenly, the waiter disappears into the night and returns moments later with a pushcart laden with an array of sweets that cause the optical nerves behind your eyes to sing, dance, and cheer with delight. The aroma enters your nasal passages, wraps itself around your neck, and whispers into your ear, "Which of us will you choose?" It's a tough choice, like deciding on what the best day of your life has been or, even harder, your favorite song. You can thank the pastry chef. He has done his job of showcasing his desserts in a convincing way. The fine details and spectacular arrangement drop you into a visual ecstasy that pushes aside your inhibitions. You drool and wiggle your fingers villainously and say, "I'll take the tiramisu." Hats off to the chef. He showcased his finest products and made it hard for you to resist.

> Gastrin, a popular dessert in ancient Greece, was similar to baklava. It contained various seeds, nuts, spices, and honey. Athenaeus, a second and third century author, mentions it in his work *Deipnosophistai* ("The Gastronomer") and credits Chrysippus of Tyana for the recipe.

Truth is, pastry chefs weren't the first to come up with the idea of showcasing. This is a tactic that God has employed in His plan to save man from rebellion and restore the relationship with Him. We see this in Romans 5:8: *"But God shows his love for us in that while we were still sinners, Christ died for us."* The word "shows" here in the Greek is *synistēsin*. One meaning of this word, particularly here, is "to set forth, demonstrate, present, bring to light." A modern way of presenting the idea is to say "showcase" or "display." You know, like fine desserts.

In Romans 5:8, Paul is writing to the Roman church about the astonishing nature of God's love. In 5:7, Paul makes the case that it's *rare* for someone to die for a good person, yet it isn't unimaginable. Though uncommon, it happens. These are acts of heroism, as when a fellow soldier takes a bullet for their comrade or when a friend donates a kidney to their bff and risks dying (and sometimes does). Yet, Paul says God's love is more astonishing because it goes a step further. Here is where Paul says that God "showcases" *His* love. God has this magnificent love, His finest product if you will, and He had a way of putting it on magnificent display for the world. He put it on the cart and wheeled it out before humanity so we could ooo and ahh over it. His hope was that we would find it hard to resist and want to indulge in it.

Have you figured out what this display looked like? A T-shaped Roman cross, with the outstretched arms of Jesus Christ upon it. It was God Himself dying the brutal death of a slave—not for His family, friends, or followers, but for His enemies, haters, and all of us who are sinners. This was the perfect showcase for perfect love. It was unheard of for an innocent man to die for his enemies. To quote the old Christian folk hymn, "What wondrous love is this?" Who could resist such an extraordinary thing? It's God's will that nobody passes it up. He wants us all to receive it with joy in our hearts, smiles on our faces, and, sometimes, tears streaming down our cheeks. It makes Him happy to see us enjoy His great gift.

Maybe you've never experienced this sort of love. Perhaps you've been involved in one-sided relationships where you were the one always giving and the other party was always taking. Maybe you are a victim of abuse or have suffered from emotional turmoil because your parents gave you up, not wanting to raise you. Or is it possible your past addictions have made you believe nobody could ever love you? The good news is the pastry chef is making his rounds. He has a display he wants you to check out. Don't shoo it away so fast. God wants you to indulge in the work of Christ.

Instead of focusing on all those who have come up short in their display of love, why not set your heart and mind on the showcase of perfect love? I guarantee you, the more you meditate on it, the more you will be able to receive it. In return, it's likely your own life will become its own showcase of this godly love. Your enemies better watch out: there's a pastry cart coming their way.

53

STIR UP: *ANASEIŌ*
(ἀνασείω)

---

*But the chief priests **stirred up** the crowd to have him release for them Barabbas instead.* (Mark 15:11)

οἱ δὲ ἀρχιερεῖς ἀνέσεισαν τὸν ὄχλον ἵνα μᾶλλον τὸν Βαραββᾶν ἀπολύσῃ αὐτοῖς. (ΚΑΤΑ ΜΑΡΚΟΝ 15:11)

Greek mythology was an absorbing subject to me in school. I found it intriguing to hear about the pagan gods that influenced Greco-Roman thought and culture, especially since the early church challenged these influences throughout the New Testament.

Poseidon is one of the most famous Greek gods. Best known as the god of the sea, he is often depicted as riding around the waters in a chariot pulled by fish-tailed horses, seahorses, or dolphins. Poseidon was known for his awful temper, so he was considered to be the most disruptive of all the Olympian gods. He was ever interrupting the plans of Zeus and he was known to trouble the sea.

Statues of Poseidon or his Roman equivalent, Neptune, are common in Europe. Perhaps the most famous ones are in Bristol, England; Prešov, Slovakia; and Berlin, Germany. These depict the troublemaking god holding his weapon, the trident (a fish spear), that he would use to demonstrate his might and take revenge by splitting rocks, causing gale-force winds, and creating overpowering walls of water.

Poseidon was also the god of earthquakes, storms, and floods. For this, he earned the nickname *ho seiōn*, or "the shaker," as Plato called him. The ancient Greek writers Aristophanes and Xenophon agreed that when the earth or sea was trembling, Poseidon was busy shaking it up.

Polyphemus's mother was Thoosa, a sea nymph who looked like a mermaid. She was associated with dangerous currents.

We see an example of this in Homer's *Odyssey*. Odysseus had blinded Poseidon's giant cyclops son, Polyphemus, by jamming a burning spear into his only eye. Then Odysseus insulted him. Poseidon took his revenge when he discovered Odysseus out to sea in a raft. He stirred up the waters with his trident and blasted Odysseus with a storm. The raft was torn to pieces and Odysseus would have drowned if he hadn't been rescued by the sea-goddess, Leukothea.

While we know that these characters and stories are simply myths, they were influential two thousand years ago. It would not be unheard of for an early Christian to read or hear the historical occurrences of the New Testament through the lens of Greek mythology. A perfect example is in Mark 15:11. Here, the crowds were urging Pilate to release a prisoner for Passover, as was his normal custom. By this time, Jesus had been arrested; Pilate asked the crowd if they wanted him to release Jesus. The text says the chief priests "stirred up" the crowd so Pilate would instead release Barabbas, another political prisoner.

The Greek word here for "stirred up" is *aneseisan*. It is a two-part word that comes from the preposition *ana*, which can mean "up," and the word *seiō* ("to shake," "to agitate," "to cause something to move back and forth rapidly and violently," "to whip something back and forth"). The nickname for Poseidon, *ho seiōn* ("the shaker"), comes from *seiō*.

When *seiō* is combined with *ana* and makes *anaseiō*, it literally means "to shake up" and denotes a very intense form of shaking up, stirring up, or whipping up. It is possible that this action by the chief priests reminded some early readers of Poseidon— stirring up the winds violently and treacherously shaking up the sea when he was angry and upset. This makes perfect sense because the religious leaders were angry at Jesus and trying to take revenge on Him for His Messianic displays of power.

So, here we have an incredible picture: the religious leaders are stirring up the crowd violently like a terrible sea storm, trying to sink the Messiah, once and for all. In this moment, we get a first-century glimpse of just how much Jesus faced during His time of trial. Here He was, the lonely Savior in the middle of a violent storm of people, none of whom cared if He should die. That's a desolate place to be. Yet, He stood strong through it all, weathered the storm, and hung on the cross.

We can rest assured that, if we want to serve Christ, we can expect that the enemy will stir up treacherous storms for us as well. Have you ever been in a place where you felt as though the enemy had shaken up the winds against you? God's Word is teaching us here that being a Christian and living for Christ can be a lonely experience, full of these types of experiences. Whether it comes in the form of people who persecute you, situations that obstruct you, or temptations that challenge you, Satan will do his best to drown your faith.

Nevertheless, the Holy Spirit has been given to us so that we can be strong during these storms and fulfill what the Lord has called us to do, despite Satan's best attempt to agitate our environment.

Has the enemy stirred up anything in particular in your life? How have you been standing against it? Ask the Lord for His help. He will give you the strength you need to outlast these storms. You can trust in the Lord to keep your head above the water and make sure you stay afloat.

Let the enemy get as angry as he wants. Let him send as many waves as he cares to send. If Christ outlasted the storm, so will you. *"He who is in you is greater than he who is in the world"* (1 John 4:4).

54

WARP: *EKSTREPHŌ*
(ἐκστρέφω)

---

*As for a person who stirs up division, after warning him once and then twice, have nothing more to do with him, knowing that such a person is **warped** and sinful; he is self-condemned.*
(Titus 3:10–11)

αἱρετικὸν ἄνθρωπον μετὰ μίαν καὶ δευτέραν νουθεσίαν παραιτοῦ, εἰδὼς ὅτι ἐξέστραπται ὁ τοιοῦτος καὶ ἁμαρτάνει ὢν αὐτοκατάκριτος. (ΠΡΟΣ ΤΙΤΟΝ 3:10–11)

Pulling clothes out of the dryer is at the top of my list of "things I hope I don't have to do in heaven." Sure, I enjoy the velvety, soft smell of dryer sheets and fresh clothes, but that doesn't make up for having to wrestle with my blue jeans and T-shirts in order to turn them right side out again.

It always seems that just about everything I pull out of the wash somehow manages to get turned inside out and is in desperate need of my untangling skills before I fold them and put them away. I have literally spent forty-five minutes just twisting clothes back to normal—the way they were when I put them into the wash. Strange things happen in the laundry room. It's a mysterious world. Forget space exploration; I'd like some insight about what's going on in the washer and dryer.

Apparently, I'm not the only one who's been tangled up. In 1993, an eighth-grader named Christie was in knots about how the laundry had been coming out of the dryer inside out. She decided to unravel the issue by doing a little research of her own. A student at Los Cerritos Intermediate School in Thousand Oaks, California, Christie charted her family's underwear in the laundry as her project for the school's science fair. For over a hundred loads, Christie made sure that her family's underwear—hers, her parents', and her seventeen-year-old sister's—were turned right side out before being tossed into the washing machine.

When her data assessment came to an end, she noted that more than 50 percent of the time, the washer, dryer, or both turned the underwear inside out. Christie figured it out—no more sleepless nights for those of us who suspect there are dryer goblins. The washer and dryer do enough tossing and tumbling to warp our clothes, especially our underwear. For solving this mystery, Christie earned first place in her division at the Ventura County Science Fair and went on to the state finals at the Museum of Science in Los Angeles.

Jockey International, a popular brand of underwear, heard about her experiment and sent each family member six packs of underwear, informing Christie that it would emerge as a superior brand of underwear in her research. If that's the case, I need to get some of those. I'm tired of dealing with things that are inside out.

In Titus 3:4, the apostle Paul writes about the inside-out minds of carnal people and their thinking. Paul is instructing Titus to avoid such people because they are divisive and only want to argue for the sake of argument. You know the type: people who think they're always right and everyone else is wrong, who won't let you get a word in edgewise without some sort of smug contradiction.

Crete is the largest Greek island, the fifth largest island in the Mediterranean Sea, and the eighty-eighth largest island in the world. Humans have inhabited Crete for at least 130,000 years.

On the island of Crete, where Titus pastored, these types of people were found among Jewish rabbis as well as Greek philosophers. Both parties were obsessed with making excessively fine distinctions about obscure philosophical and theological matters, while neglecting the basic tasks of serving God at the same time. Imagine sitting around talking about minute points of an obscure doctrine on charity, but doing nothing to help the homeless or feed the poor. This sort of thinking seems twisted, backwards, and inside-out. And that's exactly what it is.

Paul says a person who thinks this way is "warped." The Greek word for "warped" here is *exestraptai*. This is a two-part Greek word that comes from *ek* ("out of") and *strephō* ("to twist," "to turn," and "to bend.") When combined, it literally means to "turn out" or "to twist out" and was used to describe distorting something by means of turning it inside out.

Like a menacing washer or dryer, Satan had turned the minds of these particular individuals inside out so that they majored on the minors and minored on the majors. They were backwards in the way they thought about religion. The way they supposedly served God was all twisted up and tangled.

Paul advised Titus to avoid people like this. He wasn't even to try turning these people right-side out—it would be a waste of time. Titus could find better things to do. After all, they would only tell Titus that what he was doing was wrong and argue with him about everything. Sounds like endless hours of unproductive confusion. Why bother?

The problem isn't people who disagree with us, but those who just love to argue and prioritize the wrong things when it comes to serving God. Do you know people whose thinking is inside out? If so, avoid conversations with them. Like clothes in the wash, their rationale is twisted and you aren't going to find much success trying to untangle it. It's much harder than untangling a pair of jeans or underwear, believe me. Instead, use your energies to serve God in more fruitful ways, like simply praying for those individuals or showing them kindness when they want to argue.

Instead of going to war with these folks on Facebook or going back-and-forth with them in a group text, why not spend that time evangelizing the lost, feeding the poor, or serving your church? If you do, you'll discover a more fruitful and enjoyable Christian life.

55

DECEITFUL: *PLANOS* (πλάνος)

---

*Now the Spirit expressly says that in later times some will depart from the faith by devoting themselves to **deceitful** spirits and teachings of demons.* (1 Timothy 4:1)

Τὸ δὲ πνεῦμα ῥητῶς λέγει ὅτι ἐν ὑστέροις καιροῖς ἀποστήσονταί τινες τῆς πίστεως προσέχοντες πνεύμασιν πλάνοις καὶ διδασκαλίαις δαιμονίων.

(ΠΡΟΣ ΤΙΜΟΘΕΟΝ Α 4:1)

Horseback riding has never gone well for me. I've done it twice in my life and, in both instances, my horse got distracted and veered off course. The first time was when I was eight. My little horse attempted to go ahead of the rest of the horses and ended up getting kicked in the face by one of its friends. This nearly sent me sailing into the air. It kept me off horses for about twenty years.

In the Caribbean a few years back, I decided to be brave and try riding again. This time, it was worse. We were riding along on the beach, letting the horses gallop in the water. Things were going well until my horse saw a few stray dogs. Against commands, it took off and began chasing them— with me struggling on his back. While everyone was calmly walking their horses in a single file, there I was on the other side of the beach, in the middle of a wild dog chase.

Some horses get distracted and take off wherever they please. Just ask Sean Bowen, the jockey for a horse named Reckless Behavior. That horse lived up to his name one March afternoon in 2019 while at the Uttoxeter track in Staffordshire, England.

It was a typical race day. Reckless Behavior was entered in the two-and-a-half-mile handicap chase. Just as the race began, the horse tossed Bowen off his back, crashed through the guard rails, and escaped the track. Soon, Reckless Behavior was living large, wandering the streets of Uttoxeter. Witnesses said the horse trotted past a few roundabouts while a convoy of vehicles from the course attempted to track him down. He made his way to the town square and, when he was finally caught, he was hanging out next to a Domino's Pizza. When Bowen was asked about the incident, he said, "He just has his own way of thinking." A wandering mind, I guess you could say.

In 1 Timothy 4:1, God's Word talks about wandering off track. While not referring to horses, it does refer to individuals who demonstrate reckless behavior and veer from the true faith of Christ. Here, the apostle Paul has just finished discussing the true doctrines concerning Christ (see 1 Timothy 3:16) and is contrasting them with false teachers and their teachings. Paul makes it clear that these teachers have deviated from the faith because they've followed "deceitful" spirits. The Greek word here for "deceitful" is *planois*. It is an adjective describing the supernatural, evil spirits that have caused the false teachers to wander from the truth.

Planos literally means "leading astray," "causing someone to be mistaken," and "misleading." In antiquity, its cognate words were used to describe stars that appear to wander without an orbit and bees that buzz around randomly, without any particular direction. Homer used it in *The Iliad* to describe horses that wander off the race course, like Reckless Behavior.

In his biography, *The Life of Alexander the Great*, Plutarch said the king slept with a copy of *The Iliad* under his pillow at night. Historians doubt this, however, since the size of *The Iliad* on papyrus would make that impossible.

The apostle Paul was telling Timothy that wicked spirits had taken these false teachers along for a ride that led them away from the track of truth. This would have made sense to Timothy because he was pastoring in Ephesus, where people believed that malevolent spirits haunted the air and attempted to destroy people. Paul was affirming this was so. (See also Ephesians 6:12.)

The notion here is that obliging a deceitful spirit is like riding a rogue horse. It's sure to take you far away from the truth, opposite of where Christ wants you to be.

Have you ever met someone who veered from the truth in Christ? Perhaps while in college or around midlife? They might say they've been enlightened, undergone a shift in their thinking, or have found another way to practice their spirituality. While they think they're being smart or more cultured, God's Word says they're being deceived on a ride that leads away from Him.

As you move forward in your faith in Christ, realize that there will come times in your life when Satan will try to turn you off course. He has legions of wicked spirits that work through people. They will do their best to draw you away from the Word of God that has been planted in your heart.

This may happen in a philosophy class in college, where an articulate and informed professor does his or her best to make a case against the Bible. It may take place in a discussion with friends who push unconventional ideas now popular in the culture. It could even happen over time as you surf YouTube and find secular speakers who challenge the fundamental things you grew up hearing in church or Bible studies. Satan is ready to help you mount up on a crazy horse that's pawing the ground, eager to take you for a bumpy ride down the road of lies and trickery.

Keep a guard over your heart and mind. (See Proverbs 4:23.) As Paul told Timothy, *"Have nothing to do with irreverent, silly myths. Rather train yourself for godliness…as it holds promise for the present life and also for the life to come"* (1 Timothy 4:7–8).

56

STRONGHOLD: *OCHYRŌMA*
(ὀχύρωμα)

---

*For the weapons of our warfare are not of the flesh but have
divine power to destroy strongholds.* (2 Corinthians 10:4)

τὰ γὰρ ὅπλα τῆς στρατείας ἡμῶν οὐ σαρκικὰ ἀλλὰ
δυνατὰ τῷ θεῷ πρὸς καθαίρεσιν ὀχυρωμάτων, λογισμοὺς
καθαιροῦντες. (ΠΡΟΣ ΚΟΡΙΝΘΙΟΥΣ Β 10:4)

In 332 BC, Alexander the Great led one of the most vicious sieges the
world has ever known against the city of Tyre. The Siege of Tyre began
when the Tyrians refused to let Alexander sacrifice to the god Heracles in
their city. This upset Alexander and escalated into a standoff between his
forces and the Tyrian military. Despite Alexander's strength, the Tyrians
were confident they couldn't be defeated. Their city was about a half-mile

inland and was fortified by walls that were said to be 150 feet high. This made it tough for even the best armies to overcome them.

But Alexander was determined. He ordered his men to use timber, rocks, and rubble to build a causeway across the water in order to reach the city, so they could then bombard it. During this process, it occurred to Alexander that he needed more naval support. He mustered two hundred and twenty ships from Byblus, Aradus, Rhodes, Lycia, Cilicia, Macedon, and Cyprus. He also recruited 4,000 extra soldiers.

When the time came for Alexander's army to strike, he sailed toward Tyre with his fleet and took the city by surprise. Conflict ensued. After a deadly skirmish, Alexander finally got his ships up to the city walls and his men pounded on them with battering rams. The Greeks finally broke through, rushed into the city, and started killing the Tyrians and looting their property.

Alexander showed them no mercy. His army killed over 6,000 Tyrians and crucified 2,000 more on the beach. He also sold 30,000 into slavery. It was a terrible slaughter and remains one of the greatest sieges on a military stronghold from the ancient world. A seemingly impenetrable fortress was seized by an army that crushed its way in. When it was all over, after seven long months, Alexander made his sacrifice to Heracles in Tyre.

In 2 Corinthians 10:4, the apostle Paul draws this imagery in writing about overpowering a fortress. But rather than a city wall, he is referring to the fortification around the human mind.

In this letter to the Corinthians, Paul was responding to criticisms from his enemies. They'd been saying that Paul conducted his ministry from the flesh, meaning he had no supernatural demonstrations or signs to back his rhetoric. He had no revelation or miracles to show the people, they said, so his ministry was nothing more than mere human effort. (See 2 Corinthians 12:1; 11–12).

In response, Paul uses military metaphors, telling the Corinthians that he doesn't wage war as a mere human being. Rather, his warfare, his gospel ministry, comes equipped with weapons of divine power to destroy "strongholds."

The Greek word for "strongholds" here is *ochyrōmatōn*. It means "fortress," "prison," and "strong-walled place." It describes a walled place that is fully capable of fortifying people and keeping them secure from outside forces. It comes from the root word *echō*, which means "to hold firm." Like the city of Tyre, it holds its citizens safely.

> Seneca was a first-century Roman Stoic who tutored Nero in his youth and advised him when he became emperor. Nero thought Seneca was involved in a plot to kill him so he ordered Seneca's death.

In antiquity, first-century philosophers such as Seneca used *ochyrōma* figuratively to describe persuasive arguments that a person used during a philosophical disagreement with an opponent. These arguments made it nearly impossible for their reasoning to be besieged, or for such orators to be convinced by the other side.

When writing to the Corinthians, Paul uses "strongholds" figuratively to describe the arguments his opponents would use to try to wall out the gospel to keep from being converted. It's likely you've talked to someone who has built up a stronghold around their thinking in order to keep the gospel out. They may use the arguments of popular atheist teachers, erect walls using *science*, or even use ideas from their own religion to keep the truth of Christ from pouring in.

If you've had experience talking to people like this, you know how difficult it is. To persuade them about Christ is like trying to besiege a fortified Tyre. But Paul was successful. Throughout the course of his ministry, he had ripped down many strongholds by preaching the gospel and making converts of the people. (See Acts 16:30–32; Acts 19:8.)

God had supernaturally empowered Paul; his ministry wasn't just from human effort, for he had God's help behind him. How else could he do it? Convincing people to change their beliefs is nothing short of a miracle. If you aren't certain of that, it's likely you haven't talked to many people about faith and religion yet!

But the good news is, we don't have to do it on our own. God has equipped us with His supernatural abilities to knock down philosophical battlements that stand in the way of people coming to Jesus. That takes the pressure off of *you*.

Don't be intimidated by others' arguments and reasoning. Don't let the Facebook comments that the atheist leaves under your post intimidate you. Don't go to bed feeling dreadful because you have nothing to say to convince people to seek Jesus. You aren't failing God. He knows how challenging these fortifications can be to penetrate and He would never expect you to do it by yourself.

You can tap into His help by simply seeking Him. Look to Jesus and ask the Holy Spirit to give you His wisdom and His anointing to share the gospel. (See James 1:5.) Get ready to be equipped with supernatural weapons that knock down even the strongest fortifications.

57

TREASURE UP: *SYNTĒRĒO* (συντηρέω)

---

*But Mary **treasured up** all these things, pondering them in her heart.* (Luke 2:19)

ἡ δὲ Μαριὰμ πάντα συνετήρει τὰ ῥήματα ταῦτα συμβάλλουσα ἐν τῇ καρδίᾳ αὐτῆς.

(ΚΑΤΑ ΛΟΥΚΑΝ 2:19)

Ever since the beginning of time, mankind has observed the cosmos and pondered the mysteries of the universe. There's an instinctive wonder that gets stirred up when we look into the starry sky on a clear night. *How big is the universe? Is there other life out there? Why are we here?* I'm sure you've contemplated these questions and many others like them. Our musings haven't been in vain, though. They've led us to important discoveries: the fact that the earth rotates around the sun; the existence of a star, Icarus, nine billion light years from earth; organic molecules on Mars; and ice at our moon's poles. While these are incredible finds, there remain endless questions to ponder. Pondering them, we are.

Great minds are hard at work, wrestling with the most complex secrets of the cosmos, such as:

- *Is there life out there?* Considering the size of the universe, we should have found another form of intelligent life by now. But we haven't. Are we all alone?

- *What's inside of a black hole?* We know that gravity is so strong within black holes that they swallow everything around them, including light. But what happens once something passes through?

- *What is dark matter?* Dark matter is supposed to make up 85 percent of the universe and is thought to hold it together. And we have no idea what it is.

- *Where did the moon come from?* We've been there, yes, but how did it start circling the earth? Did it come from another galaxy?

- *What's going to happen to the Arecibo Message?* This radio message was sent in 1974 to the star cluster M13 with basic information about humanity. It will take 25,000 years for it to reach its destination and, if reciprocated by intelligent life, at least another 25,000 years for a reply.

- *Do "daughter universes" exist?* Quantum theory suggests that all possible outcomes do occur and they all happen within another universe. If true, another universe exists in which you are married to the person you almost married. And you are there, thinking your reality is the only one.

Scientists will keep probing the universe until they figure these things out. And I'm glad they will. Their persistent pondering in the past has paid off. Today, we know more about the universe than we ever have and it has helped us to appreciate God's creation all the more.

In Luke 2:19, we are given a picture of Mary, the mother of Jesus, pondering the birth of Jesus like an astronomer studying a star. Certain shepherds had an angelic visitation, announcing to them that the Savior, Christ the Lord, had been born in the city of Bethlehem. The shepherds immediately rushed to Bethlehem and found Jesus, lying in a manger, Mary and Joseph beside Him. The shepherds told them about the angelic visitation and explained what the angels had told them. (See Luke 2:10–14.)

When Mary heard it, she "treasured up" all these things.

The Greek word here for "treasured up" is *syneterei*. It's a two-part word made up of *syn* ("with") and *tereo* ("to observe," "to keep in view," and "to take note of.") Interestingly enough, Aristotle used the word *tereo* in his *On the Heavens* to describe Egyptian and Babylonian scientists who had been involved in humanity's earliest space exploration. They took note of the stars and planets and made observations about them.

> The ancient Greeks believed that there were four elements: earth, water, air, and fire. Aristotle believed there was a fifth element, "aether," which comes from the Greek word *aither*, meaning "upper air" or "heavenly air."

When *tereo* is combined with *syn*, the word takes on more intensity. It describes someone watching over something with great vigilance and thorough reflection. It means "to ruminate," "to continue to think about," "to carefully observe," "to ponder what something might mean." It could describe an astronomer who, with great care and intensity, works out the profound mysteries of the cosmos by paying close attention to the collected data.

In this case, it gives us a picture of a deep-thinking Mary who is taking into consideration all of the data that the shepherds gave her, as well as the rest of the happenings of the nativity, to figure out exactly what Jesus's birth meant. By wrestling with her questions and being persistent in her musings, Mary was able to come to the right understanding about the Lord Jesus.

Mary is a perfect picture of how God wants us to seek Him. God's Word tells us that we must contemplate His Word and constantly keep it in our thoughts if we want it to produce a harvest of understanding. (See Luke 8:15.)

This is exactly what Mary did. It is what we must do as we consider who Jesus is and what He wants from our lives. If we don't, we'll never get answers from God's Word and it will be no one's fault but our own. So often, people blame God for their failure to understand His Word, but the truth is, they are the ones who don't spend any time probing it for discoveries. We have to seek in order to find. (See Matthew 7:7.)

Do you spend time searching out the vast universe of God's Word? Do you make time to study the Scriptures? Do you pay attention when the pastor is preaching in church? Do you think about the sermon throughout the week?

Exploring the Bible can be just as exciting as exploring the universe.

58

SELFISH AMBITION:
ERITHEIA (ἐριθεία)

---

*Do nothing from **selfish ambition** or conceit, but in humility count others more significant than yourselves.*

(Philippians 2:3)

μηδὲν κατ᾽ ἐριθείαν μηδὲ κατὰ κενοδοξίαν ἀλλὰ τῇ ταπεινοφροσύνῃ ἀλλήλους ἡγούμενοι ὑπερέχοντας ἑαυτῶν. (ΠΡΟΣ ΦΙΛΙΠΠΗΣΙΟΥΣ 2:3)

If you've lived long enough, then you know something about the nature of elections. Politics is a ruthless enterprise, with smear campaigns, mud flinging, scare tactics, lies, and manipulation. But modern political campaigns are tame compared to the brutal American presidential election of 1800. John Adams had been elected president in 1796, with Thomas Jefferson as vice president. The two were long-time friends, having met in 1775 as delegates to the Continental Congress. They grew closer later when they both lived in Europe, serving on diplomatic assignments.

Despite their friendship, Adams and Jefferson held different ideas about the role of government. Jefferson was part of the Democratic-Republican party and maintained the conviction that stronger rights belonged to the states. Adams was part of the Federalist party and believed in a stronger centralized government. These differences grew so vast that they bitterly separated the two friends. During his tenure as vice president, Jefferson abandoned Adams and went back to Monticello to figure out how to defeat Adams in 1800.

> In the first book of *Politics*, Aristotle wrote: "It is clear that the city-state is a natural growth, and that man is by nature a political animal, and a man that is by nature and not merely by fortune [cityless] is either low in the scale of humanity or above it."

As you can imagine, the campaign of 1800 was vicious. Mud-flinging went on left and right. Jefferson accused his good friend of being a "hideous hermaphroditical character, which has neither the force and firmness of a man, nor the gentleness and sensibility of a woman."

Adams's campaign fired back, calling Jefferson "a mean-spirited, low-lived fellow, the son of a half-breed Indian squaw, sired by a Virginia mulatto father." Even Martha Washington got in on the clash, coming to Adams's defense and calling Jefferson "one of the most detestable of mankind."

Jefferson got the last word. He hired someone in the press to spread a rumor that Adams wanted to attack France—a blatant lie. It proved to be effective, however, because many Americans believed the rumor and Jefferson won the election. Adams was so upset that he refused to show up at Jefferson's inauguration. The two friends didn't talk again for twelve years.

Despite the falling-out, they eventually began writing to each other in 1812, citing their mutual respect and desire to renew their friendship. Adams wrote to Jefferson from his home in Quincy, Massachusetts, wishing him a happy new year. Writing back from Monticello, his planta-tion home in Virginia, Jefferson responded cordially. Aged and living 564 miles apart, they remained pen pals for fourteen years and exchanged a combined 158 letters.

In what might be the greatest twist of irony in American history, the friends and former rivals died on the same day: July 4, 1826, the fiftieth an-niversary of the Declaration of Independence, which they both had helped to write. It's safe to say that these two men went through it all together, including the bitter pains of division caused by selfish ambition.

In Philippians 2:3, God's Word warns us about the divisions that come from our own selfish ambitions and instructs us to avoid them. Here, Paul was writing to the Philippian church, where there had been a rivalry going on among some of the believers. Paul was making a call for unity and giving practical advice about how to end these rivalries. He says, *"Do nothing from selfish ambition…"*

The Greek word here for "selfish ambition" is *eritheian*. It means "strife," "contentiousness," and "rivalry." Implied within the word is the idea of using whatever means necessary to one-up someone and look better than they do—like Adams and Jefferson did in 1800.

Aristotle used *eritheia* in his work, *Politics*, to describe candidates get-ting into office using unethical means. Even in his day, he was aware of the manipulation, coercion, and strong-arming that politicians use to get into power.

Yet, Paul is telling us that this doesn't ensue only in politics. It happens in the church. Believers compete with one another at each other's expense in order to achieve positions of leadership, celebrity, and prominence. Paul was telling the church to stop it immediately.

There's simply no room for rivalry in the church because it causes strife and division. Christ's body must not be divided. (See 1 Corinthians 1:10, 13.) Instead of campaigning for themselves, the believers were to serve one another, the way Christ served us.

Have you ever done something out of selfish ambition that cost one of your brothers or sisters in Christ? While it's likely you haven't run a public smear campaign, maybe you *have* smeared someone's name so that you could benefit from it. Or maybe you've been serving your church with a spirit of one-upmanship in order to get a position you're after, rather than simply serving your church as unto the Lord. Behavior like this may get you ahead in the short run, but in the long run, it's certain to cause you all kinds of problems, especially with the people you hurt. Whatever it is that you are after, it's not worth competing if you have to divide God's people to get it. There's nothing that God wants us to have that we must vie with other Christians to attain it.

If you've been competing with others, why not try a new approach to promotion? Instead of putting people down like you are running a sleazy political campaign, do what Jesus did and serve those people instead. The outcome will be a win-win that leaves everyone edified, blessed, and stronger.

59

HOSPITALITY: *PHILOXENOS* (φιλόξενος)

---

*Show **hospitality** to one another without grumbling.*
(1 Peter 4:9)

φιλόξενοι εἰς ἀλλήλους ἄνευ γογγυσμοῦ.
(ΠΕΤΡΟΥ Α 4:9)

Recently, I saw a decoration at a party store that summed up how many people in today's busy American culture feel about having family, friends, and neighbors over for an evening of socializing. The gold banner featured the shocking statement, "Please Leave By 9." Just imagine. You can suspend it over the cheese and crackers and people will be sure to get the hint. I shared a photo of it on social media. It blew up, with people saying, "Yes, that's exactly how I feel. I need one of those."

Many of us want to have people over, have a few laughs, and see our company to the door before we fall over from exhaustion or the refreshments run out. I get it. Yet this attitude toward hospitality is quite different from what I've received as an evangelist in different nations of the world.

From the moment I began my peripatetic travels, I quickly found that certain cultures exhibit a greater degree of hospitality than my own. For them, showing gracious hospitality is a fundamental part of who they are—to reject it was to reject them. If I didn't allow them to host me, it would do untold damage to the relationship. I thought I was doing them a favor by insisting on staying in a hotel. At the time, if I was in their shoes, I would have wanted *them* to stay at a hotel.

But this is a slap in the face on so many levels. In their cultures, they are taught that taking care of a stranger is a way to honor God. Would I deny them this? Should they let a hotel take care of me when God had given them that responsibility?

I saw this firsthand when I was preaching in Greece, traveling with a couple of other pastors. One night, we stopped to minister at a Gypsy church in Thessaloniki. It was my hope to check into a local hotel afterward, get some rest, and be on our way.

Not so fast. The pastor absolutely insisted we sleep at his house. My Bulgarian pastor friend told me, "Don't try to fight this. You have no idea how much you will offend him if you don't stay." Well, that was that.

When we got to his house, he set up three large tables in his front yard and his family began to cook up a feast. Mind you, it was eleven o'clock at night. They made lamb, pasta, roasted vegetables—it was amazing. After we ate, the pastor's family gave up their rooms and beds for us. We were awakened in the morning by an enormous breakfast before they hugged and kissed us goodbye and sent us on our way.

If I ever have felt the love of Jesus, it was on that hot August night in that Gypsy village in Greece. They treated me the way I imagine they would have treated the Lord. *That's* hospitality.

In 1 Peter 4:9, God's Word tells us about the importance of hospitality. It's not talking about the kind of hospitality where a host puts up a "Please Leave By 9" banner. No, it's a welcome that treats guests as though they were sent by the Lord Jesus Himself. Here in 1 Peter 4, Peter is discussing the imminence of Christ's return. He urges believers to use their abilities to serve the kingdom and make disciples.

One such ability is hospitality. Peter tells them to *"show hospitality… without grumbling."* The Greek word "hospitality" here is *philoxenoi*. It is a two-part Greek word that comes from *philos* ("loving," "having special interest," "friendly") and *xenos* ("stranger," "foreigner," "alien"). Combined, it means "love for the stranger," "special interest in the foreigner," and "friendliness to the alien."

According to a 2017 study by the University of South Wales, the University of Western Australia, and the University of Sydney, strangers do a better job picking out an attractive profile picture for our social media sites than we do for ourselves.

Peter was instructing the believers to open up their homes and welcome guests in a loving way, offering them the finest care. They could do this by housing traveling missionaries who were passing through, by welcoming unbelievers in order to build relationships that would lead to opportunities to share the gospel, and volunteering their homes to be used for congregating as a church.

This sort of hospitality was essential for the early church to grow. First, it wasn't ideal for traveling missionaries to stay in inns. In the first century, inns were dirty, expensive, and notorious for prostitution. It was far better for another believer to feed and shelter the missionaries.

Secondly, Christianity spread through relationships. Showing Christian hospitality to curious unbelievers was a key strategy for evangelism and church growth.

Thirdly, there were no church buildings for the first two hundred years of church history. In order for the church to congregate, hosts homes were needed. Hence, when believers showed great hospitality to allow strangers into their homes, the gospel spread.

Have you ever thought about how hospitable you are? Have you ever thought about it in connection to growing the kingdom of God? When the

Holy Spirit fills our hearts, He gives us a genuine desire to take good care of people who are *foreign* to us.

Whether this means letting the visiting preacher stay in the guest room of your home, inviting your unsaved neighbor over for a cup of tea, or volunteering your home on a weeknight for a small group, you are advancing the kingdom of God in a genuine way.

Don't make the mistake of thinking you need some enormous spiritual gift to make an impact on the kingdom. Much can be done by simply taking five-star care of the people God sends your way.

If you have anti-social tendencies, toss those aside lest they hinder what God can accomplish through you. When you welcome others with genuine hospitality, you'll see the kingdom grow right before your eyes.

60

COWORKER: *SYNERGOS*
(συνεργός)

And we sent Timothy, our brother and God's coworker in the gospel of Christ, to establish and exhort you in your faith.

(1 Thessalonians 3:2)

καὶ ἐπέμψαμεν Τιμόθεον, τὸν ἀδελφὸν ἡμῶν καὶ συνεργὸν τοῦ θεοῦ ἐν τῷ εὐαγγελίῳ τοῦ Χριστοῦ, εἰς τὸ στηρίξαι ὑμᾶς καὶ παρακαλέσαι ὑπὲρ τῆς πίστεως ὑμῶν.

(ΠΡΟΣ ΘΕΣΣΑΛΟΝΙΚΕΙΣ Α 3:2)

If you have *any* sort of job, you understand about *coworkers*, those people you work alongside for the greater good of the company or organization. You might love some of them, but there's probably a few who need your prayers.

The kind of coworkers you have will affect *your* work as well as your employer. Good ones bring greater productivity, a happy workplace, and higher revenue. Bad ones make for decreased productivity, a tense environment, and perhaps a decline in revenue. That's why everyone hopes for good coworkers who pull their weight and take tasks by the horns instead of those who drag their feet in the mud and complain about everything they have to do.

I'm sure you can remember noble coworkers you've had over the years. Strange ones are harder to forget. In a 2012 article, *Business Insider* compiled a list of the most ridiculous and bizarre things people have ever seen their coworkers do.

A construction employee got sacked. Distraught, he went home, put on a Godzilla suit, came back to the office wearing it, and destroyed all the tiny scale model homes that this development company had set up for display.

One elementary school didn't have Wi-Fi because a teacher brought a note from her chiropractor saying she was allergic to electricity, especially Wi-Fi. If that was not enough, when she felt her condition getting worse, she'd ask coworkers to turn off their cell phones. Not sure I could deal with that.

A pizza shop worker said one of his coworkers came into work one day, made ten pepperoni pizzas, took a single slice from each one, and assembled these in a box, which he took home for himself. When confronted, he denied the whole thing. Stealing pizza has apparently become an art.

Our jobs are healthier when we have good coworkers sharing the load. Otherwise, work can be a grind.

First Thessalonians was the first epistle written by Paul, around AD 52. The Scriptures include thirteen of the apostle's letters, but it's believed that he wrote hundreds of letters during his lifetime.

In 1 Thessalonians 3:2, the apostle Paul is writing to the Thessalonians about kingdom work. He tells them something quite interesting: Timothy is *"God's coworker."* In other words, God considers His servants His "coworkers."

Before we take a look at what this word means, here's a little background: Paul wanted to visit the Thessalonian church again, but he had been unable to go. So, he sent Timothy to strengthen the Thessalonians' faith and encourage them with the Word of God. Paul wanted the Thessalonians to see Timothy as a credible and capable minister, so Paul endorsed Timothy with the title, "God's coworker."

The Greek word here for "coworker" is *synergon*, a two-part Greek word that comes from *syn* ("with," "linked together," "partnered up") and *ergon* ("task," "occupation," "labor," "undertaking"). When the words are combined to form *synergos*, it means "partnering together for a task" and "linking together for occupational purposes."

In antiquity, it defined two people who shared the same trade, like colleagues and associates. When used in a negative sense, it described an accomplice to a crime. The idea is simply two or more individuals on a mutual mission, pulling their weight, in order to accomplish the shared goal. Paul was saying that Timothy was linked with God and was working with Him to bring people to faith in Jesus Christ.

What a thought—we are *colleagues* with God. While this is exciting, it's also a great responsibility. We must decide what kind of coworker we want to be. Are we going to be the kind who pulls our weight, eagerly taking on the tasks that the Lord gives us and finishing them with excellence? Or are we going to be the kind of colleague who puts on a Godzilla suit, steals pizza, and complains about the Wi-Fi?

I, for one, want to be the kind of coworker God looks forward to working with. I don't want Him wondering what I'm going to do next. Instead, I want Him to know that when I am working for the kingdom, He's always going to get my best work, without complaints.

Is there a task that the Lord has given you to fulfill? Is there some weight that God has asked you to pull? How are you doing with it? Are you cutting corners and procrastinating, or have you been staying on top of things for the glory of the kingdom?

If you think that you could be doing better with what God has asked you to do, decide right now to become a better associate. Tell the Lord where you have failed and ask Him for His help. He will be delighted to hear your heart and will be excited to keep working with you to bring people to Jesus. The work we do alongside God is the most important work we could ever do for anyone. Let's give God our best and be a coworker He can count on.

61

HELPER: *PARAKLĒTOS* (παράκλητος)

And I will ask the Father, and he will give you another Helper, to be with you forever.   (John 14:16)

κἀγὼ ἐρωτήσω τὸν πατέρα καὶ ἄλλον παράκλητον δώσει ὑμῖν, ἵνα μεθ' ὑμῶν εἰς τὸν αἰῶνα ᾖ.
                                        (ΚΑΤΑ ΙΩΑΝΝΗΝ 14:16)

Dispatcher Antonia Bundy of Lafayette, Indiana, received an unusual call for emergency help one January afternoon in 2019. On the other end of the line was a little boy, summoning her for assistance...with his homework. That's right: the innocent student called 9-1-1 because he'd had a bad day at school and needed someone to show him how to add fractions. (I understand the little guy's pain—fractions weren't necessarily my forte in school either.) Instead of dismissing the child's problem as irrelevant, the kind dispatcher comforted him and helped him work through his problem. According *ABC News*, the conversation went like this:

Dispatcher: Nine-one-one.
Boy: Hi, um, I had a really bad day and… I just, I don't know.
Dispatcher: You had a bad day at school?
Boy: Yeah…
Dispatcher: What happened at school that made you have a bad day?
Boy: I just have tons of homework.
Dispatcher: OK. What subject do you have homework in?
Boy: Math. And it's so hard.
Dispatcher: Is there a problem you want me to help you with?
Boy: Yeah, um, what's three-fourths plus one-fourth?
Dispatcher: So, do you have your paperwork in front of you?
Boy: Yeah.
Dispatcher: OK. So if you do, three over four. Put that on your paper.
Boy: OK.
Dispatcher: And then do plus one over four.
Boy: OK.
Dispatcher: OK, so, what's three plus one?
Boy: Four.
Dispatcher: Ok and then… four over four is what?
Boy: One?
Dispatcher: Yeah. Good job.
Boy: Thank you.
Dispatcher: You're welcome. Was that your only problem?
Boy: Yeah. I'm sorry for calling, but I really needed help.
Dispatcher: You're fine. We're always here to help.

Bundy's department applauded the way she helped the young boy. Instead of scolding him for using an emergency line for homework help, she exhibited empathy and understanding, going the extra mile to make sure the little guy was taken care of. On top of that, she let the boy know that he could always count on them for help—someone cared. It must have been encouraging for him to know that he wasn't facing the wide world of math alone. If he ever happened to run into difficulty again, a faithful helper stood by. All he needed to do was call.

> If you call 9-1-1 by mistake, authorities say you should not hang up because the dispatcher may think you have an actual emergency. Instead, remain calm and explain what happened.

In John 14, we find a Helper of a different sort. While He's not an emergency dispatcher, He *is* someone who's always standing by to be called upon in time of need. Jesus introduces us to Him in John 14:16.

Here, the Lord was telling His disciples that He would be leaving them. This made them uneasy because Jesus had been their leader for three years. He had protected them from all kinds of calamity, human evil, and persecution. The thought of His departure would have frightened them and left them wondering who would help them when they next ran into trouble. Jesus answers this by saying, *"And I will ask the Father, and he will give you another Helper, to be with you forever"* (John 14:16). The disciples wouldn't be left alone to fend for themselves. A Helper was on the way.

The Greek word for "Helper" is *paraklēton*. It is a two-part Greek word and comes from *para* ("by the side of") and *kaleō* ("to call"). When combined to form *paraklētos*, it means "someone called by the side to help." In antiquity, it was used to describe legal experts who were called in to stand beside their clients and assist them as they stood before the courts. These advocates would encourage their clients and strengthen their cause, providing comfort to them during a volatile and crucial situation.

Later, the word was used more broadly to denote one who helps, consoles, and encourages, but not just in the legal sense. It was someone who did whatever was necessary to support and lift up the person they were helping. When Jesus used it to describe the Holy Spirit, He was assuring His disciples that they would be receiving a Divine Helper who would encourage them, strengthen them, protect them, lead them, teach them, give them what to say, and do whatever else was necessary to take care of them. (See John 14:26; 16:7–14; Matthew 10:19–20.) Jesus had called in the help of the Holy Spirit to assist those who lived for Him in the midst of this harsh and difficult world. All we need to do is call upon Him in times of need.

Have you been taking advantage of the Helper that the Lord has sent to be by your side? Or have you been trying to figure out life's challenges all by yourself? Like the little boy who innocently called 9-1-1 with simple faith expecting to find help, maybe you need to call upon the Holy Spirit with the expectation that He will be patient with you and give you the solution to your problem.

The fact of the matter is that life is difficult; we can often feel lonely, especially when we live taking a stand for Jesus. But God doesn't *expect* you to do it all alone. He doesn't *want* you to do it all alone. You *can't* do it all alone.

Why not renew your relationship with the Helper? Tell Him about your problem and ask Him to encourage you, protect you, guide you, lead you, and even teach you so you can come out of the difficulty on top. Just as the dispatcher promised the young boy that they'd always be there to help, so Jesus has promised that help is always available when we need it.

Don't hesitate to call upon the Holy Spirit. He's standing by, ready to assist. He has everything you need.

62

BABYLON: *BABYLŌN*
(Βαβυλών)

Fallen, fallen is Babylon the great! She has become a dwelling place for demons, a haunt for every unclean spirit, a haunt for every unclean bird, a haunt for every unclean and detestable beast. (Revelation 18:2)

καὶ ἔκραξεν ἐν ἰσχυρᾷ φωνῇ λέγων, Ἔπεσεν ἔπεσεν Βαβυλὼν ἡ μεγάλη, καὶ ἐγένετο κατοικητήριον δαιμονίων καὶ φυλακὴ παντὸς πνεύματος ἀκαθάρτου καὶ φυλακὴ παντὸς ὀρνέου ἀκαθάρτου [καὶ φυλακὴ παντὸς θηρίου ἀκαθάρτου] καὶ μεμισημένου.

(ΑΠΟΚΑΛΥΨΙΣ ΙΩΑΝΝΟΥ 18:2)

The Internet went crazy on February 26, 2015. Perhaps you recall *the dress* that was introduced to the world and the arguments over its colors. Was it blue and black, or white and gold? To this day, I haven't been able to see anything but white and gold. But according to a BuzzFeed poll, 33 percent of people surveyed swear it's blue and black. Everyone was looking at the same photo of the same dress and seeing completely different things. What a puzzle.

The whole thing began one day on the Scottish Isle of Colonsay. The mother of a bride was planning to wear the dress to her daughter's wedding, so she sent her daughter a picture of it. When her daughter showed it to her fiancé, they disagreed over the color. To solve the dispute, the daughter posted the photo on Facebook and asked people what they thought. The band playing at the wedding took notice and they, too, disagreed. For further feedback, one of the band members posted the photo to a popular fan page. That's when it went viral and broke the Internet. Taylor Swift, Justin Bieber, Kim Kardashian, and many other celebrities got in on the action.

At the height of its popularity, #thedress was being tweeted about 11,000 times a minute on Twitter and it seemed the world had split over what it was seeing. *The Washington Post* had good reason to call it drama that "divided the planet." While it's now a thing of the past, I'm sure you can mention the dress and still stir up some pretty contested conversation. It just goes to show how people see things differently.

In Revelation 18:2, we are presented with something that people have looked at differently since the beginning of time. While it's not a multi-colored dress, it is a city that eventually came to stand for a world system in opposition to God: Babylon. The Greek word here is *Babylōn*, which is a Greek translation for the Hebrew word *bābel*. To understand the meaning and significance of this word, we need to go back to Genesis 11:1–9 and the story of the tower of Babel. Here, a group of people settled in southern Mesopotamia and began to build a ziggurat, a pyramid-like tower that was dedicated to deities.

Inside the ziggurat was a staircase that led to the top, where there was a small room with a bed and table to host a deity. Behind this practice was the belief that gods traveled from their realm to Earth using the staircase. The ziggurat signified that the gods visited their town and ruled its inhabitants. As a result, this civilization called itself *Babylon*. In the ancient

Akkadian writing of the Babylonians, this was the word *babilu*, which meant "gate of the gods." They believed their city was special, that their culture was progressive and advanced.

But the people of God, the Hebrews, saw the Babylonian civilization differently. In the story, the Lord came down and took notice of the ziggurat that the Babylonians had built. (See Genesis 11:5.) He was so displeased that He came back a second time and disrupted their plans by confusing their languages. (See Genesis 11:7.) So rather than calling Babylon "the gate of the gods," the Hebrews played on the word *babilu* and called it the Hebrew word *bābel*, which means "confused" and "mixed up," referring to the place where God ended the plans of a wicked society. (See Genesis 11:9.) The Hebrews didn't see the city in the same light as the Babylonians; instead, they saw it as a culture that was distorted and desolate.

Ancient Babylon is located in modern-day Iraq, fifty-some miles southwest of Baghdad. The ruins there have been designated a United Nations World Heritage Site.

As time went on, the story of Babylon was not forgotten and the city is mentioned more than two hundred times throughout Scripture. Some saw Babylon's splendor, while others saw its despair. (See, for example, Isaiah 13:19; Jeremiah 50:23; Daniel 2). This occurs consistently until we get to the visions of the Apocalypse. John shows people who are enamored by the Babylonian culture and others who reject it. (See Revelation 17:2–5; 18:4.) In the end, Babylon is destroyed once and for all and God brings His city, the New Jerusalem, to replace it forever. (See Revelation 18:2; 21:2.)

By talking about Babylon, John is telling us something important: while the actual city of Babylon no longer exists, its culture still does. Its sins are seen in our modern cities every day—idolatry, drunkenness, sexual immorality, hatred, murder, pride in human achievement, and, at the center of it all, a rejection of the one true God. The question is, how do *we* see Babylon? Do we see its practices as a sign of forward-thinking and the advancement of humanity, or do we see them as mixed up and counter to God's laws?

In our contemplation, we must remember that Babylon is going to be judged in the end. We do ourselves a disservice of eternal proportions if we fail to see Babylon for what it is: confused, mixed up, and something to be avoided.

When you look at modern society, don't be perturbed if you see it differently than those around you. While some people might see an ad on TV and say, "Wow, that looks really great," *you* might say, "That looks disgusting."

Remember, there are two ways that people have regarded Babylon over the millennia. If your eyes ache at the sight of it, you are observing it the right way. Believe me, there is going to come a day when you are glad you see its true colors.

63

WELCOME: PROSLAMBĀNO (προσλαμβάνω)

Therefore **welcome** *one another as Christ has* **welcomed** *you, for the glory of God.* (Romans 15:7)

Διὸ προσλαμβάνεσθε ἀλλήλους, καθὼς καὶ ὁ Χριστὸς προσελάβετο ὑμᾶς εἰς δόξαν τοῦ θεοῦ.

(ΠΡΟΣ ΡΩΜΑΙΟΥΣ 15:7)

April 16, 2015, was a pretty average day for twenty-nine-year-old Jason Warnock. The construction worker was driving in Lewiston, Idaho, minding his own business, when he came upon a fallen tree in the road. What had happened? Curious, Warnock looked up the cliff next to him and noticed something shocking: a 2000 GMC Yukon hanging off, ready to plummet down the thirty-foot drop.

Matthew Sitko, age twenty-three, was trapped inside the Yukon. The only thing keeping him and his SUV from falling off the steep cliff was a weak chain-link fence. Warnock realized there wasn't much time. He had to save the driver before the fence gave out. He rushed into action. He raced across a footbridge, climbed up the precipitous hillside, and passed over an embankment to reach the vehicle. When Warnock arrived, he realized he couldn't smash the window to get Sitko out. Doing so would have shaken the SUV and sent it over the cliff.

Instead, Warnock got Sitko to calmly roll down the window. Then he said, "Give me your hand. If this thing goes, I want to have a hold of you so I can at least snag you out of there." It worked. He successfully rescued the other man.

As the two sat next to the Yukon and waited for police to arrive, Sitko told Warnock that he had just begun reading his Bible the night before. Warnock said, "That's great. Maybe God put me here at the right time."

I'd say that sounds about right. God sent Warnock to Sitko in order to lend a hand. If there's anything I know to be true about God, it's that He expects us to help one another, even if the situation isn't ideal. After all, that's what Christ did for us.

In Romans 15:7, God's Word talks about extending ourselves for the sake of the other person, especially in sensitive situations. The situation in Rome was complex, to say the least. There had been controversy over Christian liberty. Some Christians observed dietary restrictions; others didn't. Moreover, some Christians observed certain days as holier than others, while some Christians didn't differentiate and lived *all* days as holy unto the Lord. (See Romans 14.) Paul explains these differences by saying that Christians in the *same* fellowship share *different* convictions. This had become divisive.

Have you experienced this before? I certainly have. Growing up, I came from a denomination that frowned upon wine. When I was in Bible school, if a student was caught drinking a glass of wine, they would be reprimanded and a write-up would go into their file.

"Small cheer and great welcome makes a merry feast."—William Shakespeare, *The Comedy of Errors*

However, when I preached in certain countries in Europe, I discovered that if you refrain from drinking wine, you may be looked upon as self-righteous and weak-minded. Refusing to drink wine condemned those who *were* drinking it, making for a very uncomfortable time of fellowship. It even affected how the preaching was received. So who was right? They *both* had Scripture to support their beliefs. How do we handle situations similar to this?

God's Word gives us a profound answer. Paul writes, *"Welcome one another as Christ has welcomed you."* The Greek words here for "welcome/ welcomed" comes from *proslambanō*. It is a two-part Greek word that comes from *pros* ("near," "by") and *lambanō* ("to take in hand," "to grasp," "to seize"). When they come together, it means "to take near," "to grasp by the hand and bring close." It was used in antiquity to describe lending someone a hand and drawing them to your side.

Just as Warnock drew Sitko out of the wreckage by extending a hand, it means stretching yourself for the benefit of the other person, especially in a situation that is far from comfortable. Paul was telling the Roman believers to extend themselves to one another, despite their differences of convictions. They were to lend one another welcoming hands so they could live in unity and peace.

Could they put aside their differences and stretch themselves out for the sake of the other person? They should have. This is following Christ's example. Christ was patient and welcomed us by His side in the midst of our own weakness. We should do the same.

How do you treat Christians who hold convictions unlike your own? Do you cross your arms and refuse to shake their hand? Do you shun them or argue incessantly until you've beaten them into submission?

Doing this might make you feel better about your *own* convictions, but it harms your brother or sister in Christ and creates an unnecessary divide. Why not be like Jesus, stretch out your hand, and receive them? After you've done that, perhaps you can have a friendly conversation about your differences as well as the beliefs you share. That's showing them the love of Christ.

As Christians, we share different convictions about things that aren't necessarily prohibited in Scripture. Some may wear jeans to church, while others wear suits and ties, with dresses and fancy hats for the ladies. Some might watch Netflix, while others may not even have a TV. Some may eat meat, while others are ovo-lacto vegetarians.

It's pretty clear that the most important thing to God is not whether we order a medium-rare steak or an avocado salad, but whether we can get along.

64

PUT ON: *ENDYŌ* (ἐνδύω)

---

*But **put on** the Lord Jesus Christ, and make no provision for the flesh, to gratify its desires.*　　　　　　(Romans 13:14)

ἀλλ' ἐνδύσασθε τὸν κύριον Ἰησοῦν Χριστὸν καὶ τῆς σαρκὸς πρόνοιαν μὴ ποιεῖσθε εἰς ἐπιθυμίας.
　　　　　　　　　　　　　　(ΠΡΟΣ ΡΩΜΑΙΟΥΣ 13:14)

When I was a youngster, my parents always wanted me to be in the church plays. And so I was, against my will. I'd find myself at auditions, hoping I wouldn't get a major role. Thankfully, I never did, but I always ended up being cast as a supporting player, like the lead role's furtive, ill-advising friend. The director would give me a script with all of my lines highlighted and send me home with the instructions to "get into character."

For a month, I'd walk around the house trying to figure out who I was and how I was supposed to act. *Should I say it like this or like that? Do I move my hands like that or like this?* I'd wrestle with every nuance of my role so that I could bring it to life.

The final rehearsal—also our first *dress* rehearsal—was held a week before the play. We really were expected to *look the part*. Once, when I was playing the twerpy neighborhood kid, my mom took me to Target and bought me a new pair of jeans, a plain white T-shirt, a pair of Airwalks, and some hair gel. She cuffed the jeans, rolled up the T-shirt sleeves, and gelled my hair. I walked into final rehearsal not as Chris Palmer, but as Jake, the neighborhood pest.

For three hours, you wouldn't recognize me (hopefully). I was a scheming, sneaky, underhanded bully. And, quite honestly, I was pretty good at it. I got to push everyone around for a while...until my poor choices caught up with me at the end of the play.

The point is, the outfit made people forget who I was because it changed me into a different person. In fact, for months afterward, everyone around church kept calling me *Jake*, including the girl I had a crush on. I had pulled off the role nicely, thanks to the outfit that Mom bought. It just goes to show how much the things we wear affect who we are.

In Romans 13:14, God's Word talks to us about what we wear, spiritually speaking. The apostle Paul is telling the Roman Christians that the present time is crucial and Jesus is coming soon. In light of this, they were to act prepared for His return.

To do this, Paul tells them to *"put on the Lord Jesus Christ."* The Greek word here for "put on" is *endysasthe*. It is a two-part Greek word that comes from *en* ("in") and *dyō* ("to get," "to sink," "to enter"). When combined to make *endyō*, it means "to get into something," "sink into something," or "enter into something." Throughout antiquity, it was used to describe entering into or putting on clothes.

Dionysius wrote the twenty-volume *Roman Antiquities* to help connect the Greeks to Roman rule. The complete first nine books still exist today, along with most of books ten and eleven, and portions of the rest.

Dionysius of Halicarnassus, a Greek historian and teacher from the first century BC, used it in his work *Roman Antiquities* to describe playing a role. An actor would enter into his role by dressing up to resemble the part he was playing—as I did when I was *Jake*. Paul was telling the Roman Christians to act like Christ by dressing themselves the same way Christ dressed Himself.

Of course, Paul wasn't referring to outer garments. He was using a figure of speech and referring to the qualities that Christ demonstrated as our example, like goodness and love. (See Romans 13:8–14.) When we practice these, we sink into the character of Jesus and become like Him. The goal is to do this so well that people won't see us anymore; they'll see Jesus living in us.

What an amazing testimony this can be to the current culture. Through our actions, they can glimpse what Jesus is like and encounter Him in a living way. Certainly, this can convict many people to surrender their hearts to the Lord before He comes again.

What are *you* wearing today? Have you *put on* Christ and clothed yourself in His qualities? When you are interacting with others in your daily life, do people see His love, kindness, patience, and gentleness demonstrated in your actions and speech? Or do you act however you feel at the moment?

The truth is, all of us could use a change of clothes. Instead of just *doing you*, as the world says, why not *do* Jesus? People will appreciate goodness far more than Gucci and love far more than Louboutin.

Make it your prayer that God will shine through you so that people will see His light within you, rather than what brands you're wearing. The world needs to see Jesus. Won't you dress the part?

65

CORRUPTION: *PHTHORA* (φθορά)

By which he has granted to us his precious and very great promises, so that through them you may become partakers of the divine nature, having escaped from the corruption *that is in the world because of sinful desire.*   (2 Peter 1:4)

δι᾿ ὧν τὰ τίμια καὶ μέγιστα ἡμῖν ἐπαγγέλματα δεδώρηται, ἵνα διὰ τούτων γένησθε θείας κοινωνοὶ φύσεως ἀποφυγόντες τῆς ἐν τῷ κόσμῳ ἐν ἐπιθυμίᾳ φθορᾶς.
(ΠΕΤΡΟΥ Β 1:4)

Over the years, we've seen some pretty destructive hurricanes in the Atlantic: Mitch, Katrina, Andrew, Hugo, Ike, and Maria. These super storms caused billions in damage and took the lives of many innocent people.

Vicious as they were, none were as brutal as the Great Hurricane of 1780. We don't often hear of this storm because it happened nearly 250 years ago. It killed over 20,000 people and remains the deadliest hurricane of all time.

Thanks to preserved ship logs from those days, scientists were able to discover that the storm arrived in Barbados as a category 5 hurricane (sustained winds of 157 miles per hour or higher). It decimated Barbados before moving into the Lesser Antilles, tearing up islands such as Martinique and St. Lucia. It weakened as it moved up the Mona Passage and made landfall again in the Dominican Republic before turning and blowing out into the Atlantic.

The super storm lasted eleven days and left unprecedented damage. Every single property on Barbados was destroyed, including Fort Charles, a massive structure with stone walls three or four feet thick. Not only did it destroy island property, it sank many British and French warships that were fighting in the American Revolutionary War. Because the hurricane occurred before modern storm tracking technology, it was impossible to predict or escape its wrath.

Sadly, everything in that hurricane's path was left in ruins. Today, we heed the storm warnings, boarding up homes and evacuating cities to avoid as much destruction as possible.

> Meteorologists use the Saffir-Simpson Hurricane Wind Scale to determine a storm's destructive potential. The scale, based on a hurricane's sustained wind speed, ranges from Category 1, with winds of 74 to 95 mph (some damage), to Category 5, with winds of 157 mph or more (beyond catastrophic damage).

I was preaching on the island of St. Thomas in August 2010 when Hurricane Tomas began rolling through the Caribbean. When I got back to my hotel after preaching Sunday morning service, they were putting boards on the widows. The hotel manager told me that I had to get my stuff out of my room and leave. I wasn't allowed to stay there during the storm. The church pastor told me I shouldn't stick around for the storm. He drove me to the airport to put me on the last flight out before the hurricane bashed the island.

"You'd better get out of here," he said. "No telling what kind of ruin this storm may cause." He didn't get an argument from me. I preferred to escape the ruin than risk being ruined.

In 2 Peter 1:4, God's Word speaks to us about escaping the ruin that is in this world. However, instead of damaged caused by a hurricane, it's referring to corruption and moral deterioration. Peter informs believers that Jesus has called us to live a holy life. He has enabled us to do so through His precious promises, such as salvation and being filled with the Spirit, that make us *"partakers of the divine nature."* This simply means that we have been born again, filled with the Spirit, and, as a result, practice the same divine virtues as God.

Have you noticed that since you've been saved, you desire moral excellence over sinful living? Perhaps you used to swear. Now, after receiving Christ, the thought of talking that way grieves you. Maybe you used to lie and now you can't. It's because you are a partaker of the divine nature. You have received God's ethical nature through His Spirit. You have *"escaped from the corruption that is in the world because of sinful desire."*

The Greek word here for "corruption" is *phthoras*. It means "destruction," "ruin," and "deterioration." It was used in antiquity to describe the destruction of property and shipwrecks. Plato used it in his work, *Timaeus*, to describe water leading to disaster. Sounds like the perfect word to portray the results of the hurricane of 1780.

Instead, it is labeling the fallout of evil desires and sin. Like a super hurricane, evil desires rip through and leave everything worse than before. In the end, it deteriorates relationships, devastates families, and leaves one feeling that life is hopeless, meaningless, and no longer worth living.

But when we choose Jesus and He fills us with His Spirit, we escape these evil desires, along with the corruption and damage that they bring. Jesus provides our evacuation route and our plane ticket to get us away from the storm of corruption.

If you are looking for a way out of addiction, bondage, or sinful desires, and the miseries that these things bring, put your trust in Jesus. He will carry away your sins and fill you with new life. Rather than gale-force winds, pounding rain, and destruction all around you, you'll be sailing on peaceful waters under sunny skies.

66

CONTROL: *SYNECHŌ*
(συνέχω)

For the love of Christ **controls** *us, because we have concluded this: that one has died for all, therefore all have died.*

(2 Corinthians 5:14)

ἡ γὰρ ἀγάπη τοῦ Χριστοῦ συνέχει ἡμᾶς, κρίναντας τοῦτο, ὅτι εἷς ὑπὲρ πάντων ἀπέθανεν, ἄρα οἱ πάντες ἀπέθανον.

(ΠΡΟΣ ΚΟΡΙΝΘΙΟΥΣ Β 5:14)

Orchard Road, Wall Street, Via Dolorosa, and Champs-Elysées are all famous roads known around the world. Can you think of any others? How about Dashrath Manjhi Road?

While this might not be one of your answers, there's a compelling narrative behind it that makes it one of the most interesting roads in all the world. Located in Gehlaur, a village near the city of Gaya in the Indian state of Bihar, it is 360 feet long, thirty feet wide, and twenty-five feet deep. And it cuts through an entire mountain.

What makes it so special? It was dug by a single man, Dashrath Manjhi. Yes, that's right; he did it all by himself. It took him twenty-two years, from 1960 until 1982, and he used only a hammer and chisel.

Imagine spending years, working relentlessly to carve a working road through a mountain with the simplest of tools. As you might imagine, Manjhi was ridiculed at first. His peers mocked him and the government paid no attention to him. But Manjhi, known as Mountain Man, just kept working through it all. Nothing could stop him from chipping away.

At this point, I'm sure you're thinking, *Why in the world would he do this? What compelled him to keep working, day and night, for twenty-two years?* His motive was, without a doubt, the most touching part of the story.

The mountain was part of the Gehlaur hills, which stand between his village and the nearest place where villagers could receive medical attention. Without a road, villagers had to go around the hills—some forty miles—to get any sort of help. Dashrath's wife, Falguni Devi, died in 1959 because she was unable to get to care in time. Deeply saddened by the tragedy, Dashrath didn't want any of his fellow villagers to experience the same suffering. So he began laboring away.

"When I started hammering the hill," he said, "people called me a lunatic, but that steeled my resolve."

Over time, people came to respect what he was doing and gave him food and more tools to keep on working. In 1982, when his work was completed, he had shortened the distance for the villagers to receive medical attention from forty miles to *less than one mile*. Astounding. Mountain Man kept digging because his wife's death compelled him to do so. A strong enough motive has the power to make people tackle a mountain.

In 2 Corinthians 5:14, the apostle Paul talks about his motive to tackle the ministry head-on. He was responding to his critics—disruptive teachers who had influenced the Corinthian church. Paul opens up his heart and reminds the Corinthians why he does what he does, in spite of the criticism. He says, *"The love of Christ controls us."*

The Greek word here "controls" is *synechei*, which happens to be used in other places of the New Testament. In Matthew 4:24, it's translated "oppressed" and describes oppression from the devil as he controlled those he was afflicting, driving them into misbehavior. The word holds within it the idea of "driving" and "pushing." Because of this notion, the word came to mean "compel," "urge," and "overwhelm."

> It is medically possible to die from laughing too hard. Though highly unlikely, a laughing fit could put one at risk for a ruptured brain aneurysm, cardiac arrest, syncope, gelastic seizures, and even asphyxiation. However, if it's not overdone, laughter is good for you.

In this sense of the word, there is an example from antiquity. Chrysippus, the Greek philosopher, was said to have died from laughing too hard. Apparently, he saw a donkey eating figs and gave it undiluted wine to wash them down. He found this so hilarious that he fell to the ground laughing, started shaking, and guffawed until foam came out of his mouth. Diogenes Laertius, a third-century biographer, describes it as a forceful fit that *overwhelmed* Chrysippus.

Understanding this, we get a picture of why Paul continued to preach the gospel in the face of all the difficulties: he was driven, compelled, and overwhelmed to do so. He couldn't help himself. The motive behind this overwhelming compulsion was the great love that Jesus showed for human-ity on the cross.

Christ's ultimate sacrifice and display of grace toward mankind, through His work on the cross, kept the apostle going with passion and zeal. The love of Christ overpowered every challenge, trial, and difficulty that stood in Paul's way and kept him carving out a name for Jesus in ev-ery city he visited. Paul was driven and pushed by God's love—and that's enough to take any mountain head-on.

What's motivating you? You've probably discovered that much of what we do for the kingdom can go unnoticed and underappreciated; it may even seem to cause us more trouble than we need. For instance, you give 10 percent of your income to the church, but notice that the guy who doesn't believe in tithing seems to have nicer things. You share the gospel with the people in your life, but the lady who keeps quiet about her faith seems to be more popular.

If your motivation is for *stuff*, popularity, and a more comfortable life, you will soon run out of motivation. If you are going to serve Jesus for the long haul, your reason for doing so can only be one thing: the love that Jesus has for us.

When that love is what drives you, no mountain can stand in your way.

67

THE EVIL DAY:
TĒ HĒMERA TĒ PONĒRA
(τῇ ἡμέρᾳ τῇ πονηρᾷ)

Therefore take up the whole armor of God, that you may be able to withstand in the evil day, and having done all, to stand firm. (Ephesians 6:13)

διὰ τοῦτο ἀναλάβετε τὴν πανοπλίαν τοῦ θεοῦ, ἵνα δυνηθῆτε ἀντιστῆναι ἐν τῇ ἡμέρᾳ τῇ πονηρᾷ καὶ ἅπαντα κατεργασάμενοι στῆναι. (ΠΡΟΣ ΕΦΕΣΙΟΥΣ 6:13)

If you've ever been out in the middle of the ocean, you know just how intimidating it can be. Surrounded by an endless seascape of water, you feel so small, even if you're on a big ship.

The *last* thing you need after leaving port is a stroke of bad luck. Many shipwrecks throughout history have happened because one unexpected thing sent the ship and crew down into a dark, watery grave. Sailors know that they could be next. Therefore, there are all kinds of nautical superstitions that sailors practice to keep from having fatally bad luck.

Here are a few:

+ *Keep bananas off the ship*: That's right: bringing this tropical fruit on board is one of the big no-nos. Apparently, many of the ships that disappeared in the 1700s were carrying bananas. Taking them along supposedly increases your likelihood of disaster, so go with apples or oranges.

+ *Avoid the color green*: Don't paint your boat green, make sure your equipment isn't green, and keep green objects from coming aboard. Green represents the color of land and if there's too much green on your boat, you are likely to run aground.

+ *Don't whistle on board*: Sailors once believed that whistling would stir up the wind and cause a storm. Safer to sing instead.

+ *Wear earrings*: Why did pirates wear all those earrings? It wasn't for fashion. They believed that earrings healed bad eyesight, averted sea sickness, and prevented them from drowning.

+ *Pay attention to the rats*: If rats are abandoning the ship and jumping into the water, it's an indication that your boat is getting ready to plunge to the depths.

These and other superstitions are tall tale ways of keeping you safe on the water. Of course, they are *just* superstitions. I'm only listing them to point out that sailors have gone to enormous lengths to avoid having a bad day at sea.

The world's oldest intact shipwreck lies at the bottom of the Black Sea off the coast of Bulgaria. It is an ancient Greek trading vessel believed to be over 2,400 years old.

It's not just sailors who fear bad luck. Humanity has always feared the possibility of sudden, unexpected calamity. *What if they break up with me? What if I lose my job? What if my loved one dies? What if… What if… What if….* The *what ifs* stack miles high. People do all kinds of things to avoid the bad luck that would bring their worst nightmare.

God's Word acknowledges the propensity people have to fear bad fortune and gives us reassurance that the Lord will keep us safe. In Ephesians 6:13, the apostle Paul is telling the Ephesian church about the great spiritual conflict against unseen powers that were attempting to cause their demise. He urges them to put on the full armor of God (see study 2) so that they can stand in the battle and overcome. Here, Paul says that armor will help us *"withstand in the evil day."*

The Greek phrase for "the evil day" is *tē hēmera tē ponēra.* "Day," or *hēmera,* refers to "a literal day" or "period of time." "Evil" or *ponēros* has a wider meaning. It was used in a moral sense to mean "wicked," "knavish," and "malicious," but it was also used in an experiential sense and meant "sorrow," "unhappiness," "trouble which brings evil," and even "failure."

In fact, in this sense of the word, *ponēros* was used by Plato in his *Republic* to describe an "unlucky" voyage at sea. When *ponerōs* and *hēmera* are placed together to form *tē hēmera tē ponēra* or "the evil day," it refers to "a specific period of time or an actual day in which bad luck falls upon someone"—like a sailor who runs into a sudden storm that causes his boat to sink.

Imagine. Things are going well, the sun is shining, and the tropical ocean breeze tickles your nose and brings ecstasy to your soul. Suddenly, the sunshine is obliterated by malicious storm clouds and the sea goes wild and tosses your boat around like it's seeking revenge because of your green deck chair. Holding on for dear life, you realize *the evil day* has come upon you. This is what the Ephesians feared—a sudden gust of trouble that would ruin the voyage of life.

As a culture, the Ephesian people were superstitious. The believers who made up the Ephesian church converted to Christianity from various mystical influences. It's likely that many of them still suffered under some notions like astrology. At that time, the pagan culture followed horoscopes to determine a person's fate. They believed that if a person's unlucky star aligned into a position of dominance, *the evil day* was upon them and things were certain to go wrong.

This notion may have panicked some Ephesian Christians and caused them to do superstitious things to prevent it from happening. Paul countered by assuring them that they didn't have to fear the evil day or a stroke of bad luck. They had Jesus.

If they put on the armor of God by allowing the Holy Spirit to control their lives, they would be certain to overcome evil, bad luck, misfortune, the schemes of the devil, or whatever you want to call it. No need for superstition. They had God's armor.

God doesn't want you to live in fear of *the evil day*. Fear is demonic. As Christians, our faith should give us a reliance in the goodness of God, rather than a nervous anticipation of trouble ahead. That means if you want to bring bananas on your boat and whistle while you sail, go right ahead. You are sailing with the Lord.

68

EXACT IMPRINT:
CHARAKTĒR (χαρακτήρ)

He is the radiance of the glory of God and the **exact imprint** *of his nature, and he upholds the universe by the word of his power. After making purification for sins, he sat down at the right hand of the Majesty on high.* (Hebrews 1:3)

ὃς ὢν ἀπαύγασμα τῆς δόξης καὶ χαρακτὴρ τῆς ὑποστάσεως αὐτοῦ, φέρων τε τὰ πάντα τῷ ῥήματι τῆς δυνάμεως αὐτοῦ, καθαρισμὸν τῶν ἁμαρτιῶν ποιησάμενος ἐκάθισεν ἐν δεξιᾷ τῆς μεγαλωσύνης ἐν ὑψηλοῖς.
(ΠΡΟΣ ΕΒΡΑΙΟΥΣ 1:3)

The Internet is a brutal place. You can't have a bad day in peace anymore.

If social media clutches your blunder, you could go viral and be roasted for the next few weeks, especially if you're already in the public eye. Almost everything is fair game these days, from political gaffes and bad fashion to athletic losses and human error.

Just ask sculptor Emmanuel Santos. If you follow sports, particularly soccer, you might be familiar with his name. In March 2017, his sculpted bust of footballer Cristiano Ronaldo was *the* topic of discussion among sports fans on the Internet.

To be nice, let's just say it fell short of people's expectations. As a result, it showed up in all sorts of cruel memes and was mercilessly insulted for quite some time.

Critics said it looked nothing like the champion and compared it to everything from Sloth in *The Goonies* to Two-Face in *Batman Forever* to a work of socialist realism, the art of the Soviet Union from 1932 through 1988. Some called the bust a "bust," and others teased that it was created by a fan of Ronaldo's rival, Lionel Messi.

Santos had been given the job of creating the sculpture because the airport on the Portuguese island of Madeira, Ronaldo's birthplace, was being renamed in the athlete's honor. Ronaldo attended the ceremony, along with the president and prime minister of Portugal and hundreds of fans. As soon as the ceremony ended, the attack on the sculpture began.

The flurry of criticism was tough for Santos and his family to bear. But the artist defended himself. In an interview with *Bleacher Report*, he said he was initially pleased upon finishing the bust: "I was really happy and laughed with satisfaction. I felt that feeling of fulfillment that I had done my part." While creating it, he said, he had felt "through touching the clay I was transmitting the profile of someone."

Most critics, however, said the bust was an imperfect image of Ronaldo. In June 2018, it was removed from the airport and replaced with a work by a Spanish sculptor. However, you can still find Santos's sculpture on the Internet. While it falls short of what an exact imprint is, we do learn of a perfect example of one in Hebrews 1:3—Jesus. That's right, our Lord is *"the exact imprint"* of God's nature.

A wall painting dating to AD 235 is one of the earliest known depictions of Jesus Christ. *The Healing of the Paralytic* was found in 1921 in the Dura-Europos house church in Syria. It's now part of the Dura Europos collection at the Yale University Gallery of Fine Arts.

To understand what this means, we note that the writer of Hebrews begins with some vital theological statements about Jesus Christ. He does so because most of his audience included Christians who had converted from Judaism. He wanted to show them the superiority of Christ in comparison to those Old Testament figures who had come before Him, such as the angels, Moses, Joshua, and Aaron. To establish this, he starts with truths regarding Christ's divine nature, one of them being that He is the "exact imprint" of God's nature.

The Greek word here for "exact imprint" is *charaktēr*. It means "a mark or an impression placed on an object" and "an image." It was used in antiquity to describe the image stamped on a coin, which shared the same features as the model it resembled.

Hence, the word itself described distinctive marks, features, and characteristics of someone, like those you'd see on a bust or a sculpture. Just as an accurate bust reveals the qualities of the person it's been crafted after, so Jesus reveals the exact qualities of the divine nature. If you've seen Jesus, you've seen God. To see Jesus is to see the Father.

The Jewish Christians reading this would have grasped what the writer of Hebrews was saying: Jesus is God.

This is an important doctrine. It is at the foundation of our faith as Christians. Jesus isn't *somewhat* like God. He is not Santos's sculpture that *kind of* looks like Ronaldo. Nope. Jesus is an exact imprint: he embodies all the details, characteristics, and features of the divine nature.

Do you see Jesus that way? We must—because he is 100 percent perfectly divine. Believing anything short of this is parting ways with true Christianity. As the Chalcedonian Definition tells us, Jesus is "consubstantial with the Father according to the Godhead."[25] This means that

Jesus's divine nature is exactly the same as the Father's. This is what true Christianity will always maintain, as will those who practice it.

When you read the Gospels and see Jesus in action, remember that you are seeing *God in action*. When He healed the sick, cast out demons, or extended an invitation for sinners to repent, He was displaying the divine nature right before His followers' eyes.

When you read the Bible and listen to Jesus talk about loving your enemies, helping the poor, and forgiving those who cause you injustice, you are hearing the very heart of God whisper to your soul.

69

BREATHED OUT BY GOD: *THEOPNEUSTOS* (θεόπνευστος)

All Scripture is **breathed out by God** and *profitable for teaching, for reproof, for correction, and for training in righteousness.* (2 Timothy 3:16)

πᾶσα γραφὴ θεόπνευστος καὶ ὠφέλιμος πρὸς διδασκαλίαν, πρὸς ἐλεγμόν, πρὸς ἐπανόρθωσιν, πρὸς παιδείαν τὴν ἐν δικαιοσύνῃ. (ΠΡΟΣ ΤΙΜΟΘΕΟΝ Β 3:16)

Is there a public speaker you admire, someone who has a way of speaking so effectively that it inspires people to act? They could say what someone else has just said, but when *they* say it, it resonates with the soul.

What's behind their effectiveness? What makes their words so powerful?

Harvard Business Review says it's something you might never have guessed. I'll give you a hint: you do it 17,000 times a day. Give up? It's taking a breath. Writing for the magazine, Allison Shapira suggests that proper breathing is essential for effective communication.

She uses Margaret Thatcher as an example. The prime minister of the United Kingdom from 1979 through 1990, Thatcher was also the first female ever to be elected as a head of government in Europe. Among many other high achievements, she played a major part in ending the Cold War. It helped that she was a powerful communicator.

Shapira points out that when Thatcher became prime minister, she took voice lessons to enhance her speaking abilities. These lessons helped her develop a richer, more resonant voice. As a result, she came across as strong and confident.

Her example shows the interconnectedness of words and breathing. When we speak, our words come out on top of our breath. Try an experiment. Take a deep breath in and, as you exhale, let your words out with the air from your lungs. If you can keep your words in sync with your exhalations, you should really see the effectiveness of your speaking improve.

In 2 Timothy 3:16, God's Word talks about the connection that words have with breath. Here, Paul tells Timothy that false teachers will continue to increase and as they do, they will leave the Scriptures in search of something new. Timothy was to be unbending in the face of this. Paul urged him to keep preaching the Scriptures the way he had learned them as a child, instead of trying to fabricate new doctrines. To exhort Timothy further along these lines, Paul reminds Timothy of Scripture's the authority and effectiveness, noting, *"All Scripture is breathed out by God."*

> Unlike English, there are no silent consonants in Koine Greek. Thus, if you're saying the word *pneuma*, the *p* should be pronounced.

The Greek word here for "breathed out by God' is *theopneustos*. It is a two-part Greek word that comes from *theos* ("God") and *pneuma* ("spirit," "breath," "wind," "inner life"). When these words are combined to make *theopneustos*, it means "God breathed" or "breath that comes out of God."

Because breath and words go hand in hand, saying "breathed out by God" is a metaphor for saying "spoken by God."

The living God breathed and spoke to mankind. When we read Scripture, we are reading God's Word that came to us with the very breath of His divine self. No wonder we feel so alive after spending time reading the Word of God. It is full of His life.

Hearing this confirmed to Timothy the profitability of God's Word. It transforms, leads to eternal life, and meets our needs from slightest to greatest.

Not so with the teachings of the false teachers: those had only been breathed out by man and didn't contain an ounce of divine life. Timothy was on the right track. There was no need for him to go elsewhere.

It's extremely important for us to know that the Bible is the only book that is "breathed out by God." Failure to understand this might lead us to go on a fruitless search.

The fact is, the situation in 2 Timothy is very real, even today. People often veer from God's Word. Over the years, I've seen individuals from church put down their Bibles and pick up materials that teach Zen, New Age, or whatever else the spiritual gurus are saying at the moment, including trends and fads like Hygge, feng shui, yoga, crystals, and sound baths. While it may seem exciting at first to explore something new, it's going to leave you feeling empty inside, so you end up trying the next thing and the next thing after that.

Instead of looking around for something new, why not become better acquainted with the only words that have been breathed out by God and try new ways to explore them?

I personally have changed my Bible study methods a number of different times, but I'm always studying the same Bible. I've been at it for decades, but I've never come close to exhausting everything God has said.

His Word is an endless breath that will continue blowing fresh life upon all of those who need to be refreshed. Don't look the other way. Don't think you need to find something new. Instead, turn your face to God's Word. When you do, the Lord will speak to you—or, I should say, breathe upon you, and fill you with new life.

70

REFRESH: *ANAPSYCHŌ* (ἀναψύχω)

May the Lord grant mercy to the household of Onesiphorus, for he often refreshed me and was not ashamed of my chains.
(2 Timothy 1:16)

δῴη ἔλεος ὁ κύριος τῷ Ὀνησιφόρου οἴκῳ, ὅτι πολλάκις με ἀνέψυξεν καὶ τὴν ἅλυσίν μου οὐκ ἐπαισχύνθη.
(ΠΡΟΣ ΤΙΜΟΘΕΟΝ Β 1:16)

Is there someone who cheers you up when you're hurting? Who walks through the door and their presence signals something deep within your soul that everything is going to be all right? They put you at ease without saying much, if they say anything at all. As long as they are there, that's enough.

We could say that these individuals "refresh" us, like a thunderstorm that invigorates the skies, or rainfall that washes away the grime. They hydrate, give life, and fill you with joy until your emotions spill over the brim with gladness. Have you identified that person in your life? Maybe a pastor, a friend at church, a spouse, or possibly even a mentor?

I certainly hope you have someone, or more than one person, like this. Often, we can experience God's presence in and among other people. God designed it this way so we can grow together as a Christian community. Therefore, when God wants to refresh you with His presence, He sends a person into your life. We see an example of this in 2 Timothy 1:16.

> Tourists in Rome can visit the Mamertine Prison, which is located at the foot of the Capitoline Hill near the Forum. The San Giuseppe dei Falegnami Catholic Church (the Church of Saint Joseph of the Carpenters) is built on top of the prison.

Paul was in prison again and this time, he wasn't getting out. Unlike his house arrest in Acts 28:16, the apostle was in the Mamertine Prison in Rome. This was a grueling sentence. The prison was originally built as a cistern around 600 BC, but by Paul's time, it had devolved into part of the sewer system. It was dark, damp, chilly, and foul-smelling. Sallust, a Roman historian during the first century BC, said it was "disgusting and vile by reason of filth, the darkness and stench."

Prisoners were lowered into the dungeon through a small hole and were left alone to starve, or were brought up to face execution. An iron door connected the dungeon to the sewer; those who died in the dungeon were often dumped into the sewer and ended up in the Tiber River. Paul was imprisoned here while he was writing 2 Timothy. Paul knew that, this time, he was finished. Acquittal wasn't happening. This was the end of his race. (See 2 Timothy 4:7.)

If things weren't bad enough, it was extremely dangerous for anyone to give sustenance to a Mamertine prisoner. Their kindness might suggest that they approved of the prisoner's crime and would emulate it, if they hadn't already. For this reason, many of Paul's companions had abandoned him, including Phygelus, Hermogenes, and Demas. (See 2 Timothy 1:15;

4:10.) Yet, there was one man who had been faithful to Paul, despite the risk of supporting him. His name was Onesiphorus.

Unlike those who had abandoned Paul, Onesiphorus worked hard to find him when he arrived in Rome. It wasn't easy to unearth the whereabouts of prisoners. Onesiphorus could have given up and said, "I tried." But he kept searching and searching until he found Paul, despite the danger this triggered. Imagine the heart Onesiphorus had for his friend in chains. Talk about loyalty and faithfulness. Paul said Onesiphorus's presence "refreshed" him.

The Greek word for "refreshed" here is *anepsyxen*. It means "revive," "cool," and "give relief." This word was used to describe a number of things in Greco-Roman days. Primarily, it described a breath of fresh air, like a revitalizing breeze that gusts through the window and purifies the room. It makes perfect sense why Paul would describe Onesiphorus's presence like this. Paul had been in a noxious dungeon for quite some time. It had been a long time since he had smelled anything pleasant. The constant fetid odor had become his norm. Yet, when Onesiphorus got to Paul, it was like a pure, refreshing breeze had entered the prison.

Anapsychō was also used in antiquity to describe how a wound was treated. When bandaging a broken limb, the doctor would leave the wound uncovered so that the air might dry it out. Back then, doctors believed that a wound would heal faster if it was not covered.[26] Hence, *anapsychō* came to be associated with healing, renewal, and revitalization.

Here, God's Word is showing us that sometimes, God doesn't change the circumstances to help us. Instead, He sends someone into our lives who can bring His refreshing presence and revitalize our joy, endurance, peace, and hope. Notice that Paul never got out of prison. According to historians, the Emperor Nero beheaded Paul shortly after he wrote 2 Timothy. But God *did* sustain Paul with His presence, in his darkest hour, using the help of another believer who was full of the Holy Spirit.

You may be in the darkest situation of your life—a condition where you feel that you cannot endure it on your own—but God has placed those around you who can be a breath of fresh, healing air. Or maybe *you* aren't going through a difficult time but you know *someone* who is. Then, God has placed *you* in *their* life so *you* can be that breath of fresh air to them. That means, don't just pray for them. Show up in their life and do something to give them hope.

Let me give you an example. When our worship leader and his wife were expecting their second child, she got a dreadful case of shingles about halfway through the pregnancy. Everyday life became a challenge. Our worship leader was working overtime while his wife stayed at home and watched their active two-year-old. I was out of town, so I called to pray with them, but after I hung up, I felt convicted that prayer wasn't enough. They needed something else to refresh them, something tangible. So, our church called a catering company and, within two hours, we had sent over $300 worth of already-prepared meals to their home. It was enough to last them for quite some time. This became a turning point in the expectant mother's recovery. They were refreshed and revitalized.

God refreshes us through people. He will either send someone to you, or send you to someone else. When you notice this, thank God that He is wafting through the lives of those He loves.

71

SCOFFER: *EMPAIKTĒS* (ἐμπαίκτης)

Knowing this first of all, that scoffers *will come in the last days with scoffing, following their own sinful desires.* (2 Peter 3:3)

τοῦτο πρῶτον γινώσκοντες ὅτι ἐλεύσονται ἐπ᾽ ἐσχάτων τῶν ἡμερῶν ἐν ἐμπαιγμονῇ ἐμπαῖκται κατὰ τὰς ἰδίας ἐπιθυμίας αὐτῶν πορευόμενοι. (ΠΕΤΡΟΥ Β 3:3)

The *Sandlot* is one of my favorite movies of all time. It's a 1993 coming-of-age comedy about nine boys who spend the summer of 1962 playing baseball and getting into harmless mischief. Their misadventures include getting sick at a carnival, being thrown out of the neighborhood pool, campouts in a treehouse, and running from an enormous, angry dog. Perhaps one of the funniest and most well-known scenes in the movie is when the overweight and most outlandish kid in the bunch, Hamilton "Ham" Porter, gets into an insult contest with Phillips, a boy on a rival baseball team. It's classic, gut-busting childhood humor at its best. It's a perfect example how twelve-year-olds act, especially when they disagree with one another:

> Phillips: You shouldn't be allowed to touch a baseball. You're all an insult to the game.
> Ham: Come on. We'll take you on, right here. Right now. Come on.
> Phillips: We play on a real diamond, Porter. You ain't good enough to lick the dust off our cleats.
> Ham: Watch it, jerk.
> Phillips: Shut up, idiot.
> Ham: Moron.
> Phillips: Scab eater.

The taunts get more and more ridiculous until Ham hits Phillips with the knockout blow: "You play ball like a girl."

The kids gasp. Phillips is devastated by this insult of all insults. He can't say anything to top that. Mortified, Phillips rides away on his bike with his tail between his legs, while all of Ham's friends pat him on the back like he's a hero. Hats off to the directors for doing an excellent job at portraying *childishness.*

Name-calling and bullying are all-too-common examples of typical childish behavior. Instead of seeking to understand each other, the two baseball rivals mocked each other's personal traits and disrespected one another's abilities. I suppose it's funny to watch twelve-year-olds do it in the context of a movie, but the truth is *adults* behave like this toward one another *all the time.* And *that's* not funny.

Have you ever seen an adult making fun of and mocking another adult? I don't mean harmless jest. I am talking about outright attacks on their personal life, values, beliefs, and things they hold sacred. It's not so humorous, is it? Unfortunately, our society is filled with this sort of disrespect.

In 2 Peter 3:3, we see this kind of derision within first century Christianity. Peter was writing to arouse believers about the second coming of the Lord. It is certain and near, he says, having been spoken of by the Old Testament prophets, by Christ himself, and by Christ's apostles. In light of this, believers were to live holy lives and remain faithful to God's Word.

But Peter warns them that there would be those who would mock and live lives of sensuality. Peter calls these individuals "scoffers." The Greek word here for "scoffers" is *empaiktai*. This is a two-part Greek word that comes from *en* ("in" or "with") and *paizō* ("to play like a child").

> "It is ill to speak words light as wind."   —Homer, *The Odyssey*

Paizō was used to describe a lack of seriousness toward something, how people act when they are joking around, having fun, and being lighthearted or frivolous. In fact, Homer uses it in the *Odyssey* to describe maidens playing a game with a ball. The idea is to treat something without any real care, as when children play at the park or amuse themselves with their toys.

When *en* is combined with *paizō* to make *empaiktēs*, it means "a person who plays with" and describes "a person who makes fun of someone or something," or "one who plays around at another's expense," like a kid who mocks someone in a disrespectful and demeaning way.

Peter was saying these "scoffers" would treat the second coming of Christ carelessly. They were going to ridicule it, make jokes about it, and disrespect those who believed in it. Like a childish bully getting in an opponent's face, belittling and name-calling, they would taunt the Christians and laugh at their convictions and beliefs. They'd rather deride the Christians for believing there was going to be a final judgment than become accountable for the way they lived. Peter implored the believers to carry on in holiness despite the childish attacks because the day of the Lord is certain to come soon.

Peter had his scoffers then—and we have ours now. Have you ever seen someone on TV or YouTube having a good ol' time making fun of the Lord's return? They joke, "It's been over 2,000 years, where's He at? Wasn't He supposed to come soon?" And *then* the scoffers endorse an anything-goes lifestyle, letting Christians know just how much fun they're missing by being *holy* and *old-fashioned*.

Don't let these childish attacks get to you. Instead of returning fire, pray for their souls and ask the Holy Spirit to open their eyes to the truth. Pray that they will experience conviction so they can see the need for salvation. Pray unconditionally for the Lord's love and blessing on them. Someone has to be the bigger person. Let it be you.

72

TAKE HEART: *THARSEŌ* (θαρσέω)

I have said these things to you, that in me you may have peace. In the world you will have tribulation. But take heart*; I have overcome the world.* (John 16:33)

ταῦτα λελάληκα ὑμῖν ἵνα ἐν ἐμοὶ εἰρήνην ἔχητε· ἐν τῷ κόσμῳ θλῖψιν ἔχετε· ἀλλὰ θαρσεῖτε, ἐγὼ νενίκηκα τὸν κόσμον. (ΚΑΤΑ ΙΩΑΝΝΗΝ 16:33)

You were made for this…. Good luck…. Break a leg…. Knock 'em dead…. You'll do great.

I'm sure these sound familiar to you. They're popular phrases used to exhort and inspire. If you're paying attention, you may also hear "Have fun,"

"Be safe," or "God bless." These short encouragements are power-packed with idiomatic meaning that says all that needs to be said. At the core, they are conveying cheer.

We don't have to look far to find examples of popular phrases that have been become iconic. How about *hakuna-matata*, which goes back to the 1994 Disney blockbuster *The Lion King*. It was Timon and Pumbaa's favorite phrase and means "no worries." They taught it to Simba after his father died to help him overcome his troubled past.

Since we are talking movies, we can't forget, *"May the Force be with you."* This expression is used all throughout the *Star Wars* movies to wish one another good luck. If you are friends with a *Star Wars* fan, they are likely to smile and tell you this at some point, like on your wedding day, before a job interview, or maybe when you have to go home to face an angry spouse.

On February 20, 1962, the phrase "Godspeed" became well-known when astronaut Scott Carpenter wished this for astronaut John Glenn as the latter became the first American launched into space. Nowadays, we say "Godspeed" to wish someone success when they are going away. In fact, I often say it to friends when I drop them off at the airport.

Popular phrases go all the way back into the annals of history. A Latin phrase from the fourth century AD—*felicior Augusto, melior Traiano*—was used by the Roman Senate to inaugurate new Roman emperors. It basically means, "Be more fortunate than Augustus and better than Trajan." Both men had successful reigns, so this was just another way of wishing the emperors good luck.

The next time someone is about to take on a task, try telling them, *Felicio Augusto, melior Traiano*. It would be funny if you said that before they did something mundane, like cutting the lawn or shoveling snow. Millennial humor, I suppose. Can you think of any other phrases you like to use?

Some famous Latin phrases that we still use today include *carpe diem* ("seize the day"); *amor vincit omnia*: ("love conquers all things"); *semper fidelis* ("always faithful"); and *caveat emptor* ("let the buyer beware").

Jesus had a favorite phrase that He often used: *tharseite*.[27] He uses it a total of seven times in Matthew, Mark, John, and the Acts.[28] It gets translated as either "take heart" or "take courage."

In antiquity, it meant "to dare," "to be bold," and "to be firm in the face of danger," "do not fear." Plato, in his work *Phaedo*, uses it to describe confidence in the face of death. In the Greek Old Testament, LXX, it is used to exhort men to be courageous during times of danger and emergency.

Moses uses it in Exodus 14:13 to encourage the children of Israel when faced with the imminent threat of the fast-approaching Egyptians: "*And Moses said to the people, "Fear not* [tharseite], *stand firm, and see the salvation of the* LORD, *which he will work for you today. For the Egyptians whom you see today, you shall never see again."*

Elijah uses it in 1 Kings 17:13 to encourage the widow of Zarephath who was running out of food: "*And Elijah said to her, 'Do not fear* [tharsei]; *go and do as you have said. But first make me a little cake of it and bring it to me, and afterward make something for yourself and your son.'"*

Tharseite is a phrase to dispel anxiety and fill hearers with notions of victory and cheer. In John 16:33, Jesus uses *tharseite* to strengthen His disciples. They had just received bad news, learning Jesus would be leaving them. Even worse, Jesus told them that they would be persecuted just as He was. (See John 15:8–16:4.) That means they would be hated and even put to death.

Can you imagine how the disciples felt after hearing this? Think about how *you* feel when you get sudden, unexpected bad news. I know that when this happens to me, my stomach drops, I start to sweat, and my legs turn into rubber. I imagine that's how the disciples were feeling when Jesus told them how things were going to go after His death.

In the midst of this, Jesus says *tharseite* or "take heart." He told His disciples to trust Him and be bold in the face of the trials that were about to come. And this they could do because Jesus had "overcome the world." All of the opposition Jesus faced from His persecutors could not hinder Him from fulfilling what God had sent Him to do. The disciples could expect the Lord to strengthen them so that they could overcome their own troubles, as had Jesus. The Lord was backing them. They were to face the world with boldness and courage.

While you may not be facing deadly persecution today, it's probable you are facing trouble that you need to face with courage. Maybe you have to talk to someone who is difficult to face. Perhaps you need to tell the truth about something to someone you've been hiding it from. Or maybe you work in an environment in which it's intimidating to be a Christian.

God hasn't called you to live in fear. If He is leading you, you can trust that He is backing you and has supplied you with the strength you need to go forward with assurance.

Be bold. Go get 'em. Godspeed. Hakuna-matata. May the Force be with you. Tharseite.

73

DEPARTURE: *ANALYSIS*
(ἀνάλυσις)

For I am already being poured out as a drink offering, and the time of my departure *has come.*　　　(2 Timothy 4:6)

Ἐγὼ γὰρ ἤδη σπένδομαι, καὶ ὁ καιρὸς τῆς ἀναλύσεώς μου ἐφέστηκεν.　　　(ΠΡΟΣ ΤΙΜΟΘΕΟΝ Β 4:6)

When I was a little boy, I often cried when the weekend was over. Weekends were the best, especially when my cousins spent Friday and Saturday nights visiting us. We'd stay up late, watch movies, eat pizza, and play 8-bit Nintendo. What more can a nine-year-old boy ask? It was life the way I wanted it to be, and that's why I'd get so sad when we took my cousins home on Sunday afternoon. I have a very vivid memory of moping around on Sunday night after they were gone, looking out the widow and thinking, *If only I could turn back time forty-eight hours to Friday night.*

Mom interrupted my adolescent musings and told me to stop sulking. "You know, Chris, you have to stop being so sad every time your cousins leave. Nothing lasts forever."

Nothing lasts forever? This was a hard concept for my nine-year-old mind to assimilate. But I didn't have to understand what she meant right then and there. I had my whole life in front of me to figure it out.

My next lesson in this came when I graduated from high school. I thought I'd be happy, but when I woke up the morning after graduation, I realized high school was now just a memory. It was over, both the good times and the bad ones. The little gnawing in my stomach reminded me of the feeling I used to have when my cousins left after a visit. Except it wasn't just a weekend that was over, but an entire chapter of my life. Sitting beside my bed, I remembered Mom's words: "Nothing lasts forever."

I didn't hear these words again until tragedy struck a few years later, when a good friend died after a long battle with leukemia. I had never had a friend die before; I had never even *thought* about losing a friend. We played on the soccer team together. He was funny, liked to play with fire, and was a good drummer. I thought we'd always be friends. But now he was gone. This wasn't just a chapter of my life that had ended; a close friendship was suddenly gone. Sitting beside my bed after getting the news, I heard Mom's words again: "Nothing lasts forever."

Since then, I've seen chapters close on all sorts of things: romances, relationships, seasons of success, and even ventures I had hoped would last a lot longer. But now, when it happens, I beat Mom to the punch: "I know, Mom, *nothing lasts forever.*"

According to the Central Intelligence Agency, Monaco has the highest average life expectancy at 89.4 years, while Chad has the lowest at 50.6 years. The average life expectancy in the United States is 80 years.

Though sobering and serious, God's Word doesn't hide this truth from us either. There are plenty of places where Scripture points out the brevity of human life. (See, for example, Matthew 6:19–20; Mark 8:36; James 4:14.) As Christians, we should not ignore these passages.

In 2 Timothy 4:6, the apostle Paul is in prison and is nearing his end. It's clear he understands that his earthly life and ministry won't last forever and, actually, has now reached its conclusion. Knowing this, Paul tells Timothy, *"The time of my departure has come."*

The Greek word here for "departure" is *analyseōs*. It means "loosing," "untying," and "breaking up." In antiquity, it was used to describe a number of things such as: untying a ship from its moorings, unyoking an animal from a cart, breaking up a campsite, and freeing someone from chains or fetters. By using this word, Paul was making it abundantly clear that his hard work was done. It was time for him to set sail. He was packing up and soon he'd be liberated from this life.

After all, nothing lasts forever, not even a lifetime of ministry for the Lord. But this didn't bother the apostle Paul. Though *this* life won't last forever, the next life will. And Paul was looking forward to leaving behind the temporary so that he could enter into the eternal. Imagine a life where you *never* have to say goodbye, a life where *everything* lasts forever.

Are you prepared for that kind of life? Do you live your life respectful of the fact that one day, you will have to pack it all up and head into eternity? Oh, I know it's something that you don't want to think about right now and hopefully it's a long time from today. But the time *will* come. Your work *will* stop. Your ship *will* set sail. And at that point, you'll pack up your campsite and head toward your eternal home.

If you live your life the way God has told you how to live it, when that time comes, you'll have no reason to sulk or fear. It won't be depressing or sad. Instead, it will be peaceful and joyful, definitely *not* a hopeless goodbye, but rather a confident, "See you soon."

Take an inventory of your life and take advantage of your remaining time. If you need to make any changes, make them today. You never know when your day of departure will be here. Like my mom said, nothing lasts forever.

74

FORBEARANCE: *ANOCHĒ* (ἀνοχή)

Or do you presume on the riches of his kindness and forbearance and patience, not knowing that God's kindness is meant to lead you to repentance? (Romans 2:4)

ἢ τοῦ πλούτου τῆς χρηστότητος αὐτοῦ καὶ τῆς ἀνοχῆς καὶ τῆς μακροθυμίας καταφρονεῖς, ἀγνοῶν ὅτι τὸ χρηστὸν τοῦ θεοῦ εἰς μετάνοιάν σε ἄγει.

(ΠΡΟΣ ΡΩΜΑΙΟΥΣ 2:4)

World War I was, without a doubt, one of the bloodiest and deadliest wars the world has ever known. Fought between the Allied and Central Powers from 1914 to 1918, over 25 million people were either wounded or killed.

It is said that, on average, over two hundred soldiers died for every *hour* of fighting. Over 57.6 percent of all those who fought became casualties of the war. That means, going in, the odds of survival weren't in your favor. It was a horrible time in human history.

> On June 28, 1914, the assassination of Archduke Franz Ferdinand of Austria and his pregnant wife, Sophie, by Gavrilo Princip, a Bosnian Serb revolutionary, triggered the start of World War I.

But amid the horror, there is a story that shows that goodness still existed, even in the blood-spattered trenches of gruesome fighting.

It happened on December 24, 1914. Yes, that's right, Christmas Eve. Around 8:30 p.m., the Germans (Central Powers) illuminated their trenches, began singing, and wished the British soldiers (Allied Powers) across the way, "Merry Christmas." After this, the two sides began to sing Christmas carols to one another. The Germans sang "Silent Night" to the British and the British sang "The First Noel" back to the Germans.

When Christmas Day dawned, the German soldiers came out of their trenches, crossed Allied lines, began hollering, "Merry Christmas" in English, and shook hands with the British soldiers in a friendly manner. The two sides then exchanged gifts—mainly cigarettes and plum pudding. Some soldiers even played a game of soccer together.

This unplanned and spontaneous truce, known as the *Christmas Truce of 1914*, lasted most of the day until dusk, when both sides returned to their trenches. But before the fighting picked back up, one German solider told an Allied soldier, "Today, we have peace. Tomorrow, you fight for your country, I fight for mine. Good luck."

Christmas Day 1914 was likely the only bright, shining day during the four years of WWI. It was a time of truce, cease-fire, goodness, and mercy. Although it wasn't long, it was merry while it lasted.

In Romans 2:4, we find a truce of a different kind—one from God. Here, the apostle Paul is writing to the church in Rome about God's justice and kindness, as well as the need for humanity to repent. Paul points out that the purpose of God's kindness is to lead us to Him.

One of the ways this kindness is displayed is through God's "forbearance." The Greek word here for "forbearance" is *anochēs*. It means "a temporary cessation," "a pause," "an armistice," and even "a truce." In antiquity, it was used to describe hostiles holding back their forces—like the British and German soldiers during Christmas 1914. In essence, it is telling us that God shows His kindness by putting up with our sin and not wiping us out the moment we do something to offend His sacredness.

You aren't struck by lightning when you do something wrong because God calls a cease-fire, a truce. He gives us an opportunity to surrender to Him. Considering that He is infinitely holy and we are the agitators in the conflict, this is exceptionally kind. What a patient and wonderful God we have!

However, we need to keep in mind that like many truces or cease-fires, it is only temporary. Because God is just, He is going to have to call an end to the truce at some point and judge those who refused to accept His invitation to repent and submit to Him. (See Romans 2:5.) In light of this, we must take advantage of the truce God has made with us.

Have you seized upon God's cease-fire? Are you still in conflict with Him? It would serve you well to surrender to God so He doesn't have to judge you for those things that you refuse to deliver up to Him. God has called a truce because He loves you and wants to reconcile with you. But it has to be on His terms, not yours. If you haven't surrendered, what are you waiting for?

While this verse is ultimately talking about salvation, it can also be applied toward something in your personal life. Perhaps you *have* given your heart to Jesus, but there is still something going on that does not please the Lord. Up to this point, you might not have reaped any consequences. Count that as God's forbearance—He's putting up with it for a little while so you can come to Him. You won't be able to get away with it forever. There will be a time when what you are doing catches up. The good news is, you are in a time of truce right now.

Be grateful for God's kindness and forbearance. Be thankful that He didn't blast you the moment you did something wrong. Instead, He has approached you, blessed you, and extended His hand toward you to be His friend. Don't stay in your trench. Reach up and accept God's love and mercy.

75

VIOLENT: *PLĒKTĒS* (πλήκτης)

For an overseer, as God's steward, must be above reproach. He must not be arrogant or quick-tempered or a drunkard or vio-lent or greedy for gain. (Titus 1:7)

δεῖ γὰρ τὸν ἐπίσκοπον ἀνέγκλητον εἶναι ὡς θεοῦ οἰκονόμον, μὴ αὐθάδη, μὴ ὀργίλον, μὴ πάροινον, μὴ πλήκτην, μὴ αἰσχροκερδῆ. (ΠΡΟΣ ΤΙΤΟΝ 1:7)

As a fisherman, I have seen my fair share of lightning strikes over the years. Nothing ruins a day on the water more than lightning. Cold weather? No worries; just wear a coat. Rain? A little water never hurt anyone. Thunder? Just the angels bowling.

But lightning? First bolt I see, I'm outta there. I'll quickly reel in my line, pull up the anchor, and get to cover as fast as I can. There's something about standing in the middle of a lake with a metal rod in my hand that seems like a bad idea during a lightning storm. Plus, I have watched too many storm shows to know that lightning is *not* my friend.

National Geographic confirms this. They say that over 2,000 people are killed every year by lightning. That seems like a lot to me.

The average American has a one in 5,000 chance of being struck in their lifetime. While it *is* possible to survive a lightning strike, there are long-term side effects, such as memory loss, dizziness, weakness, and numbness. So it's nothing you want to mess around with while trying to catch some fish.

But more than just deadly, lightning is extremely powerful. It's 54,000 degrees Fahrenheit or five times hotter than the surface of the sun. Unbelievable, right? But true. One bolt releases enough energy to power a 100-watt light bulb for three months straight. And if *that* weren't enough, the electrical impulse in lightning travels at a speed of 136,000 mph.

Considering all this, it's safe to say that you don't want to get hit. Pack up your picnic, stop dribbling the ball, and get inside the next time you see those flashes of heat dancing angrily in the sky. If one gets too close, it will flatten you out.

In Titus 1:7, we see another form of "lightning." Though not an electrical charge that snakes through the sky, it's a hazardous personality trait that devastates people and causes a lot of damage.

Here, Paul has commissioned Titus to appoint elders in the Cretan church. It was important for Titus to entrust the right sort of godly leaders, so Paul gives Titus benchmarks to look for when making his selections. One criterion is that such individuals could not be "violent."

This is an interesting word in the Greek. Here it is the noun *plēktēn*. It means "a pernicious person," "a quarrelsome individual," and "a bully." It comes from another Greek word, the verb *plēssō*, which means "to strike with force," "to smite," and "to sting."

In antiquity, Hesiod, a Greek poet from around 750 BC to 650 BC, used *plēssō* in his work *Theogony* to describe the angry Zeus striking down his opponent, Typhoeus, with bolts of lightning. Hence, the idea behind "violent" or the noun *plēktēs* refers to "intense, spiteful anger," like the kind Zeus exhibited when he zapped his enemy.

> In *Theogony*, Hesiod wrote about three Cyclopes, the brothers Brontes, Steropes, and Arges, who forged Zeus's lightning bolts for him. In *Alcestis* by Euripides, Apollo killed them because they had made the lightning bolt that Zeus used to kill Apollo's son, Asclepius.

Paul was telling Titus to make sure that whoever he picked didn't have a capacity for this sort of rage. It would be devastating to the church to have a leader who went around bullying people and blasting them with bolts of anger. God's leaders were to look like Jesus, not Zeus.

I learned this lesson the hard way. In the early days of my ministry, I thought that leadership strength meant using an iron fist. A ministry team member came with me on an overseas trip. I had given him a set of rules and I expected him to comply.

One particular night after service, this individual decided it would be nice to pick up the bill for the whole table. This included myself, the pastor, the pastor's family, and some members from the church. When the check came, he explained that he had already paid. Everyone was blown away by his kindness and generosity. That is, everyone except for me.

In my thinking, this was breaking the rules. He was supposed to run everything he did by me, including something like this. That night, when we got back to the hotel, I scorched him until he was well-done. Like Zeus, I had lightning coming out of my eyes, my hands, and my throat: "Now, you listen to me. You don't just go doing stuff. I don't care how nice you think it is. What's more important, being a good guy or my rules? You don't think these people have any money of their own? If you want to pay for dinner, you can go on your own trip and do that. But when you are on *my* trips, you do what *I* say. Got it?"

I'm still shocked that he didn't punch me in the face. I would have deserved it. What a jerk I was.

The next morning, I woke up and felt awful. *I* was the *leader.* I heard the Holy Spirit say to me, "Is that how I treat you when *you* do something that *I* don't like?" Conviction gripped my heart. I found myself asking for this individual's forgiveness, which he was happy to extend to me. In that moment, I realized that being "violent" has no place in the body of Christ, especially among God's leaders. Since then, I've tried my best to leave the lightning alone.

How about you? Do you throw lightning bolts to get people to do what you want? Or do you treat them the way Jesus would? We need to use gentleness with others. After all, we don't want them to pack up and run for the hills every time they see us coming.

76

INNOCENT: *AKERAIOUS*
(ἀκέραιος)

---

*For your obedience is known to all, so that I rejoice over you,
but I want you to be wise as to what is good and* **innocent** *as to
what is evil.* (Romans 16:19)

ἡ γὰρ ὑμῶν ὑπακοὴ εἰς πάντας ἀφίκετο· ἐφ᾽ ὑμῖν οὖν
χαίρω, θέλω δὲ ὑμᾶς σοφοὺς εἶναι εἰς τὸ ἀγαθόν, ἀκεραίους
δὲ εἰς τὸ κακόν. (ΠΡΟΣ ΡΩΜΑΙΟΥΣ 16:19)

Tornadoes have always churned up public interest. You can't turn on
Netflix or cable TV without seeing some kind of special about them.
In fact, you can find bands of storm chasers on YouTube, out there with
the latest technology and trying to collect more data about these raging,
whirling storms.

I've seen three tornadoes. As a kid, I watched one in terror while eating at a Wendy's restaurant. Another time, I was on a hotel balcony in Myrtle Beach and saw a funnel drop from the sky, plunge into the ocean, and turn into a water spout. Still later, I was driving to preach at a youth conference in Wisconsin when, in my rearview mirror, I witnessed a twister drop from the clouds and devastate farmland behind me. As a third-time eyewitness, I'm relieved that I've never been in a twister's path.

According to *National Geographic*, tornadoes cause $400 million worth of damage every single year. With rushing winds of up to 250 mph, they have been known to carve a path of destruction a mile wide and fifty miles long.

Every so often, stories of phenomenal survival emerge after a tornado has ripped its way through an area. One such tale surfaced after March 3, 2019, when a deadly tornado touched down in Lee County in eastern Alabama. It killed twenty-three people and left copious damage. It tore across the west Georgia state line into the town of Waverly Hall, where it ripped apart houses and snapped trees in half.

But there was one home *directly* in the tornado's path that was untouched. Drone footage of the storm's path, marked by fallen trees and debris, shows a lone house standing in the middle of all the devastation. The twister apparently just hopped right over the roof. While everything around the house bent, broke, and fell, the house stood as though it had conquered the storm, uncorrupted by its power.

In Romans 16:19, God's Word tells us that we, too, can be safe from the power of a storm. It's not talking about whirlwinds and cyclones, but the powers of evil that stir in this world. Here, the apostle Paul is concluding his letter to the Roman church, leaving them with a final, vital exhortation to be *"innocent as to what is evil."*

The Greek word here for "innocent" is *akeraious.* It can mean "unharmed," "unravaged," "untouched," and "not corrupted." In antiquity, it was used to describe cities that had not been devastated and ravaged by war. It was also used to describe an estate that remained intact, untouched by trouble, and in good condition, like that house in Waverly Hall, Georgia.

The idea behind *akeraious* is to be pure and uninfluenced by surrounding calamity or devastation. Christians must not be influenced by the sinful storms of society or the churning cyclones of culture. While the rest of the world is bending to evil, the believer should remain strong and stalwart, without compromise and unhindered by corruption.

> Emperor worship began with Julius Caesar. During his lifetime, a statue was erected to him with the words *Deo Invicto* (to the unconquered god). This was likely just flattery. After his death, however, he was given the title *Divus*, "the deified," and a temple was erected for his worship.

This would have been well-understood by the Christians in Rome. Their society was full of sensuality and emperor worship. Each day, these influences rolled right over top of them and challenged them to snap. But Paul was admonishing them to stay strong. This was a feasible request. God had built them to withstand the storm. They just had to make the decision to remain firm and not bend.

The fact is, the gales of wickedness swirl in our society today. You may be right in their path. When you go to work, does wickedness run over top of you? While you are hanging around on campus, do gusts of evil blast in your direction? As long as we live in this world, there are going to be times when we simply can't avoid the path of the storm.

But that's okay. God's Word has made it clear that we have been built to last and emerge untouched. It's possible to sit in your cubicle and not become like the people who share your workspace. You can attend college and not bend your worldview to conform to those who challenge God. When you are grounded in God's Word, nothing can move you. You will remain unscathed, uncorrupted, and innocent before the Lord.

If you find yourself in a situation you can't avoid, don't bend or compromise. You will find that the power of the Holy Spirit sustains you and keeps you from harm. When push comes to shove, you will emerge victorious, unscathed by sin. Give God praise that He has built you to remain innocent and stormproof.

77

SEAR: *KAUSTRĒIAZO*
(καυστηριάζω)

Through the insincerity of liars whose consciences are seared.
(1 Timothy 4:2)

ἐν ὑποκρίσει ψευδολόγων, κεκαυστηριασμένων τὴν ἰδίαν συνείδησιν.   (ΠΡΟΣ ΤΙΜΟΘΕΟΝ Α 4:2)

Are you a steak-eater? I sure am. In fact, I'm a steak fanatic. Take the explore page on my Instagram for example. Every time I look at it, I'm met by tomahawk ribeyes being salted, tossed onto the grill, and sizzling with splendor. Yum!

I've tried many of the methods and recipes I've seen over the years and have become a self-taught grill master. My steaks would make your mouth water—and I've posted the videos to prove it.

But it wasn't always so. When I first began, I thought all you had to do was slap a steak on the grill, turn it on, and let it cook. Just thinking about this now makes me want to go back in time, shake my younger self by the shoulders, and shout, "You're wasting a good cut of meat!" You should never *ever* put a steak on a cold grill. It should be at least 450 degrees or even 600 degrees.

> Beef was not eaten often in the ancient world. Cows were raised for their milk and bulls were used as draft animals, so by the time either was no longer useful for those purposes, their meat was old and tough.

You *must* sear it; that is, you must cook the outside of the meat at a high temperature. If you do this right, something called the *Maillard reaction* occurs—a browning effect that makes the meat look caramelized. But there's always the chance you can sear it too long. If that happens, you'll end up with a charred, black lump of steak that no one wants.

This was the case when I first tried to sear a steak in a stainless steel pan on the stove. The pan was so hot that it turned purple. No exaggeration. That pan was nearly 500 degrees. I had smothered my steak in olive oil...not realizing that smoke point of olive oil is 410 degrees. As soon as I placed the beef in the pan, a billow of smoke engulfed my kitchen, immediately followed by a flame high enough to kiss the stove light.

I was in the early stages of burning my house down. It was either abandon my steak or let the flames keep climbing. I had no choice but to extinguish the flames and ruin the beef, but at least I survived to tell the tale. Afterward, I looked at the steak and sure enough, in that short time, it had been scorched black. I remember saying to myself, "Wow, that is some kind of heat. This whole searing thing is serious business."

God's Word, too, says something about searing. Only it refers to searing the soul. In 1 Timothy 4, the apostle Paul is writing to Timothy about the nature of false teachers. He says they are in collusion with demonic spirits (verse 1) and their *"consciences are seared."* The conscience refers to the faculty of the soul that recognizes right from wrong. It is the moral and ethical compass of human existence. Paul said theirs were "seared," kind of like my incinerated steak.

The Greek word for "seared" here is *kekaustēriasmenōn*. It means "to burn something with a hot iron" or "to brand with a red-hot iron." It is part of a word family that describes things like cauterizing a sore, the burning of the sun, and scorching hot wind. This is not an average temperature, or even a hot temperature. It is the extreme heat you get from turning your stove up so high that your pan turns purple. It chars the life out of whatever it touches.

Because the false teachers practiced habitual sin, demonic spirits had taken their consciences and put them on high heat. They seared them until they were black, lifeless, and good for nothing. Their consciences had become incapable of telling the difference between right and wrong. They'd grown oblivious to moral virtue, were hardened, and were no longer sensitive to what is godly. These were all the result of persisting in sin without turning to God in repentance.

Wickedness damages our souls. Every time we compromise with sin and temptation, we are putting our conscience into the pan and turning up the heat. We may not even notice it at first, but the longer we stay near the heat, the more it's going to cook. If we don't pull away, our conscience will blacken until it's charred and no good.

Think about it. Have you ever been hesitant to do something at first, like trying illegal drugs, gambling, viewing pornography, or lying? After doing it once, you notice it becomes easier to do it the next time. Do you realize what's happening? Your conscience is being cooked by the devil. If you don't do something to stop it, you won't even think twice about sinning any more. In fact, it could even get to the point where you call what you are doing *good*. This is chef Satan at work.

Keep your soul off the devil's grill. Stay out of hell's kitchen. If you need to pull your conscience from the flames, you can do that right now by asking the Lord to forgive you and restore you. You can trust that the Holy Spirit will begin that process.

From here on out, remember to sear your steaks, not your soul.

78

DEEPLY MOVED: *EMBRIMAOMAI* (ἐμβριμάομαι)

---

*Then Jesus, **deeply moved** again, came to the tomb. It was a cave, and a stone lay against it.* (John 11:38)

Ἰησοῦς οὖν πάλιν ἐμβριμώμενος ἐν ἑαυτῷ ἔρχεται εἰς τὸ μνημεῖον· ἦν δὲ σπήλαιον καὶ λίθος ἐπέκειτο ἐπ' αὐτῷ.
(ΚΑΤΑ ΙΩΑΝΝΗΝ 11:38)

Not all heroes wear capes. This is especially true of Kerry Gold, a horse that unexpectedly saved its owner's life one day.

Kerry's owner, dairy farmer Fiona Boyd, was separating a calf from its mother. Cows are usually easygoing about this normal routine. Yet, on this particular day, the calf began to bellow and cry. Sensing its despair, its mother charged toward Boyd and ploughed into her side, slamming her to the ground. Helpless, she tried to get back on her feet, but the mother cow wouldn't let her. Instead, the 1,300-pound beast continued to ram her head against Boyd, pushing her back down. Unable to escape, the farmer tucked herself into a ball with her arms protecting her neck and face. She knew it was only a matter of time before the cow crushed her to death.

Suddenly, sensing her owner was in danger, Kerry Gold rushed to the scene. She kicked the enraged cow with her back hooves, forcing it back. The horse continued to attack the cow, allowing Boyd to crawl away to safety under an electric fence about fifteen feet away. Kerry Gold watched over her until she made it through. This brilliant horse became an immediate hero for moving so swiftly and rescuing her owner from certain death.

> Alexander the Great rode a Thessalian horse named Bucephalus. The breed is now extinct. Julius Caesar rode a horse named Genitor. Rome's augurs predicted that whoever rode Genitor would dominate the world, so Caesar never let anyone else ride him.

In John 11:38, we find another hero: Jesus, who rushes in to save the life of his friend Lazarus. John tells us that Lazarus had fallen sick and Jesus had been notified. Yet, by the time Jesus arrived, Lazarus had already been dead for four days. (See John 11:17.) As you might imagine, it was a sad scene, with people mourning and distraught. (See John 11:17–21.)

What's fascinating about this account is that John shows it to us from Jesus's perspective. John doesn't just describe what is going on; he describes what is going on *inside Jesus*. John tells us that Jesus notices the weeping, the sadness, and all the heartache caused by the death of Lazarus, and how all of this makes the Lord feel. (See John 11:33.) John chooses a fascinating Greek word to convey his emotion: *enebrimēsato*. John drops this word a second time, in verse 38 (*embrimōmenos*), once again describing how Jesus felt. Only this time, it was how Jesus felt when He was taken to the actual tomb of His friend, Lazarus.

In both instances, the ESV has translated the word as "deeply moved." That definition does the job, but unfortunately, it is a little vague to English speakers. "Deeply moved" could mean anger, frustration, hopelessness, excitement—who knows? It's not until we find out how the word was used historically that the light goes on. *Embrimaomai* was associated with "extreme concern," accompanied with an indignation to make things right. In antiquity, it was used to describe the bellowing of a horse before it stormed the enemy in battle. When we see this word, it's easy to picture Kerry Gold: concerned, indignant, and charging to the scene to rescue someone in distress. But here, Jesus is being depicted as a war horse, plunging Himself into the thick of the battle.

Jesus was angry at death. He had witnessed how it had destroyed the life of Lazarus and broken the hearts of those whom he loved most. Now, the Lord was launching a war on death. He was preparing to meet the foe of mankind in battle. The narrative tells us that Jesus had the stone of the tomb rolled away and commanded Lazarus to come back from the dead. And Lazarus rose. Jesus battled death and overcame it, setting Lazarus and those brokenhearted free from its heinous grip. He didn't just sit back passively and allow death to have its way. No, Jesus rushed into battle and overcame the enemy.

God doesn't sit back untouched and indifferent toward the hardship that death causes the human race. He is moved every time there is a mass school shooting. His heart becomes heavy when He witnesses the genocides that take place all over the world. He weeps when a family loses a child or a child loses a parent. He sorrows when innocent blood is shed. Death is God's enemy and He is outraged by how this foe has so devastated the lives of His creation from the beginning of time.

Despite all this, the word *embrimaomai* signals to us that God has done something about death through Jesus Christ. Jesus stormed it, defeated it, and has promised us freedom from it if we believe on Him. You see, the raising of Lazarus was the last miracle of Jesus that John records. It was also Jesus's greatest miracle in the Gospel of John, as it foreshadowed Christ's own death and resurrection. Jesus would rise just like Lazarus and we who believe on Jesus have the promise that we, too, will one day rise again. (See 1 Corinthians 15:51–57.)

When you see the disasters and calamities caused by death, think of a charging horse, outraged at its foe. Jesus has rushed to humanity's side and has secured for us victory over death. Thankfully, we serve a God who is deeply moved by the things that cause us harm—and who has taken action to get us out of harm's way.

79

MANIFESTATION:
PHANERŌSIS
(φανέρωσις)

To each is given the *manifestation* of the Spirit for the common good. (1 Corinthians 12:7)

ἑκάστῳ δὲ δίδοται ἡ φανέρωσις τοῦ πνεύματος πρὸς τὸ συμφέρον. (ΠΡΟΣ ΚΟΡΙΝΘΙΟΥΣ Α 12:7)

There are few individuals from the twentieth century who deserve as much respect as the late evangelist Billy Graham. While growing up, I wanted to be like him, preach like him, and save souls like him. Every single one of us preachers did. Graham was a man of integrity, without scandal, and a lover of Jesus and the lost, a modern-day apostle Paul.

When he passed away on February 21, 2018, social media erupted with tributes commemorating his race well run. His body was placed in honor in the U.S. Capitol Rotunda so people could pay their respects.

Graham had preached the gospel to more people than anyone else, ever—over 200 million people in over 185 countries and territories all over the world. Considered the "pastor to the presidents," he nurtured every president from Harry Truman to Barack Obama. Graham received the Presidential Medal of Freedom, the Congressional Gold Medal, an honorary knighthood from the British Empire, and even a star on the Hollywood Walk of Fame.

But where did it all begin for Billy Graham? How did he become so visible to the public eye?

It all happened in 1949 when he was a young man holding a tent crusade in Los Angeles. A media mogul by the name of William Randolph Hearst, impressed by Billy's preaching, sent word back to his national network of editors: "Puff Graham." That was the signal to write praiseworthy stories about the evangelist. Suddenly, flashbulbs began popping.

Graham appeared in *Life*, *Newsweek*, and *Time* magazines, as well as newspapers all over the country. He became a national star. Graham pulled a reporter aside to find out why they were making him so visible. To Graham's surprise, the reporter told him what Hearst had said. Graham never had the opportunity to speak to Hearst to find out why he decided to "puff" him.

Graham became the most influential preacher of our time and was under a spotlight that kept shining on him even after his death. Of course, Billy Graham's incorruptibility and Christ-filled life had something to do with that, too. But Hearst helped.

> "Christ not only died for all; he died for each."   —Billy Graham

In 1 Corinthians 12:7, the Holy Spirit is put under a spotlight. Here, the apostle Paul is writing to the Corinthian church about the exercise and use of spiritual gifts. These gifts are supernatural abilities, coming from the Holy Spirit, which edify the body of Christ and bring glory to Jesus.

Nine of them are listed in 1 Corinthians 12:7–10: the utterance of wisdom; the utterance of knowledge; faith; gifts of healing; the working of miracles; prophecy; distinguishing between spirits; tongues; and interpretation of tongues.

If you have ever seen these gifts properly used, then you know what a blessing they are. People are edified, healed, delivered from the power of Satan, and brought to salvation in Christ. Paul tells us that when they are being implemented, it is proof that the Holy Spirit is working in our midst. To communicate this, he calls them the "manifestation" of the Spirit.

The Greek word here for "manifestation" is *phanerōsis*. This is interesting because it comes from the Greek word *phōs*, which means "light." It makes sense why *phanerōsis* means "a making visible" and "exposure." That's what light does. Moreover, Hyperides, a political leader from the fourth century BC, used it in a speech to describe "publicity."

Hence, *phanerōsis* implies the idea of a bright light shining on someone that makes them noticeable, like flashbulbs popping on Billy Graham. God's Word is telling us that when we see the gifts of the Spirit exercised in our church services, they are making the Holy Spirit visible to us.

How do we know the Holy Spirit is present with us? The spiritual gifts shine a bright light upon Him and give Him the attention He deserves. After all, *He* is the one who heals, delivers, and points people to Christ. He deserves publicity. And no better way for Him to get it than through His gifts.

If you are a pastor or a ministry leader, do you allow the gifts of the Holy Spirit to manifest in your communal gatherings? Do you pray for the sick, prophecy, and allow tongues and interpretation of tongues to be exercised? When you do, you bring the right kind of attention to the Holy Spirit. And when people see Him, He will point them to Jesus.

Perhaps you aren't in a leadership position in the church. You can still exercise the gifts of the Spirit when you are comforting a friend, talking to someone about salvation in Christ, or praying for an individual who is battling sickness. When these gifts bless the individual you are ministering to, the bulbs will pop, and they will see that there is someone greater working through you.

I've learned this from experience. A man came to our church with a leg issue. This was the first time he had ever been to a church service where the pastor believed in healing, so he didn't know what to expect. At the end of the service, our team laid hands on him and prayed for him, and he was instantly healed. He began to walk on his leg and kept saying, "What did you do to my leg? What did you do to my leg?" I explained to him that it was the Holy Spirit who had touched him and that we hadn't done anything at all——except pray.

The man was dumbfounded. He had never experienced the power of the Spirit because he'd known nothing about it. When that healing took place, the flash bulb went off, and the Spirit got the attention He deserved. With that, the man gave his heart to Jesus and went home a new man, with a new leg. What a great honor and blessing it is to have the Holy Spirit present in our midst.

With that said, the key to effective ministry is simple: "Puff the Spirit" and make room for His gifts.

80

SYMPATHETIC: *SYMPATHĒS* (συμπαθής)

Finally, all of you, have unity of mind, sympathy, brotherly love, a tender heart, and a humble mind. (1 Peter 3:8)

Τὸ δὲ τέλος πάντες ὁμόφρονες, συμπαθεῖς, φιλάδελφοι, εὔσπλαγχνοι, ταπεινόφρονες. (ΠΕΤΡΟΥ Α 3:8)

If anyone knows a thing or two about sympathy, it's George Agate and John Whybrow. At the time of this writing, they hold the Guinness World Record for the fastest around-the-world ride on a tandem bicycle. They accomplished this incredible feat in 290 days, seven hours, and thirty-six minutes, from June 8, 2016, until March 25, 2017. They biked a grand total of 18,608.07 miles together.

Their quest began in the United Kingdom and took them through France, Belgium, the Netherlands, Germany, Czech Republic, Austria, Slovakia, Hungary, Serbia, Romania, Bulgaria, Turkey, Georgia, Azerbaijan, Iran, Afghanistan, Pakistan, India, Thailand, Malaysia, Singapore, Australia, New Zealand, the United States, Mexico, Guatemala, El Salvador, Honduras, Nicaragua, Costa Rica, Panama, and finally back to the UK.

The two men called it "an ultimate test of team work."

Whybrow was "the captain," the rider in the front, and Agate was the "stoker," the rider in the back. The captain is in charge of steering, braking, and warning of any upcoming hazards like potholes. The stoker is responsible for adding extra power when needed, maintaining the bicycle's equilibrium, and map reading. The captain has to be mindful of the fact that his teammate has a bumpier ride and can't brake. Both riders need to trust and understand each other, taking each other's difficulties into consideration.

Whybrow and Agate were sympathetic toward each other. Because of this, they were able to man the tandem bike successfully to reach their goal. Indeed, their effort was a perfect example of teamwork and sympathy.

In 1 Peter 3:8, God's Word talks a little about showing sympathy and tells us that it is extremely important for working together in the body of Christ. Here, Peter is giving instruction on how believers should relate to one another. He lists ways of treating each other that bring about God's blessings.

According to Hallmark Cards Inc., Americans buy more than 90 million sympathy cards every year. About 90 percent of those cards are purchased by people over age forty.

One of these ways is being "sympathetic." Sometimes, in English, sympathy is often thought of undesirably, like pity or feeling sorry for someone. Here, it is positive and contains a much stronger meaning than simply making a show over someone's misfortunes.

We can see this by looking at the Greek word for "sympathetic."[29] Here, it is *sympatheis*. This is a two-part Greek word and comes from *syn* ("with") and *paschō* ("to suffer," "to experience something unpleasant," "to go through something evil"). In antiquity, *paschō* was often used to describe those who suffered some sort of blow or experienced an unfortunate twist of fate, such as punishment or sickness. When *paschō* is combined with *syn* to make *sympathēs*, it means "suffering a blow together," "experiencing something unpleasant with," "going through something troublesome together." The idea is two or more people working together within the same trial, like tandem bicyclists.

Peter is saying that suffering with each other is one of the greatest essentials to serving each other in the body of Christ. This goes deeper than sending a Hallmark card or writing on someone's Facebook wall when they are going through times of trouble. While that's a nice gesture, truly showing sympathy is actually entering into that person's world and walking alongside them through the darkness of life. That might mean spending long hours with the sufferer at the hospital, reading Scripture to them. It could mean doing their errands until they are themselves again. It might even mean helping them out financially so they can get back on their feet.

You get the picture. Extending sympathy toward someone means you are going to have to trouble yourself in the process. But that's what Jesus did for us, isn't it? He looked upon our misery and brokenness, robed Himself in flesh, and experienced the trials of humanity. (See Philippians 2:6–8.)

I learned a lot about this sort of sympathy when I was in my first year of pastoring. Three months after I started our church, a dear member's eighteen-year-old son tragically passed away. She was a single mother and her son was her whole life. There isn't a more difficult thing for a pastor to see a person in his congregation experience—it was devastating.

As a young pastor, I wasn't sure how to approach this. One thing I quickly realized, though, was that helping this precious woman wasn't something our church could do overnight. Instead, we had to share her sufferings over time and this lasted several years.

Many times, she would come to church saddened and we had to lift her up. She'd talk about her son and we'd be a listening ear. When the anniversary of her son's death came, we were there for her. I even remember spending time in court beside her as she testified about what happened to her son. I was just a presence so she didn't fall apart.

As time marched on, I began to see the crucial importance of being sympathetic. True love means inconveniencing yourself by entering into someone's pain and going straight through it with them, no matter how long it takes or how much it costs. That's Jesus's model for us.

One day, years after her son died, she pulled me aside and said, "Pastor, if it wasn't for you and the church during those times, I may have ended my life." It's the most humbling thing anyone has ever told me.

Are you showing others sympathy by suffering with them through difficult times? Are you committed to riding with them on tough roads and during all of life's ups and downs? If you want to experience the profound blessings of God, serve others with sympathy. Joining with others in their joy and suffering is what the Christian life is all about.

81

CHEERFUL: *HILAROS*
(ἱλαρός)

Each one must give as he has decided in his heart, not reluctantly or under compulsion, for God loves a cheerful giver.

(2 Corinthians 9:7)

ἕκαστος καθὼς προῄρηται τῇ καρδίᾳ, μὴ ἐκ λύπης ἢ ἐξ ἀνάγκης· ἱλαρὸν γὰρ δότην ἀγαπᾷ ὁ θεός.

(ΠΡΟΣ ΚΟΡΙΝΘΙΟΥΣ Β 9:7)

Oh, pastors—they're always talking about money." That's a common complaint.

While I'm not denying that there *have* been abuses in the past, as with anything, God's Word *does* give fiscal instruction that needs to be taught despite any human abuses. It's said that there are over 2,000 verses in the Bible that instruct concerning finances. If ministers are going to preach the full Word of God, it's impossible to avoid talking about money, especially since money plays such an important role in life. The truth is, if believers do what God's Word says concerning money, they will live with abundant blessing and there will be peace in their finances.

We find one of these instructions in 2 Corinthians 9:7. Here, the apostle Paul is taking up an offering. That's right. Paul talked about money and passed the plate or basket around. You see, in Galatians 2:10, James, Peter, and John had admonished Paul to help the poor believers throughout the course of his ministry. Some of these poor believers included the Christians in Jerusalem. As a result, Paul made a special point to take up an offering for them from the churches in Macedonia and Corinth. At first, the Corinthians were delighted to help. (See 1 Corinthians 16:1–4.) However, by the time Paul wrote 2 Corinthians, they had fallen behind on their commitment. Paul needed to motivate them to continue their giving. So, Paul tells them about the Macedonian church's enthusiasm to give and uses an agricultural illustration to explain that giving is like sowing a seed that brings forth a harvest. (See 2 Corinthians 8:1–5; 9:6–15.) It is at this point that Paul lets the Corinthians in on a very important truth: *"God loves a cheerful giver."*

The Greek word here for "cheerful" is *hilaron*. This word should sound familiar to you; from it, we get the English word "hilarious," meaning "boisterously merry." When you think of "hilarious," you think of someone bursting with laughter, glowing with amusement. This imagery comes from the Greek *hilaros*, which means "glad," "happy," and "joyful." It was used in antiquity to describe bright shining things such as daylight and the color gold turns after it is heated in a furnace. The idea is that something *hilaros* shines with splendor and burns with brilliance. When used here in 2 Corinthians 9:7 in the context of giving, it depicts a person giving to God with a face that shines with joy like the noonday sun. God loves it when we give like this because *He* is that kind of giver.

This is the way God provides for us. He doesn't meet our needs with a bland and begrudged look on His face. He does it with excitement and enthusiasm. And God delights when *we* give like this because we are acting like Him. We aren't only supposed to give *to* God. We are supposed to give *like* God. This doesn't change just because someone has taken advantage of God's people in the past.

> A study conducted by the *Journal of Personality* determined that 7 p.m. is the time of day when people are the happiest.

I first learned about cheerful giving when I was just a young man, fresh out of Bible school. I was attending a church conference and the Holy Spirit prompted me to give a certain amount in the offering. I wasn't happy about it.

First, if I gave it, it would be the largest check that I, at age twenty-two, had ever written. And second, I thought, *This church is huge. I certainly need the money more than they need it.* Nevertheless, the Holy Spirit kept prompting me to give that same amount. By the last night of the conference, I knew I had to give it or I would end up being disobedient to the Lord.

I made a decision to go for it, but I also came up with a plan. I'd drop the offering in the bucket as fast as I could. If I didn't give it fast, I might relent. I wanted to get it over with.

However, it didn't seem that the Holy Spirit was fond of my plan. Shortly before the offering was taken, He corrected me. It dawned on me that if I didn't give *joyfully* then I wasn't giving with the heart of God. Suddenly, I changed my plan. By faith, I told the Lord that I was thankful that I could give into His kingdom. As the bucket made its way down my row, I began to praise the Lord. I made myself smile as big as I could. I wasn't going to just give *to* God, I was going to give *like* God. My face was going to shine bright and be *hilaros*.

After I gave my offering, the joy of the Lord came over me and my heart stirred with excitement. I went from dreading to give to being glad to give. That *hilaros* brightness stayed on my countenance the whole night, as my heart had changed toward giving to the Lord.

But the story gets even better. A few weeks later, an unexpected ministry position was offered to me—my very first. The salary happened to be exactly one hundred times what I had given. What a blessing from the Lord! What made it more exceptional was that I knew the Lord had given it to me cheerfully, with gladness, happiness, and joy. After all, He's a giver.

Don't let anyone spoil your joy of giving to the Lord. If you have a scowl on your face the next time you are supposed to give, remember that God shines with splendor and burns with brilliance every time He gives to you. The least you can do is turn that frown upside down and give with a *hilaros* heart.

82

ENDURANCE: *HYPOMONĒ*
(ὑπομονή)

For you have need of endurance, *so that when you have done the will of God you may receive what is promised.*

(Hebrews 10:36)

ὑπομονῆς γὰρ ἔχετε χρείαν ἵνα τὸ θέλημα τοῦ θεοῦ ποιήσαντες κομίσησθε τὴν ἐπαγγελίαν.

(ΠΡΟΣ ΕΒΡΑΙΟΥΣ 10:36)

If you are a younger sibling, like me, you may have had your fair share of beatdowns during your childhood years. At least, I did. As the older of two boys, my brother used his fists more than once to remind me who was the boss. (I'm sure he meant it with love.)

No matter how much brawling toughened me up, I was still far from being a professional fighter. Those guys take punch after punch and keep on ticking. How is it that the more punches they can take, the more fights they are likely to win? This is the kind of stamina and endurance that make fighters great, especially one of the greatest of them all, Muhammad Ali.

In his book *Ali: A Life*, Jonathan Eig points out something about the champ that many people may not have realized. According to statistical data compiled from his fights, prior to 1970, Ali did 61.4 percent of the hitting against his opponents. After 1970, something changed. He became a different fighter. Eig says:

> Over the course of the rest of his career, however, Ali took as much punishment if not more than he gave. He hit opponents 5,705 times and got hit 5,506 times. In other words, the man often regarded as the greatest heavyweight of all time was being struck almost as often [sic] he was striking his opponents. Even the 50-50 ratio wasn't as good as it seemed, because the overwhelming majority of Ali's punches were jabs, while his opponents employed more hooks and uppercuts, which tend to do greater damage.

It can be tempting to think that a champion always easily outdoes his opponents as an obvious overpowering force. But Ali's case shows something different. Winning has a lot to do with how many punches you can take. "But it ain't about how hard ya hit; it's about how hard you can get hit and keep moving forward." At least, that's what the "Italian Stallion," Rocky Balboa, says in *Rocky VI*. "How much you can take and keep moving forward. That's how winning is done."

Ali proves Rocky's point perfectly. Winning is enduring.

We find this principle in Scripture. In Hebrews 10:36, the writer of Hebrews tells his audience, *"For you have need of endurance."* The believers in Hebrews had already been through a lot of difficulty. Early on in their conversion, they had suffered persecution, with thieves plundering their homes and their opponents treating them with loathing and vicious hostility. Some believers were even imprisoned. The Hebrew Christians had endured these punches in the past and were facing more discouragement. They wanted to give up because Christ hadn't returned. They wanted their reward. Since they hadn't received it, they were ready to throw in the towel. But the writer of Hebrews encourages them and says they need more "endurance."

The Greek word "endurance" here is *hypomonēs*. It is a two-part Greek word and comes from *hypo* ("under") and *menō* ("to stay," "to remain," "to wait"). When the two words are conjoined, it means "staying under" or "remaining under" something. In antiquity, it described a strong sword outlasting the blows of a battle. The idea is to have enough strength to stay and wait under a hostile attack until the assault is over. In the Hebrews' case, it meant to remain under the persecution and discouragement until they survived it. Just like Muhammed Ali, who would stay in the ring, withstanding the punches, until he won the fight.

> Theagenes of Thasos, who lived during the fifth century BC, was a famous Greek Olympian boxer, the Muhammad Ali of his day. He is said to have won more than 1,300 bouts during his career.

It's clear that if we are going to be successful Christians, we have to be prepared to last until the final round is over, no matter how hard the punches are. Giving up is simply not an option. We are called to endure. The Hebrew Christians were urged to carry on—and we must do the same.

Are you in a vicious fight today? Are the punches coming harder and more frequently than before? If that's the case, the Lord wants to give you the fortitude to stand under it until you outlast it. Maybe you are believing God to pay off some debt and are feeling the force of financial pressure. If so, God will supply you with the strength not to be overcome with worry and fear. Perhaps you are undergoing a temptation that is bullying you to act in a manner that you would eventually regret. The Lord will give you the power you need to stand your ground and keep punching back until it gives up and relents.

Remember, you are in Christ and He is the one who stands behind you. You are equipped to stand as long as you have to until the dust settles and you emerge as the champ. No matter what fight you face today, ask the Holy Spirit to strengthen your stance and build up your endurance so that you can be the fighter that God wants you to be—one who can stand toe-to-toe with the enemy, take his best punches, and go all the way to the final bell.

83

EAGER LONGING:
APOKARADOKIA
(ἀποκαραδοκία)

For the creation waits with eager longing *for the revealing of the sons of God.* (Romans 8:19)

ἡ γὰρ ἀποκαραδοκία τῆς κτίσεως τὴν ἀποκάλυψιν τῶν υἱῶν τοῦ θεοῦ ἀπεκδέχεται. (ΠΡΟΣ ΡΩΜΑΙΟΥΣ 8:19)

Waiting sounds like such drudgery. It usually is, considering most of the things we wait around for in life. Our phone to charge. The coffee to brew. The movie to begin.

Among our most toe-tapping waits is the one we endure as the traffic light goes so slowly from red to green. Statistics show we spend a major portion of our lives just sitting at red lights. Let's say you begin driving at the age of fifteen and finish at the age of eighty. You'll have spent about 3,809 hours of your life sitting at a traffic light. That's 159 days—about five months—just waiting there, doing whatever you do until the light turns green.

Five months is a lot of time. That's longer than it took to write this book. And that's *just* waiting at red lights. That doesn't include waiting in line at the grocery store, waiting at the gate to board your plane, or waiting for your spouse to get ready to go someplace.

Sometimes waiting isn't so bad. There are times when it can be quite exhilarating. Gentlemen, think about how excited you were when you were standing at the altar, waiting for the doors to open and your bride to start walking down the aisle. That was better than waiting in line at Walmart. Or what about waiting for the sunset while sitting on the beach in Hawaii? That's better than waiting for your number to be called at the Department of Motor Vehicles.

One of the most pleasurable things to wait for is a parade. When I was a little boy, Dad would take my brother and me to the Thanksgiving Day parade in downtown Detroit. As we stood on Woodward Avenue, we'd lean over the partitions and stretch our little necks as far as they could go to see what float was coming down the street. I'm sure anyone who saw our enthusiastic faces could tell that we were waiting eagerly for the next delight the parade had to offer.

> A giraffe's neck—six to eight feet long—is the longest of any animal. With its head so high in the air, a giraffe can keep a good lookout for predators. Julius Caesar brought the first giraffe to Rome from Egypt in 46 BC and it was called a "camelopardalis" (a camel-leopard).

So, waiting isn't always a drudgery. It comes down to what you are waiting for. If it happens to be the right thing, you'll wait eagerly and excitedly, neck outstretched, like a six-year-old child at a parade.

We see an example of excited waiting in Romans 8:19. Remarkably, the apostle Paul had been writing to the Roman Christians concerning suffering. As mortals, it is something that we cannot avoid, especially as Christian mortals who share in the sufferings of Christ. Yet, this suffering is just temporary.

God's Word tells us that a day is coming when we will share in the glory of Christ, which includes a glorified body like the Lord's. (See Romans 8:17.) At this time, God will restore to human beings the glory they once had and put an end to all of our sorrows. He will *also* restore the glory that creation has lost. It doesn't take much to figure out that the created world has experienced the effect of man's fall, which includes death and decay. But when we are glorified, the creation will be restored along with us.

The result will be a renewed world, free from corruption. To communicate the majesty of the event, Paul anthropomorphizes creation, saying it *"waits with eager longing"* for the day of its liberation from the effects of sin and death. The Greek word here for "eager longing" is *apokaradokia*. It is made up of the Greek words *apo* ("from"), *karā* ("head"), and *dokeuo* ("to spy" or "to watch"). Together, these three words mean "to spy on something using the head." It gives us a picture of someone sticking their neck out, with excitement, in suspense—like a bridegroom eagerly tipping his head to get the first glimpse of his bride when she comes down the aisle. I've seen this happen at nearly every wedding I've officiated. As soon as I tell the guests to stand for the bride, the groom always tilts his head and looks down the aisle, anticipating his bride walking through the doors. He can't wait for the first glimpse of their new lives together.

This is similar to the picture we get here of creation, neck stretched with excited hope, seeking the day of the Lord to come so that it can enter a new state. The fact is, the earth is going to become a far more beautiful world and creation is counting the days until it happens.

If creation is looking forward to the day when Jesus replaces chaos with glory, then so should we. We shouldn't freak out with the rest of the world when they talk about the earth being destroyed by nuclear war, climate change, or some sudden epidemic. While these issues deserve to be addressed and have their place in our political discussions, as believers, we should never allow them to make us fearful, troublesome, or afraid. God has promised us that He will deliver creation from the fall. That includes these issues and more. Instead of sitting around waiting in fear for some cataclysmic event to destroy the population, we should join the earth in rejoicing that Jesus is coming. He will deliver the earth from any apparent threat or any certain chaos.

As Christians, we believe in the hope of Christ's return and we wait for His restoration with excitement. We know that when He comes, He is going to make everything right. He will disarm the nuclear threat, free us from any potential threat of disease or climate change (if there even *is* one), and will make this beautiful planet all the more stunning. Instead of waiting around in fear for the day to come when things go off the rails, we should wait in excitement for Jesus to make the world the kind of place we all dream for it to be.

Creation has stretched out its head and is looking for that day with a smile on its face. We should do likewise. Something marvelous is coming.

84

THEOPHILUS: *THEOPHILOS* (Θεόφιλος)

It seemed good to me also, having followed all things closely for some time past, to write an orderly account for you, most excellent Theophilus, *that you may have certainty concerning the things you have been taught.* (Luke 1:3–4)

ἔδοξεν κἀμοὶ παρηκολουθηκότι ἄνωθεν πᾶσιν ἀκριβῶς καθεξῆς σοι γράψαι, κράτιστε Θεόφιλε, ἵνα ἐπιγνῷς περὶ ὧν κατηχήθης λόγων τὴν ἀσφάλειαν.

(ΚΑΤΑ ΛΟΥΚΑΝ 1:3–4)

Have you ever met someone who loves the Lord, but still has doubts about certain things? Living a life of faith often comes with a lot of questions, even deep uncertainties. Statistics from Barna Research in 2017 suggest that many Christians go through these times of significant doubt. Who knows? You may be experiencing this even now.

The fact is, about 65 percent of those in the United States who self-identify as Christians or former Christians say they have questioned what they believe about God. Twenty-six percent say they still experience doubt, while 40 percent say they have worked through the uncertainty. Only 35 percent say they have never experienced doubt about religion or God.

One thing we can gather from these statistics is that it *is* possible to love God and serve Him while experiencing certain doubts. That seems to describe a lot of the Christians in the U.S. But that's okay. If you are going through doubt, God still loves you and you're in good company.

There were those in New Testament times who loved God, but still had pressing questions about their faith. They needed answers in order to overcome. One such person is Theophilus, who we find in Luke 1:3 and Acts 1:1. Both the Gospel of Luke and the Acts of the Apostles were written by Luke to Theophilus, a Gentile believer who likely had a high-ranking social status.[30] Theophilus was sincere in his faith. In fact, it would seem likely that he was in charge of publishing Luke's accounts, including paying for them to be copied and distributed to a wide audience. His sincerity and love for God made his given name fitting because "Theophilus" means "lover of God." His name is the Greek word *Theophilos*[31] which comes from the words *theos* ("God") and *philos* ("loving" or "having special interest"). It gives us a picture of someone who loves God and has a special interest in Him—enough to pay for and distribute literature about God.

Despite Theophilus's interest and love for God, he had been struggling with his faith. Christianity, at first, seemed like a Jewish movement and he was a Gentile. He might have been wondering why he was following something that was Jewish. Maybe he felt out of place. Further, he knew that many Jews had rejected Jesus. Did those Jews know something about Jesus that he didn't?

Some notable individuals named Theophilus from modern times include Theophilus Eugene "Bull" Connor (1897–1973), a segregationist from Alabama; and Theophilus "Theo" Martins, a hip hop artist, record producer, actor, DJ, and fashion designer born in 1987. It's also the name of the title character of the last novel written by Thornton Wilder, *Theophilus North*.

Like all of us, Theophilus loved God and was eager to do things for Him, but still had reservations. Isn't it interesting that God's Word presents us with a man whose literal name is "lover of God," but who was, at the same time, full of serious questions about the God he served? God's Word is telling us that it *is* possible to love the Lord and still have areas of uncertainty in your life.

Does that sound like you? Maybe you volunteer at your church, yet you have seen some things in the news lately that have made you wonder where God is. Perhaps you are a pastor and some of the arguments against Christianity have made your faith a bit shaky. This doesn't mean you've stopped loving God. It just means that you need some more answers. And God has them for you.

In light of Theophilus's questions, the Holy Spirit put it into Luke's heart to write a two-volume account about Jesus's life and teachings. This would get right to the bottom of Theophilus's inquiries and give him answers to strengthen his faith. But why would God do this? The answer goes back to Theophilus's name. The Greek word *Theophilos* not only means "lover of God," but it just as sincerely means "beloved by God," "the one whom God loves," or "the one in whom God has a special interest in." Despite all of Theophilus's questions and uncertainties, God loved him. God saw him doing his best to figure out the faith, pondering who Jesus is and how he could make sense of the things he had heard about the Lord. Theophilus was seeking. God never leaves a sincere seeker without answers.

As a result, through Luke, God gave His dear son Theophilus a whole two-volume set about Jesus, full of enough detail to show Theophilus why the Jews rejected Jesus and how the Gentiles fit into the plan of God. If that weren't blessing enough, He used the eager Theophilus to publish it and spread it around so the rest of us could have it for thousands of years.

God must have known we'd have the same doubts and uncertainties as Theophilus.

The fact is, all of us who love God and serve Him by faith will have our questions and concerns. There will be times when we flat out don't understand. But God has provided His Word to us as an answer. The Bible is God's blueprint for developing a faith that stands firm upon the Lord and is a resource for answers in times of our most extreme doubt.

No matter how acute your uncertainty might be today, be like Theophilus and get into the Word. I'm certain it will dispel your insecurities about following the Lord, with answers that will make you sure and strong.

85

GREATLY ANNOYED:
DIAPONEOMAI
(διαπονέομαι)

And this she kept doing for many days. Paul, having become greatly annoyed, turned and said to the spirit, "I command you in the name of Jesus Christ to come out of her." And it came out that very hour. (Acts 16:18)

τοῦτο δὲ ἐποίει ἐπὶ πολλὰς ἡμέρας. διαπονηθεὶς δὲ Παῦλος καὶ ἐπιστρέψας τῷ πνεύματι εἶπεν, Παραγγέλλω σοι ἐν ὀνόματι Ἰησοῦ Χριστοῦ ἐξελθεῖν ἀπ' αὐτῆς καὶ ἐξῆλθεν αὐτῇ τῇ ὥρᾳ. (ΠΡΑΞΕΙΣ ΑΠΟΣΤΟΛΩΝ 16:18)

Many people have a favorite pair of jeans, a pair that fits *so* well that wearing any other pants seems like a crime. A good pair of jeans can last for years. I've had my fair share of them. Perhaps my best was a pair I had in my late twenties. They were lightweight, with just a tiny bit of stretch. They fit me perfectly at the waist and cuff—probably the best $45 I ever spent.

Those bad boys would hug my legs and remind me that I'm loved. I could wear them with my Nike AirMax sneakers and a T-shirt, *or* I could dress them up with some Kenneth Cole loafers, an Oxford shirt, and a blazer. I traveled in those jeans, preached in them, fished in them, laid around the house in them, and even went on a few dates in them. In fact, I was hoping that when Jesus returned, He'd rapture me to heaven in them.

But something happened one day that stopped my world. A hole appeared in the worst possible place. Some holey jeans can be considered cool (although I've never been much of a fan), but not a hole *there*. At first, it was small and not noticeable. Over time, however, the hole grew bigger and more obvious. No longer could I wear them with the same dignity and respect for myself that I had in the past. Soon, they became *around the house* jeans. Maybe I'd do an errand or two in them…while wearing a coat that hid the hole.

Finally, the hole got so big that I had to retire those jeans forever. They were simply worn out. The denim could take no more. They were tired, spent, and fed up with all that I had put them through. What could I do? They refused to carry on any longer.

Have you ever felt like an old pair of jeans, tired and worn out from everything you've been through? So tired that you refused to go on anymore? Like my old favorite jeans, did you get to a place where enough was enough, once and for all? If so, then you are like the apostle Paul in Acts 16.

The term "denim" comes from the French term "serge de Nimes"—meaning a sturdy fabric from Nimes, France. Unlike other cotton fabrics, denim has a diagonal ribbing pattern that makes it both soft and strong.

The apostle was in Philippi, where he encountered a slave girl who was possessed by a spirit of divination. This fortune-teller followed Paul and his missionary team around, declaring, *"These men are servants of the Most High God, who proclaim to you the way of salvation"* (Acts 16:16–17). Seems like a nice thing to say, right? Wrong.

330 GREEK WORD STUDY

The people of Philippi knew this girl was possessed with an evil spirit. Her endorsement gave them the impression that Paul was in league with her. This discredited him and all of his efforts to preach the gospel. After putting up with this slave girl for days, in Acts 16:18, Paul finally became so "greatly annoyed" with her that he cast the evil spirit right out of her. He couldn't take it anymore.

The Greek word here for "greatly annoyed" is *diaponētheis*. It is a two-part Greek word that comes from *dia* ("through") and *ponos* ("work," or "hard labor"). When combined to form *diaponeomai*, it means "to work through" in the sense of "to wear out." In antiquity, it described something that had been thoroughly developed with intense strain, often to the point of exhausting it or wearing it out—like my favorite pair of jeans. In Acts 16:18, it meant that the slave girl's constant derision became so intense that it wore Paul thin. He was annoyed, worn out, and fed up. He couldn't continue to let her follow him around. He finally did something about it and cast the devil out of her. Paul had reached his breaking point and it prodded him into action.

How about you? Is there something unhealthy in your life that is wearing you thin and exhausting your energies? It may not be a devil-filled soothsayer following you around. Perhaps it's an unhealthy relationship that God has told you not to be in. Maybe it's a habit you have developed, like watching pornography, smoking, or even bending the truth. Perhaps it's an endeavor that God hasn't told you to take up.

Whatever it is, there has to be a point where you get so fed up you finally break with it and refuse to go on any longer. God doesn't want to see this thing to take advantage of you. He wants you free of it. Aren't you tired of it wearing you thin?

If you are being vexed by it, that's a good thing. In fact, that annoyance is the Holy Spirit telling you it's time to toss this detrimental thing. Are you willing? I hope so. Otherwise, it will keep wearing holes in your life.

God doesn't want that for you and I'm sure you don't want that for yourself. Instead of ignoring what's annoying you, use that annoyance to break free. When you do, your life will become a lot more holy, as opposed to holey.

86

ROOT: *RHIZOŌ* (ῥιζόω)

Therefore, as you received Christ Jesus the Lord, so walk in him, rooted and built up in him and established in the faith, just as you were taught, abounding in thanksgiving.

(Colossians 2:6–7)

Ὡς οὖν παρελάβετε τὸν Χριστὸν Ἰησοῦν τὸν κύριον, ἐν αὐτῷ περιπατεῖτε, ἐρριζωμένοι καὶ ἐποικοδομούμενοι ἐν αὐτῷ καὶ βεβαιούμενοι τῇ πίστει καθὼς ἐδιδάχθητε, περισσεύοντες ἐν εὐχαριστίᾳ.

(ΠΡΟΣ ΚΟΛΟΣΣΑΕΙΣ 2:6–7)

On March 15, 2018, tragedy struck Florida International University and the city of Sweetwater, Florida. A $14.5 million pedestrian bridge—which weighed 950 tons and spanned 174 feet—collapsed into a busy intersection and crushed eight cars. Six people were killed and eight were injured.

The collapse came just after the university had hailed the bridge as a "construction marvel" and an "outstanding example" of the Accelerated Bridge Construction (ABC) method. Yet after the bridge fell, the university had to delete a tweet that quoted its president saying, "FIU is about building bridges and student safety. This project accomplishes our mission beautifully." Apparently, it had not.

Prior to the collapse, the bridge had been lauded as a prime example of the ABC method, a bridge-building technology that's supposed to make installation more efficient. Prior to the collapse, the university said, "This method of construction reduces potential risks to workers, commuters, and pedestrians and minimizes traffic interruptions." The main span of the bridge, it reported, "was installed in a few hours with limited disruption to traffic over the weekend."

A *few* hours? That *would* have been impressive…except the bridge fell.

After reviewing over 2,000 pages of bridge calculations at the request of *The Miami Herald*, three independent structural engineers concluded that the unconventional placement of supports along the bridge created a weakness at a key connection point. In their opinion, the builders misjudged the amount of weight a strut on the north end of the bridge could handle. When too much weight was placed on the strut, it gave out, and down came the bridge. This sad accident proves it's better to take your time when you build something rather than work fast and risk making a crucial error.

In Colossians 2:6–7, God's Word tells us the same thing, spiritually speaking. Here, the apostle Paul is writing to the saints in Colosse about Christian maturity. He shares with them that being mature meant looking to Jesus for all of their spiritual needs, instead of searching in other places. (See verse 10.) This was an important exhortation. At that time, false teachers had come along and were seeking to sway the Colossians away from the true doctrines of Christ.

A wild fig tree that grows at the Echo Caves near Ohrigstad, Mpumalanga, South Africa, was found to have the deepest roots ever discovered. They go down about 400 feet.

To resist these deceptions, Paul told the Colossians that they needed to be "rooted" in Christ. The Greek word here for "rooted" is *errizōmenoi*. It means "to fix firmly," "to put on a firm foundation," and "to be strengthened." It was used in antiquity to describe something that had been built sound and secure—like the proper way to build a bridge. Hence, "rooted" describes something that has been built correctly and fixed firmly in place so that it doesn't give out or collapse when weight, pressure, and tension are placed upon it.

Paul was exhorting the Colossians to fix themselves firmly upon the Word of God so that false teachings couldn't cause their faith to fold. This meant they had to do what was necessary to get a better grasp on Christianity. They had to think more deeply about the Scriptures and their meaning. This would take time and a constant, intentional effort. But the more the Colossians did this, the more rooted they would become in the doctrines of Christ and the harder it would be for false teachers to sway them away from God's truths.

All of us can benefit from Paul's words. Are you doing things that root you firmly in the Lord? Are you studying the things that make your faith stronger and more secure? Or are you just coasting along, at surface level, with ideas that make you feel good, but don't give you the fortitude to stand against any real intellectual challenge?

The proliferation of information (both true and false) and opinions (both noble and cringeworthy), from every quarter, continues at such a pace that no one really knows how big the Internet is, or even how many apps there are. What we *do* know is that Christians will be confronted by more attacks from atheists, agnostics, other world religions, and worse. Many of their arguments may seem compelling and put a lot of pressure on the critical thinking of Christian believers. Will these arguments cause a collapse? Not if you spend careful time examining the Scriptures in a manner that will help you discover a deeper understanding of Christ's message. Doing this requires a commitment of time; it cannot be done overnight. However, this is a commitment you'll make if firmly establishing your faith is important to you.

Challenge yourself. Don't settle for "bless me" messages and books that tell you how great your life can be. Don't let hip-sounding Christian music be the extent of your biblical understanding. And certainly don't go to church just to hear what God is going to do for you next. God is not a heavenly bellboy—and none of these superficial things take any real time. They won't make you strong or enable you to bear the pressure of intellectual challenges bearing down upon your Christian faith.

Instead, push yourself to grasp the brilliant philosophical meaning that is contained in the Word of God. Study the great Christian thinkers. Go into the annals of church history and discover how the church fathers answered the questions that you are facing now. Attend Sunday school or Bible study at your church so you're not only inspired, but educated.

Although these practices take time, you will be fixing your faith strongly and you won't collapse when the weight of the world comes against you.

87

SUPPLEMENT: *EPICHORĒGEŌ* (ἐπιχορηγέω)

For this very reason, make every effort to supplement your faith with virtue, and virtue with knowledge, and knowledge with self-control, and self-control with steadfastness, and steadfastness with godliness, and godliness with brotherly affection, and brotherly affection with love. (2 Peter 1:5–7)

καὶ αὐτὸ τοῦτο δὲ σπουδὴν πᾶσαν παρεισενέγκαντες ἐπιχορηγήσατε ἐν τῇ πίστει ὑμῶν τὴν ἀρετήν, ἐν δὲ τῇ ἀρετῇ τὴν γνῶσιν, ἐν δὲ τῇ γνώσει τὴν ἐγκράτειαν, ἐν δὲ τῇ ἐγκρατείᾳ τὴν ὑπομονήν, ἐν δὲ τῇ ὑπομονῇ τὴν εὐσέβειαν, ἐν δὲ τῇ εὐσεβείᾳ τὴν φιλαδελφίαν, ἐν δὲ τῇ φιλαδελφίᾳ τὴν ἀγάπην. (ΠΕΤΡΟΥ Β 1:5–7)

One day around Thanksgiving, a man wearing a New England Patriots jacket walked into Walmart in Darby, Vermont. Shoppers soon discovered that he wasn't there to shop for himself. He entered that particular Walmart specifically to pick up the tab for other shoppers—with his own money.

The act of unusual generosity took place when many people were plac-ing Christmas presents on layaway. The mystery man approached the lay-away counter and asked shoppers if he could pay for their goods. People were in shock; some were even skeptical. After all, who does that sort of thing? One woman said to the mystery man in disbelief, "This can't be. Who can afford to pay for everyone's layaway?"

Desiring to remain anonymous, he told the woman, "Santa Claus can."

Santa Claus must have paid a hefty price. Although Walmart could not disclose how much he spent in total, the shoppers interviewed said there were people in line who had $800 and $900 items on layaway. On top of that, the man also paid for all of the other layaway items in the storage room. No balance due for anyone. Shoppers were able to take everything home that night. Talk about spreading Christmas cheer.

However, the shoppers said it wasn't about the *stuff*. What touched them profoundly was the man's kindness and extravagant generosity toward complete strangers. I agree. Hats off to this mysterious layaway benefactor.

While many of us may never be able to be *this* magnanimous, in 1 Peter 1:5–7, we hear about another sort of funding that all of us can do that is pleasing to the Lord. In talking about living an effective Christian life, Peter says authentic faith in Christ is demonstrated in practical ways. In other words, we can't say we have faith in Christ, then kick back, satis-fied, without any real proof of change that has come from our faith.

Real faith requires real change—and this requires effort on our part. To describe this effort, Peter says, *"Make every effort to supplement your faith with virtue."* He continues with other characteristics that we are to add to our Christian lives, such as self-control and brotherly affection.

The most interesting part of what Peter is saying is found in the word "supplement." Here, it is the Greek word *epichorēgēsate*. It means "to grant," "to fund," and "to supply at one's own expense." This word comes from the Greek word *choros*, which meant "a band of dancers and singers," which today we might call a "chorus." Seems sort of odd, doesn't it? What does funding have to do with a chorus? Allow me to explain.

When *epichorēgeō* was first used, it was a symbolic term that meant "to fund the expenses of a chorus." Back in ancient Athens, a rich individual was often appointed by the state to fund most of or all of the expenses of a stage production where a *chorus* performed. This benefactor was known as the *chorēgos*. It cost the *chorēgos* a lot of money, at his own expense—like the mystery man who paid for everyone's layaways at Walmart.

> Typically, in Greek theater, a chorus offered background informa-
> tion to the audience and gave actors time for scene changes. Cho-
> ruses could consist of twelve to fifty people.

Later, *epichorēgeō* came to mean "to put on an expensive event" or "to fund a costly project." Finally, it came to mean "to supplement," "to supply," or "to provide." Yet, the idea of providing, at one's own expense and with one's own money, remained intact.

Peter's audience would have understood that adding virtue to their faith, as well as all the other characteristics on the list, would require an expensive effort on their part. The point is, if we want to grow in faith, we can't sit back and expect this to happen magically. No, we need to make an extensive effort to grow, which includes doing practical things that make our faith effective. This is supplementing and funding our Christian lives. This pleases the Lord.

Consider your Christian life for a moment. How have you been fund-ing its growth? Like the mystery man at Walmart, have you paid the price to gain knowledge from the Word of God? Has it cost you to live with self-control? Do you have to make an intentional effort to live committed to Jesus? It might take a lot to be kind and loving to some of the people in your family or at your workplace, especially the ones who have ruffled your feathers in the past.

Don't be a cheapskate when it comes to your faith. Fund it. Supplement it. Put some effort behind it. Don't fire back when you are insulted. Refrain from feeding the flesh. Stay committed to Christian disciplines like pray-ing, reading the Word, and going to church.

You are the *chorēgos* of this operation. Decide in your heart that you are going to give your best effort to make it a success. When you do, God will bless you in return—both in this life and on layaway, waiting just for you, in the next one.

88

IDLENESS: *ATAKTŌS*
(ἄτακτος)

For we hear that some among you walk in idleness, *not busy at work, but busybodies.* (2 Thessalonians 3:11)

ἀκούομεν γάρ τινας περιπατοῦντας ἐν ὑμῖν ἀτάκτως μηδὲν ἐργαζομένους ἀλλὰ περιεργαζομένους.
(ΠΡΟΣ ΘΕΣΣΑΛΟΝΙΚΕΙΣ Β 3:11)

Many years ago, when I was in the eighth grade, I was a saxophonist in the junior high band. I wasn't that bad either. Name a song and I could pipe it out—"Mary Had a Little Lamb," "Sawmill Creek," and even Christmas specials like "Hark, the Herald Angels Sing" and "We Three Kings." The saxophone was a serious thing to me. I can't remember why. Maybe it was because I aspired to be the next Kenny G.

More likely, it's because my mom made me practice every day and told me I *had* to get an A. My parents had paid *good money* for my alto sax. They weren't investing in my musical skills for me to let them *all go to waste*. So, every day, I'd drag that sax into school, set it up, and go over my notes and sheet music. I had no choice. My parents were coming to the junior high concert to see how their little saxophonist was doing.

Finally, the big night arrived. All my band friends gathered in the music room to warm up before the show, dressed up in our Bugle Boy shirts and ties. In just a few minutes, we were tuned and ready to put on a concert extravaganza. We sounded good. I felt confident and prepared. It was going to be a great night.

After we took the stage, the school principal, Larry Krueger, took the mic and did a little emceeing before we began our first piece. He welcomed the parents, talked about the band, and made what must have been *the* corniest joke in the history of the world. (I wish I could remember it!) He was a serial corny joke-teller and this one outdid anything I'd ever heard. The audience was almost booing, it was so bad.

A trumpet player to my left mumbled, "Mr. Krueger and his lousy jokes." Another trumpet player beside him heard that remark and began to laugh hysterically. This wasn't a chuckle. It was a "he's going to be laughing for the next ten minutes" sort of laugh.

The concert was now in jeopardy. The conductor raised his arms and the first piece began. Nearly fifteen seconds into the piece, I noticed out of the corner of my eye that the laughing trumpeter wasn't even trying to play. He had his head on the stand, his trumpet on the floor, and was laughing out loud, uncontrollably, while the rest of us put on the concert. Suddenly, he lifted his trumpet and tried to perform. Bad idea. He blared the wrong note, gave up, and put his head down and laughed even harder. It looked like he was going to spend the whole concert convulsing in chortles.

When the first piece was over, the conductor thrust his finger in the trumpeter's direction and yelled, "Knock it off!" His tomato-red face and deadly tone scared the daylights out of the kid. I guess that's all it took to get him back in order. We finished the second and third pieces just fine.

But that first piece had been hard for the rest of us to get through because the trumpet player was acting disorderly and out of sorts. You've got to love junior high.

> The most popular Greek musical instruments included the lyre, a small stringed instrument that looked like a U-shaped harp; aulos, two wooden wind instruments played together; and a syrinx, a set of panpipes.

Although this is a juvenile example of disorderly behavior, God's Word in 2 Thessalonians 3 mentions adults being disorderly in the Christian community. Paul was writing to the Thessalonians about living lives marked by godly discipline. There were those within the church who were lazy freeloaders who refused to work. Instead of providing a living for themselves, they expected others in the church to take care of them.

We don't know why they refused to work. Some scholars believe these Thessalonians thought working was pointless since the coming of Christ was so near. While that's a strong possibility, it's also possible that they disliked manual labor, as this was a familiar sentiment among Greek culture in those days.

It's also possible that these individuals in Thessalonica just flat out thought they were too spiritual to work. If you've been around the body of Christ long enough, then it's likely you've run into people whose heads are so far in the clouds that they think they are above going to work. They have to fast, pray, and street witness all day—no time to make a living. They expect other Christians to give them money instead.

Besides being blatantly lazy, these Thessalonians wound up with too much time on their hands. Because they had no business of their own, they got into everyone else's. As you can imagine, this created a mess. God's Word calls all of this *"idleness"* (2 Thessalonians 3:11).

Here, "idleness" is the Greek word *ataktōs*. It comes from the Greek word *tassō*, which means "to order," "to arrange," and "to put in place." However, the alpha privative in front nullifies it so that it means "against order," "disarranged," and "out of place."

In fact, this word can be translated "without rhythm." It was used in antiquity to describe a musician who was offbeat. I imagine it could describe my junior high school friend who was out of control while the rest of us played our instruments.

Paul was telling the church in Thessalonica that the lazy people who were freeloading in the community had gotten out of rhythm with God's plan for their lives—and they needed to knock it off. God wanted them to work hard to make their own living. They could get back into rhythm by getting their own jobs and minding their own business.

If we want to serve God in an orderly way, we need to do the same. While it may not seem lofty, it *is* certainly godly and spiritual. Yes, there are seasons of prayer when we get away and seek the Lord. But prayer isn't the only thing you should do. Street witnessing is important, but if it doesn't pay the bills, you need to find a job.

The fact is, God expects us to be honorable and provide for ourselves using the strength and skills He's given us. It sure beats acting out of sorts.

89

REWARD: *MISTHOS* (μισθός)

Watch yourselves, so that you may not lose what we have worked for, but may win a full reward. (2 John 1:8)

βλέπετε ἑαυτούς, ἵνα μὴ ἀπολέσητε ἃ εἰργασάμεθα ἀλλὰ μισθὸν πλήρη ἀπολάβητε. (ΙΩΑΝΝΟΥ Β 1:8)

Football players work hard to grow in their sport, especially those who want to become professionals. Even when they are young and touch the pigskin for the first time, they go through intense training.

Such training includes everything from strength conditioning to high-endurance workouts to extremely strict diets. They bust up tackle dummies, go full throttle in scrimmages, lug around medicine balls, carry weight plates, and then bandage themselves up so they can do it all over again the next day. When you see these players on the field, you know they are pushing their bodies to the limit.

For instance, Russell Wilson, who began his first year as quarterback for the Seattle Seahawks in 2012, includes boxing as part of his workout routine. The key word here is *part*. Wilson also swims, cycles on a stationary bike, lifts weights, box jumps, tosses a medicine ball, and does agility and shoulder exercises plus yoga.

Wide receiver Odell Beckham Jr. has been considered one of the hardest working players in the National Football League. His trainer said Beckham once landed from a flight at midnight and called him up, wanting to work out. Said workout went from 2 a.m. to 4 a.m.

> The median salary of a National Football League player is around $860,000. The average career length for NFL players is only 3.3 years.

Need I say more? To make it in the NFL, you have to put in a lot of effort. So, yes, some players make millions of dollars, but they are at it 24/7, not just on game day. Being named Most Valuable Player, earning a Super Bowl ring, receiving a Rookie of the Year award—it's the glory and reward that comes from brutally putting your body through its paces. I imagine that's why some of these guys weep when they finally hold what they've punished themselves to get.

That being said, can you imagine holding up a trophy as your own and then, one day, having it all taken away?

It seems unfathomable, but it happened. Just ask Reggie Bush, a former running back and Super Bowl champ who played in the NFL from 2006 to 2016. Prior to his pro career, Bush played for the University of Southern California from 2003 to 2005 and was part of USC's championship teams in 2003 and 2004.

In 2005, he won the Heisman Trophy, the highest award in college football. It's given to the player who exhibits the greatest ability, along with diligence, perseverance, and hard work. Some past winners include football greats like Tony Dorsett, Herschel Walker, and Bo Jackson.

But in 2006, it was reported that Bush had been receiving "improper benefits" as a student athlete. It took the National Collegiate Athletic

Association four years to investigate. In the end, the NCAA concluded that Bush should have been ineligible as an athlete in the 2005 season. Before the Heisman Trophy Trust made the decision to revoke the award, Bush gave it back. All that hard work. All those yards run. All those hours in the gym. And now, no Heisman to show for it.

It's true that most of us are not football players with a Heisman Trophy on our shelf, but there *is* an eternal reward waiting for us in heaven. God's Word tells us that we need to be careful because unless we work for it properly, it can be taken from us. I know this isn't the kind of stuff that makes people shout hallelujah in church. However, we need to remember that God's Word contains warnings for us that are just as important as the stuff that makes us want to get up and dance around the sanctuary.

In 2 John 1:8, the apostle was cautioning his audience about false teachers who were seeking to turn believers away from the truth. These false teachers were travelling around and John didn't want his audience to allow them into their community. If they heeded these imposter teachers and their false doctrines, they'd end up compromising their faith and could lose the full "reward" of their service to the Lord. The Greek word here for "reward" is *misthon*. It means "a workman's wage" or "recompense." In antiquity, it described a rightful payment for honest work.

The Heisman Trophy could be considered a *misthos* for all the hard work a college football player puts in. For John's audience, a *misthos* referred to the heavenly reward that awaited them for serving the Lord in an honest manner. However, if they listened to the false teachers, they'd end up corrupting this honest work and put their reward in jeopardy. It could be taken from them.

Think about that for a second. Here you are, a Christian who has done all this work for the gospel. You've walked in love, shown charity, ministered to the poor, and sacrificed yourself to serve others. Yet because you started following the wrong crowd, you lose the reward for your service. It's heartbreaking.

As Christians, we need to remember not to get complacent, as if our reward is already locked away in a glass case. It awaits us in heaven *if* we continue to work honestly for the Lord. Keep that in mind when you're doing your spiritual workout. Refuse to get involved with anyone or anything that could take your *misthos* away.

90

REDEEM: *EXAGORAZŌ*
(ἐξαγοράζω)

Christ **redeemed** *us from the curse of the law by becoming a curse for us—for it is written, "Cursed is everyone who is hanged on a tree"—so that in Christ Jesus the blessing of Abraham might come to the Gentiles, so that we might receive the promised Spirit through faith.* (Galatians 3:13–14)

Χριστὸς ἡμᾶς ἐξηγόρασεν ἐκ τῆς κατάρας τοῦ νόμου γενόμενος ὑπὲρ ἡμῶν κατάρα, ὅτι γέγραπται, Ἐπικατάρατος πᾶς ὁ κρεμάμενος ἐπὶ ξύλου, ἵνα εἰς τὰ ἔθνη ἡ εὐλογία τοῦ Ἀβραὰμ γένηται ἐν Χριστῷ Ἰησοῦ, ἵνα τὴν ἐπαγγελίαν τοῦ πνεύματος λάβωμεν διὰ τῆς πίστεως. (ΠΡΟΣ ΓΑΛΑΤΑΣ 3:13–14)

My visit to the Yad Vashem, the World Holocaust Remembrance Center in Jerusalem, Israel, was one of the most important four hours of my entire life. In that short time, I learned more about the facets of life—history, suffering, hatred, death, war, heroism, good, and evil—than I ever did in any classroom. I remember walking through the exhibits with horror, terror, and a bit of shame for my own ignorance. As my mouth hung open, parched and dry from being too shocked to swallow, I looked at as many artifacts as I could and attempted to imagine them belonging to a person who was just as real and alive as I. Oh, the value of a single human's life!

During the Holocaust, a German businessman understood this, although he was a Nazi. Oskar Schindler became a hero for saving the lives of over 1,200 Jews. In 1940, Schindler acquired an enamelware factory that was close to the Jewish ghettos of Kraków, Poland. Using his business savvy and his own money, he employed Jews who were destined for German concentration camps rather than Poles.

The Academy Award-winning movie, *Schindler's List*, based on a novel about Schindler's efforts, contains one of the most dramatic scenes in cinematic history. Schindler, portrayed by Liam Neeson, is thanked by the Jewish workers he has saved and is given a ring with a quote from the Talmud engraved on it: "Whoever saves one life saves the world entire." Schindler breaks down. He feels as though he could have saved more people.

"I could have got more out. I could have got more… If I'd made more money. I threw away so much money. You have no idea. If I'd just…I didn't do enough! This car. Goeth would have bought this car. Why did I keep the car? Ten people right there. Ten people. Ten more people.…" Schindler falls to his knees, crying, as the Jewish workers console his heavy heart.

Today, Oskar Schindler is honored at Yad Vashem. His efforts to save the Jewish people from genocide using his own money is a perfect picture of the concept of "redemption," an important biblical theme.

One of the places we find this theme is in Galatians 3. Here, Paul is telling the Galatians that Christ has redeemed us from a horrible existence through His work on the cross. To convey this, he says, *"Christ has redeemed us from the curse of the law."* The "curse of the law" refers to separation from God. (See Deuteronomy 27:26.) It is a life of guilt, misery, depression, slavery to sin, and, in the end, eternal death. But Christ "redeemed" us from this.

The Greek word "redeemed" here is *exēgorasen*. This interesting word comes from the noun *agora*, which meant "a marketplace." Hence, *exagorazō* means "to buy from out of the marketplace."

> Agoraphobia is a fear of crowded places. It comes from the Greek words *agora* "marketplace" and *phobos* "fear." Hence, it is "fear of the marketplace."

The idea behind it in Galatians 3:13 is that we were bound to a wretched existence. Hope was dim. Yet, Jesus bought our freedom with His sacrifice on the cross—just as Schindler bought the safety of 1,200 Jewish lives using his own welfare. Now, by simply placing our faith in Christ and what He has done, we can experience a new life. We're no longer slaves and oppressed. Hope is bright.

As we go through life, it's imperative to remember *what* Jesus has done *for us. He* paid the price of our redemption. *He* picked up the bill. No matter how good and Christ-like we try to be, our own effort is simply not enough to purchase our salvation and give us a new reality. Yes, it's great to help the homeless, feed orphans, visit prisoners, care for the elderly, tithe, go on mission trips, and contribute to a cleaner environment, but *none* of these things can set us free from being slaves to sin.

I imagine that some philanthropists who help the world might cheat on their spouses. Some community leaders may lie on their tax returns. Some people who work at a food bank might take a few things home. Some people who faithfully go to church every week might curse other drivers in traffic.

We *all* need our Redeemer, Jesus Christ. *He* purchased our salvation so we can live free from sin. Doesn't redemption sound good? Isn't it wonderful that the Lord cared enough about us to give all He had in order buy us out from an awful existence?

If you are trying to obtain your own freedom from something that is holding you in bondage, just remember your freedom has already been purchased by Jesus. All you need to do is put your faith in what He has done and receive.

FINAL WORD

Greek Word Study was written to enhance your understanding of God's Word using word studies from Koine Greek, the original language of the New Testament. It is my hope that the ninety studies within this volume have made God's Word simpler and more practical for you to understand. It's my prayer that it draws you closer to our Lord and Savior, Jesus Christ. There is tremendous philosophical value in God's Word that we can use as a lens to conceptualize the times we face, as well as practical insight for living our everyday lives. Hopefully, this volume has delivered just a little bit of that to you and continues to do so as you meditate on these studies again and again.

GREEK – ENGLISH INDEX

Agōn (ἀγών): competition; contest; deadly struggle (Study 23)

Agora (ἀγορά): marketplace (Study 90)

Ana (ἀνά): up; again (Studies 10, 53)

Analysis (ἀνάλυσις): departure; loosing; untying; breaking up (Study 73)

Anapsychō (ἀναψύχω): refresh; revive; cool; give relief (Study 70)

Anaseiō (ἀνασείω): stir up; shake up (Study 53)

Anazōpyreō (ἀναζωπυρέω): fan into flame; stir up the ember; rekindle the flame (Study 10)

Anexichniastos (ανεξιχνίαστος): unsearchable; unable to search something; unable to figure something out; impossible to get to the bottom of something; incomprehensible; impossible to fully understand (Study 4)

Anochē (ἀνοχή): forbearance; temporary cessation; pause; armistice; truce (Study 74)

Andreas (Ἀνδρέας): Andrew; a Greek name; one of Jesus's twelve disciples (Study 37)

Akathartos (ἀκάθαρτος): unclean; containing impurities; foul; infected (Study 22)

Akeraious (ἀκέραιος): innocent; unharmed; unravaged; untouched; not corrupted (Study 76)

Apo (ἀπό): from (Study 83)

Apokalypsis (ἀποκάλυψις): revelation; uncovering; disclosure; discovery (Study 24)

Apekdyomai (ἀπεκδύομαι): disarm; strip clothes off; undress; disrobe (Study 27)

Apokaradokia (ἀποκαραδοκία): eager longing; spy on something using the head (Study 83)

Arsēn (ἄρσην): male (Study 33)

Arsenokoitēs (ἀρσενοκοίτης): sodomite; a male who lies down with another male; dominant partner in a homosexual relationship (Study 33)

Asōtia (ἀσωτία): debauchery; reckless abandon; wild, undisciplined living; conduct of someone when the mind is absent (Study 8)

Ataktōs (ἄτακτος): idleness: against order; disarranged; out of place (Study 88)

Babylōn (Βαβυλών): Babylon; a city in ancient Meopotamia; a world system in opposition to God (Study 62)

Ballō (βάλλω): throw; cast (Study 12)

Blaptikos (Βλαπτικός): hurtful; injurious (Study 40)

Blasphēmeō: (βλασφημέω): utter hurtful words; slander (Study 40)

Chalepos (χαλεπός): difficult; fierce; violent; dangerous; troublesome (Study 18)

Charaktēr (χαρακτήρ): exact imprint; mark, impression placed on an object; image (Study 68)

Chorēgos (χορηγός): leader (of a chorus); a rich individual appointed by the state to fund most or all of the expenses of a stage production where a chorus performed (Study 87)

Choros (χορός): band (of dancers and singers) (Study 87)

Daimonizomai (δαιμονίζομαι): demon-possessed; taken over by a hostile spirit; indwelt by a demon (Study 29)

Deilos (δειλός): cowardly; timid; afraid; one who always runs away; one who runs away at nothing (Study 19)

Dia (διά): through (Study 85)

Diaponeomai (διαπονέομαι): greatly annoyed; work through; wear out (Study 85)

Diōkō (διώκω): press on; pursue; chase; follow something in haste; move quickly and definitively toward something; march; set in swift motion; harass (Study 21)

Dokeuo (δοκεύω): spy; watch (Study 83)

Dyō: (δύω): get; sink; enter (Study 64)

Echō (ἔχω): hold firm (Study 56)

Ek (ἐκ): out of; from (Studies 4, 54)

Ekstrephō (ἐκστρέφω): warp; turn out; twist out (Study 54)

Ektenes (ἐκτενής): earnest; outstretched; extended (Study 7)

Embrimaomai (ἐμβριμάομαι): deeply moved; be extremely concerned (Study 78)

Empaiktēs (ἐμπαίκτης): scoffer; a person who plays with; a person who makes fun of someone or something; one who plays around at another's expense (Study 71)

Emplekō (ἐμπλέκω): get entangled in; scuffle with; intertwine; ensnare (Study 50)

Entynchanō (ἐντυγχάνω): hit; strike (Study 31)

En (ἐν): in; with (Studies 64, 71)

Endyō (ἐνδύω): put on; get into something, sink into something; enter into something (Study 64)

Epagōnizomai (ἐπαγωνίζομαι): contend; carry on a competiton, contest, or struggle (Study 23)

Epichorēgeō (ἐπιχορηγέω): supplement: grant; fund; supply at one's own expense; fund the expenses of a chorus; put on an expensive event; fund a costly project (Study 87)

Ergon (ἔργον): task; occupation; labor; undertaking (Study 60)

Eritheia (ἐριθεία): selfish ambition; strife; contentiousness; rivalry (Study 58)

Exēcheō (ἐξηχέω): sound forth; ring out (Study 6)

Exagorazō (ἐξαγοράζω): redeem: buy from out of the marketplace (Study 90)

Exichniazo (εξιχνιάζω): trace from; track out; search something out, explore something thoroughly; get to the bottom of something; resolve a police case (Study 4)

Ginomai (γίνομαι): be; become; take place; be born (Study 25)

Hēmera (ἡμέρα): day (literal); period of time (Study 67)

Hilaros (ἱλαρός): cheerful; glad; happy; joyful (Study 81)

Hoplōn (ὅπλον): armor; weaponry used for military purposes (Study 2)

Ho Hagios Tou Theou (ὁ ἅγιος τοῦ θεοῦ): the Holy One of God; a title ascribed to Jesus in the Gospels affirming his messianic work (Study 44)

Hyper (ὑπέρ): above, over, beyond, more than (Studies 12, 31)

Hyperballō (ὑπερβάλλω): immeasureable; throw beyond; surpass (Study 12)

Hyperentynchanō (ὑπερεντυγχάνω): intercede; hit the mark over and above (Study 31)

Hypo (ὑπό): under (Study 82)

Hypokritēs (ὑποκριτής): hypocrite; actor; pretender; interpretation (Study 42)

Hypomonē (ὑπομονή): endurance; staying under; remaining under (Study 82)

Ichnos (ἴχνος): footstep; footprint (Study 4)

Kaleō (καλέω): call (Study 61)

Kara (κάρα): head (Study 83)

Kollaō (κολλάω): join; bind closely; glue together; cement together (Study 43)

Kapēleuō (καπηλεύω): **peddle;** to be a peddler; hawk goods; to be a retailer (Study 16)

Kata (κατά): down; down from; against; through (Studies 32, 41)

Katanyssomai: (κατανύσσομαι): cut; poke totally through; stab all the way in; gouge (Study 32)

Katapinō (καταπίνω): drink down; swallow up; fully consume (Study 41)

Katharos (καθαρός): clean; innocent; morally pure (Study 22)

Kaustrēiazo (καυστηριάζω): sear; burn or brand with a hot iron; cauterize; scorch (Study 77)

Keimai (κεῖμαι): lie down (Study 33)

Kryptos: (κρυπτός): secret; hidden (Study 5)

Lambanō: (λαμβάνω): take (in hand); grasp; seize (Study 63)

Lypeō (λυπέω): grieve; annoy; cause pain; cause mental and emotional distress; make sad; hurt someone's feelings; harass (Study 20)

Malakos (μαλακός): soft; tender; delicate; effeminate, passive partner in a homosexual relationship (Study 33)

Memphomai (μέμφομαι): blame; find fault (Study 9)

Mempsimoiros (μεμψίμοιρος): malcontent; complainer; grumbler; someone constantly finding fault; one who always thinks they are on the losing side of things (Study 9)

Menō (μένω): stay; remain; wait (Study 82)

Merimnaō (μεριμνάω): anxious; occupied; enormously concerned; engaged in something with extreme care (Study 34)

Mimētēs (μιμητής): imitator; model; impersonator (Study 1)

Misthos (μισθός): reward; workman's wage; recompense (Study 89)

Moira (μοῖρα): lot (in life); fate (Study 9)

Nekroō (νεκρόω): put to death; deaden; mortify; kill; cause to cease completely (Study 39)

Nēphō (νήφω): **sober-minded;** well balanced; self-controlled (Study 36)

Nyssō (νύσσω): nudge; poke; prick (Study 32)

Ochyrōma (ὀχύρωμα): stronghold; fortress; prison; strong-walled place (Study 56)

Oligopsychos (ὀλιγόψυχος): fainthearted; discouraged; having only a little bit of soul left within (Study 46)

Oligos (ὀλίγος): little (Study 46)

Osmē (ὀσμή): fragrance; smell; odor; something that stimulates a sense of smell; perfume; scent (Study 15)

Pagis (παγίς): snare; net; trap; pit; trick; strategy (Study 38)

Paizō (παίζω): play (like a child) (Study 71)

Palin (πάλιν): again (Study 25)

Palingenesia (παλιγγενεσία): regeneration; become again; be born again; have life again; a new genesis (Study 25)

Panoplia (πανοπλία): whole armor; all equipment and weapons required for battle; the full set of a soldier's armor (Study 2)

Para (παρά): by (the side of) (Study 61)

Paraklētos (παράκλητος): helper; someone called by the side to help (Study 61)

Pareisdyō (παρεισδύω): creep in unnoticed; slip in covertly; secretly penetrate; worm one's way into (Study 26)

Parrēsia (παρρησία): confidence; frankness; outspokenness; fearlessness; freedom of speech (Study 5)

Pas (πᾶς): all; every (Study 2)

Paschō (πάσχω): suffer; experience something unpleasant; go through something evil (Study 80)

Peirasmos (πειρασμός): temptation; an extensive test that tries the nature or character of someone or something (Study 13)

Phanerōsis (φανέρωσις): manifestation; a making visible; exposure; publicity (Study 79)

Phēmi (φημί): utter; say (Study 40)

Pheugō (φεύγω): flee; escape; take flight; get away (Study 30)

Philippos (Φίλιππος): Philip; a Greek name; one of Jesus's twelve disciples (Study 37)

Philos (φίλος): loving; having special interest; friendly (Studies 59, 84)

Philoxenos (φιλόξενος): hospitality; love for the stranger; special interest in the foreigner; friendliness to the alien (Study 59)

Phōs (φῶς): light (Study 79)

Phrissō (φρίσσω): shudder; quiver; tremble; be extremely fearful; bristle; rise up on end (Study 51)

Phthora (φθορά): corruption; destruction; ruin; deterioration (Study 65)

Pinō (πίνω): drink; take in a liquid (Study 41)

Planos (πλάνος): deceitful; leading astray; causing someone to be mistaken; misleading (Study 55)

Plēktēs (πλήκτης): violent; a pernicious person; a quarrelsome individual; a bully (Study 75)

Plēssō (πλήσσω): strike (with force); smite; sting (Study 75)

Pneuma (πνεῦμα): spirit; breath; wind; inner life (Study 69)

Poiēma (ποίημα): workmanship; creation; invention; thing produced by an artist (Study 17)

Ponēros (πονηρός): evil; wicked; knavish; malicious; sorrow; unhappiness; trouble that brings evil; failure; bad luck (Study 67)

Ponos (πόνος): work; hard labor (Study 85)

Pros (πρός): near; by (Study 63)

Proslambāno (προσλαμβάνω): welcome; take near; grasp by the hand and bring close (Study 63)

Psychē (ψυχή): soul; breath of life (Study 46)

Rhizoō (ῥιζόω): root: fix firmly; put on a firm foundation; be strengthened (Study 86)

Rhyomai (ῥύομαι): rescue; snatch from; ward off; show defensive power (Study 11)

Sapros (σαπρὸς): corrupt; putrid; decayed; rancid (Study 45)

Seiō (σείω): shake; agitate; cause something to move back and forth rapidly and violently (Study 53)

Sōzō (σῴζω): save (Study 8)

Skybalon (σκύβαλον): rubbish; dung; excrement (Study 48)

Splanchnizomai (σπλαγχνίζομαι): moved with pity; touched in the inward parts; compassion (Study 47)

Strateia (στρατεία): warfare; military campaign or engagement; expedition of an army; military service (Study 28)

Stērizō (στηρίζω): establish, fix firmly in place; strengthen; support (Study 14)

Strephō (στρέφω): twist; turn; bend (Study 54)

Sympathēs (συμπαθής): sympathetic; suffering a blow together; experiencing something unpleasant with; going through something troublesome together (Study 80)

Syn (σύν): with; emphasizes accompaniment, association, assistance; linked together; partnered up (Studies 3, 57, 60, 80)

Synechō (συνέχω): control; compel; urge; overwhelm (Study 66)

Synergos (συνεργός): coworker; partnering together for a task; linking together for occupational purposes (Study 60)

Synistēmi (συνίστημι): show; showcase; set forth; demonstrate; display (Study 52)

Syntēreō (συντηρέω): treasure up; ruminate; continue to think about; carefully observe; ponder what something might mean (Study 57)

Tassō (τάσσω): order; arrange; put in place (Study 88)

Tē Hēmera Tē Ponēra (τῇ ἡμέρᾳ τῇ πονηρᾷ): the evil day; a specific period of time or an actual day in which bad luck falls upon someone (Study 67)

Tēreō (τηρέω): observe; keep in view; take note of (Study 57)

Tetelestai (τετέλεσται): it is finished; it is completed, accomplished, fulfilled, brought to an end (Study 35)

Tharseō (θαρσέω): take heart; take courage; dare; be bold; be firm in the face of danger (Study 72)

Theophilos (Θεόφιλος): Theophilus; a Greek name; recipient of the books of Luke and Acts (Study 84)

Theopneustos (θεόπνευστος): breathed out by God; breath that comes out of God; spoken by God (Study 69)

Theos (θεός): God (Studies 69, 84)

Topos (τόπος): opportunity; defined place; area; land; neighborhood (Study 49)

Xenos (ξένος): stranger; foreigner; alien (Study 59)

Zopyron (ζώπυρον): ember; spark; hot coal (Study 10)

ENGLISH – GREEK INDEX

Above: *Hyper* (ὑπέρ): over; beyond; more than (Studies 12, 31)

Again: *Palin* (πάλιν): again (Study 25)

All: *Pas* (πᾶς): every (Study 2)

Andrew: *Andreas* (Ἀνδρέας): a Greek name; one of Jesus's twelve disciples (Study 37)

Anxious: *Merimnaō* (μεριμνάω): occupied; enormously concerned; engaged in something with extreme care (Study 34)

Armor: *Hoplōn* (ὅπλον): weaponry used for military purposes (Study 2)

Babylon: *Babylōn* (Βαβυλών): a city in ancient Mesopotamia; a world system in opposition to God (Study 62)

Band (Of Dancers and Singers): *Choros* (χορός): band (of dancers and singers) (Study 87)

Be: *Ginomai* (γίνομαι): become; take place; be born (Study 25)

Breathed Out By God: *Theopneustos* (θεόπνευστος): breath that comes out of God; spoken by God (Study 69)

By (the Side Of): *Para* (παρά): by (the side of) (Study 61)

Blame: *Memphomai* (μέμφομαι): find fault (Study 9)

Call *Kaleō* (καλέω): call (Study 61)

Cheerful: *Hilaros* (ἱλαρός): glad; happy; joyful (Study 81)

Clean: *Katharos* (καθαρός): innocent; morally pure (Study 22)

Competition: *Agōn* (ἀγών): contest, deadly struggle (Study 23)

Confidence: *Parrēsia* (παρρησία): frankness; outspokenness; fearlessness; freedom of speech (Study 5)

Contend: *Epagōnizomai* (ἐπαγωνίζομαι): carry on a competiton, contest, or struggle (Study 23)

Control: *Synechō* (συνέχω): compel; urge; overwhelm (Study 66)

Corrupt: *Sapros* (σαπρὸς): putrid; decayed; rancid (Study 45)

Corruption: *Phthora* (φθορά): destruction; ruin; deterioration (Study 65)

Cowardly: *Deilos* (δειλός): timid; afraid; one who always runs away; one who runs away at nothing (Study 19)

Coworker: *Synergos* (συνεργός): partnering together for a task; linking together for occupational purposes (Study 60)

Creep in Unnoticed: *Pareisdyō* (παρεισδύω): slip in covertly; secretly penetrate; worm one's way into (Study 26)

Cut: *Katanyssomai*: (κατανύσσομαι): poke totally through; stab all the way in; gouge (Study 32)

Day (literal): *Hēmera* (ἡμέρα): period of time (Study 67)

Debauchery: *Asōtia* (ἀσωτία): reckless abandon; wild, undisciplined living; conduct of someone when the mind is absent (Study 8)

Deceitful: *Planos* (πλάνος): leading astray; causing someone to be mistaken; misleading (Study 55)

Deeply Moved: *Embrimaomai* (ἐμβριμάομαι): extremely concerned (Study 78)

Demon-Possessed: *Daimonizomai* (δαιμονίζομαι): taken over by a hostile spirit; indwelt by a demon (Study 29)

Departure: *Analysis* (ἀνάλυσις): loosing; untying; breaking up (Study 73)

Difficult: *Chalepos* (χαλεπός): fierce; violent; dangerous; troublesome (Study 18)

Disarm: *Apekdyomai* (ἀπεκδύομαι): strip clothes off; undress; disrobe (Study 27)

Down: *Kata* (κατά): down from; against; through (Study 32; 41)

Drink: *Pinō* (πίνω): take in a liquid (Study 41)

Drink Down: *Katapinō* (καταπίνω): swallow up; fully consume (Study 41)

Earnest: *Ektenes* (ἐκτενής): outstretched; extended (Study 7)

Ember: *Zopyron* (ζώπυρον): spark; hot coal (Study 10)

Endurance: *Hypomonē* (ὑπομονή): staying under; remaining under (Study 82)

Establish: *Stērizō* (στηρίζω): fix firmly in place; strengthen; support (Study 14)

Evil: *Ponēros* (πονηρός): wicked; knavish; malicious; sorrow; unhappiness; trouble that brings evil; failure; bad luck (Study 67)

Fainthearted: *Oligopsychos* (ὀλιγόψυχος): discouraged; having only a little bit of soul left within (Study 46)

Fan into Flame: *Anazōpyreō* (ἀναζωπυρέω): stir up the ember; rekindle the flame (Study 10)

Flee: *Pheugō* (φεύγω): escape; take flight; get away (Study 30)

Forbearance: *Anochē* (ἀνοχή): temporary cessation; pause; armistice; truce (Study 74)

Footstep: *Ichnos* (ἴχνος): footprint (Study 4)

Fragrance: *Osmē* (ὀσμή): smell; odor; something that stimulates a sense of smell; perfume; scent (Study 15)

From: *Apo* (ἀπό): from (Study 83)

Eager Longing: *Apokaradokia* (ἀποκαραδοκία): spy on something using the head (Study 83)

Exact Imprint: *Charaktēr* (χαρακτήρ): mark, impression placed on an object; image (Study 68)

Join: *Kollaō* (κολλάω): bind closely; glue together; cement together (Study 43)

Leader (Of a Chorus): *Chorēgos* (χορηγός): a rich individual appointed by the state to fund most or all of the expenses of a stage production where a chorus performed (Study 87)

Lie Down: *Keimai* (κεῖμαι): lie down (Study 33)

Light: *Phōs* (φῶς): light (Study 79)

Little: *Oligos* (ὀλίγος): little (Study 46)

Lot (In Life): *Moira* (μοῖρα): fate (Study 9)

Loving: *Philos* (φίλος): having special interest; friendly (Studies 59, 84)

Malcontent: *Mempsimoiros* (μεμψίμοιρος): complainer; grumbler; someone constantly finding fault; one who always thinks they are on the losing side of things (Study 9)

Male: *Arsēn* (ἄρσην): male (Study 33)

Manifestation: *Phanerōsis* (φανέρωσις): a making visible; exposure; publicity (Study 79)

Marketplace: *Agora* (ἀγορά): marketplace (Study 90)

Men (Who Practice Homosexuality): *Malakos/Arsenokoitēs* (μαλακός/ἀρσενοκοίτης): see *soft* and *sodomite* (Study 33)

Moved with Pity: *Splanchnizomai* (σπλαγχνίζομαι): touched in the inward parts; compassion (Study 47)

Near: *Pros* (πρός): by (Study 63)

Nudge: *Nyssō* (νύσσω): poke; prick (Study 32)

Observe: *Tēreō* (τηρέω): keep in view; take note of (Study 57)

Opportunity: *Topos* (τόπος): defined place; area; land; neighborhood (Study 49)

Order: *Tassō* (τάσσω): arrange; put in place (Study 88)

Out Of: *Ek* (ἐκ): from (Study 4; 54)

Peddle: *Kapēleuō* (καπηλεύω): to be a peddler; to hawk goods; to be a retailer (Study 16)

Philip: *Philippos* (Φίλιππος): a Greek name; one of Jesus's twelve disciples (Study 37)

Play (Like a Child): *Paizō* (παίζω): play (like a child) (Study 71)

Press On: *Diōkō* (διώκω): pursue; chase; follow something in haste; move quickly and definitively toward something; march; set in swift motion; harass (Study 21)

Put On: *Endyō* (ἐνδύω): get into something; sink into something; enter into something (Study 64)

Put to Death: *Nekroō* (νεκρόω): deaden; mortify; kill; cause to cease completely (Study 39)

Redeem: *Exagorazō* (ἐξαγοράζω): buy from out of the marketplace (Study 90)

Refresh: *Anapsychō* (ἀναψύχω): revive; cool; give relief (Study 70)

Regeneration: *Palingenesia* (παλιγγενεσία): become again; be born again; have life again; a new genesis (Study 25)

Rescue: *Rhyomai* (ῥύομαι): snatch from; ward off; show defensive power (Study 11)

Revelation: *Apokalypsis* (ἀποκάλυψις): uncovering; disclosure; discovery (Study 24)

Reward: *Misthos* (μισθός): workman's wage; recompense (Study 89)

Root: *Rhizoō* (ῥιζόω): fix firmly; put on a firm foundation; be strengthened (Study 86)

Rubbish: *Skybalon* (σκύβαλον): dung; excrement (Study 48)

Save: *Sōzō* (σῴζω): save (Study 8)

Scoffer: *Empaiktēs* (ἐμπαίκτης): a person who plays with; a person who makes fun of someone or something; one who plays around at another's expense (Study 71)

Sear: *Kaustrēiazo* (καυστηριάζω): burn or brand with a hot iron; cauterize; scorch (Study 77)

Secret: *Kryptos*: (κρυπτός): hidden (Study 5)

Selfish Ambition: *Eritheia* (ἐριθεία): strife; contentiousness; rivalry (Study 58)

Shake: *Seiō* (σείω): agitate; cause something to move back and forth rapidly and violently (Study 53)

Shudder: *Phrissō* (φρίσσω): quiver; tremble; be extremely fearful; bristle; rise up on end (Study 51)

Show: *Synistēmi* (συνίστημι): showcase; set forth; demonstrate; display (Study 52)

Snare: *Pagis* (παγίς): net; trap; pit; trick; strategy (Study 38)

Sober-minded: *Nēphō* (νήφω): well-balanced; be self-controlled (Study 36)

Sodomite: *Arsenokoitēs* (ἀρσενοκοίτης): a male who lies down with another male; dominant partner in a homosexual relationship (Study 33)

Soft: *Malakos* (μαλακός): tender; delicate; effeminate, passive partner in a homosexual relationship (Study 33)

Soul: *Psychē* (ψυχή): breath of life (Study 46)

Sound Forth: *Exēcheō* (ἐξηχέω): ring out (Study 6)

Spirit: *Pneuma* (πνεῦμα): breath; wind; inner life (Study 69)

Spy: *Dokeuo* (δοκεύω): watch (Study 83)

Stay: *Menō* (μένω): remain; wait (Study 82)

Stir Up: *Anaseiō* (ἀνασείω): shake up (Study 53)

Stranger: *Xenos* (ξένος): foreigner; alien (Study 59)

Strike (With Force): *Plēssō* (πλήσσω): smite; sting (Study 75)

Stronghold: *Ochyrōma* (ὀχύρωμα): fortress; prison; strong-walled place (Study 56)

Suffer: *Paschō* (πάσχω): experience something unpleasant; go through something evil (Study 80)

Supplement: *Epichorēgeō* (ἐπιχορηγέω): grant; fund; supply at one's own expense; fund the expenses of a chorus; put on an expensive event; fund a costly project (Study 87)

Sympathetic: *Sympathēs* (συμπαθής): suffering a blow together; experiencing something unpleasant with; going through something troublesome together (Study 80)

Take (In Hand): *Lambanō*: (λαμβάνω): grasp; seize (Study 63)

Take Heart: *Tharseō* (θαρσέω): take courage; dare; be bold; be firm in the face of danger (Study 72)

Task: *Ergon* (ἔργον): occupation; labor; undertaking (Study 60)

Temptation: *Peirasmos* (πειρασμός): an extensive test that tries the nature or character of someone or something (Study 13)

The Evil Day: *Tē Hēmera Tē Ponēra* (τῇ ἡμέρᾳ τῇ πονηρᾷ): a specific period of time or an actual day in which bad luck falls upon someone (Study 67)

The Holy One of God: *Ho Hagios Tou Theou* (ὁ ἅγιος τοῦ θεοῦ): a title ascribed to Jesus in the Gospels affirming his messianic work (Study 44)

Theophilus: *Theophilos* (Θεόφιλος): a Greek name; recipient of the books of Luke and Acts (Study 84)

Through: *Dia* (διά): through (Study 85)

Throw: *Ballō* (βάλλω): cast (Study 12)

Trace From: *Exichniazo* (εξιχνιάζω): track out; search something out, explore something thoroughly; get to the bottom of something; resolve a police case (Study 4)

Treasure Up: *Syntēreō* (συντηρέω): ruminate; continue to think about; carefully observe; ponder what something might mean (Study 57)

Twist: *Strephō* (στρέφω): turn; bend (Study 54)

Unclean: *Akathartos* (ἀκάθαρτος): containing impurities; foul; infected (Study 22)

Under: *Hypo* (ὑπό): under (Study 82)

Up: *Ana* (ἀνά): again (Studies 10, 53)

Unsearchable: *Anexichniastos* (ανεξιχνίαστος): unable to search something; unable to figure something out; impossible to get to the bottom of something; incomprehensible; impossible to fully understand (Study 4)

Utter: *Phēmi* (φημί): say (Study 40)

Utter Hurtful Words: *Blasphēmeō* (βλασφημέω): slander (Study 40)

Violent: *Plēktēs* (πλήκτης): a pernicious person; a quarrelsome individual; a bully (Study 75)

Warfare: *Strateia* (στρατεία): military campaign or engagement; expedition of an army; military service (Study 28)

Warp: *Ekstrephō* (ἐκστρέφω): turn out; twist out (Study 54)

Welcome: *Proslambāno* (προσλαμβάνω): take near; grasp by the hand and bring close (Study 63)

Whole Armor: *Panoplia* (πανοπλία): all equipment and weapons required for battle; the full set of a soldier's armor (Study 2)

With: *Syn* (σύν): emphasizes accompaniment, association, assistance; linked together; partnered up (Studies 3, 57, 60, 80)

Work: *Ponos* (πόνος): hard labor (Study 85)

Workmanship: *Poiēma* (ποίημα): creation; invention; thing produced by an artist (Study 17)

BIBLIOGRAPHY

"10 surprising sex statistics"; www.nbcnews.com/id/37853719/ns/health-sexual_health/t/surprising-sex-statistics/#.XicjES2ZOYU (accessed January 20, 2020).

Abbate, Emily, "The Real-Life Diet of Russell Wilson, Who Plans to Play Football Until He's 45"; www.gq.com/story/russell-wilson-real-life-diet (accessed March 11, 2020).

"About Derek Redmond"; derekredmond.com/about (accessed April 19, 2019).

"About Leeches"; www.leechestherapy.com/about-leeches (accessed July 11, 2019).

Aland, Barbara, Kurt Aland, Johannes Karavidopoulos, Carlo M. Martini, and Bruce M. Metzger, eds. *The Greek New Testament*. Fifth Revised Edition. Stuttgart, Germany: Deutsche Bibelgesellschaft, 2014.

Almsay, Steve, "$236,000 unpaid toll bill for one duo"; www.cnn.com/2013/10/17/us/texas-unpaid-toll-violators/index.html (accessed January 18, 2020).

Andrews, Evan, "What Was the Gordian Knot?"; www.history.com/news/what-was-the-gordian-knot (accessed January 18, 2020).

Arndt, William, Frederick W. Danker, and Walter Bauer. *A Greek-English Lexicon of the New Testament and Other Early Christian Literature.* Chicago: University of Chicago Press, 2000.

Auslander, Shalom, "Meet the Man Who Spent Christmas Eve Stuck Upside Down in a Septic Tank"; www.gq.com/story/man-spent-christmas-eve-in-septic-tank (accessed June 27, 2019).

Bagley, Mary, "Krakatoa Volcano: Facts About 1883 Eruption"; www.livescience.com/28186-krakatoa.html (accessed July 1, 2019).

Balz, Horst and Gerhard Schneider, eds. *Exegetical Dictionary of the New Testament.* Edinburgh, Scotland: T&T Clark LTD, 1990.

Barry, John. D *The Lexham Bible* Dictionary. Bellingham, WA: Lexham Press, 2016.

Bejan, Teresa M., "The Two Clashing Meanings of 'Free Speech'"; www.theatlantic.com/politics/archive/2017/12/two-concepts-of-freedom-of-speech/546791.

"Bloodhound"; dogtime.com/dog-breeds/bloodhound#/slide/1 (accessed July 15, 2019).

"The Bloodhound's Amazing Sense of Smell"; www.pbs.org/wnet/nature/underdogs-the-bloodhounds-amazing-sense-of-smell/350 (accessed July 15, 2019).

Bottinelli, Stef, "Sailing superstitions: 13 things never to do at sea!"; www.ybw.com/features/sailing-superstitions-13-things-never-done-at-sea-43670 (accessed July 29, 2019).

Bovson, Mara, "Prison Break? Calling Most Famous Canine Detective Nick Carter"; www.akc.org/expert-advice/news/prison-break-calling-most-famous-canine-detective-nick-carter (accessed July 16, 2019).

Bricker, Tom, "Top 10 Disney World Scents"; www.disneytouristblog.com/disney-world-scents (accessed July 9, 2019).

Browne, Alex, "11 Facts About World War One Casualties"; www.historyhit.com/facts-about-world-war-one-casualties (accessed August 3, 2019).

Bruce, F.F. *Romans*. Tyndale New Testament Commentaries Volume 6. Downers Grove, IL: InterVarsity Press, 1985.

Burton, Henry Fairfield. "The Worship of Roman Emperors." *The Biblical World 40*, no.2 (1912). 80-91.

"A Canadian sniper breaks the record for longest confirmed kill shot – but how?" www.bbc.co.uk/newsbeat/article/40381047/a-canadian-sniper-breaks-the-record-for-the-longest-confirmed-kill-shot---but-how (accessed July 12, 2019).

Carson, D.A. *The Gospel According to John*. The Pillar New Testament Commentary. Grand Rapids, MI: William B. Eerdmans Publishing Company, 1991.

Carter, Joe, "9 Things You Should Know About Billy Graham (1918-2018)"; www.thegospelcoalition.org/article/9-things-know-billy-graham (accessed August 7, 2019).

Cartwright, Mark, "Centurion"; www.ancient.eu/Centurion (accessed January 19, 2020).

Cartwright, Mark, "Poseidon"; www.ancient.eu/poseidon (accessed July 17, 2019).

Cheeky Kid, "100+ Alternative Ways to Say 'Good Luck!'"; pairedlife.com/etiquette/Ways-to-Say-Good-Luck (August 2, 2019).

Ciampa, Roy E. and Brian S. Rosner. *The First Letter to the Corinthians*. The Pillar New Testament Commentary. Grand Rapids, MI: William B. Eerdmans Publishing Company, 2010.

Cole, R. Alan. *Mark*. Tyndale New Testament Commentaries Volume 2. Downers Grove, IL: InterVarsity Press, 1989.

Crew, Bec, "The World's Loudest Sounds Caused Shock Waves 10,000 Times That of a Hydrogen Bomb"; www.sciencealert.com/worlds-loudest-sound-krakatoa-shock-waves-10000-more-hydrogen-bomb (accessed July 1, 2019).

Crow, Sarah, "50 Things You Do Everyday That Annoy Other People"; bestlifeonline.com/annoying-things-everyone-does (accessed June 25, 2019).

Crow, Sarah, "You'll Spend This Much of Your Life Waiting at Red Lights"; bestlifeonline.com/red-lights (accessed August 18, 2019).

Daniel, Alex, "21 Mysteries About Space No One Can Explain"; bestlifeonline.com/space-mysteries (accessed July 20, 2019).

Dash, Mike, "The Story of the WWI Christmas Truce"; www.smithso-nianmag.com/history/the-story-of-the-wwi-christmas-truce-11972213 (accessed August 4, 2019).

"Dashrath Manjhi Road"; www.atlasobscura.com/places/dashrath-man-jhi-road (accessed July 27, 2019).

Davids, Peter H. *The Letters of 2 Peter and Jude*. The Pillar New Testament Commentary. Grand Rapids, MI: William B. Eerdmans Publishing Company, 2006.

Davidson, Robert. *Genesis 1-11*. The Cambridge Bible Commentary Series. Cambridge: Cambridge University Press, 1973.

Deseret News, "Septic tank mishap ruins Christmas Eve"; www.deseret.com/2007/12/27/20061422/septic-tank-mishap-ruins-christmas-eve (accessed June 27, 2019).

Donnelly, Tim, "The proof that 3 men survived their escape from Alcatraz"; nypost.com/2015/10/10/relatives-have-proof-alcatraz-escap-ees-are-still-alive (accessed July 11, 2019).

Dwyer, Colin, "Cristiano Ronaldo's New Bronze Bust Is Turning Heads"; www.npr.org/sections/thetwo-way/2017/03/29/521940923/cristiano-ronaldos-new-bronze-bust-is-turning-heads (accessed July 30, 2019).

Easton, M.G. *Easton's Bible Dictionary*. New York, NY: Harper & Brothers, 1893.

Edwards, James R. *The Gospel According to Luke*. The Pillar New Testament Commentary. Grand Rapids, MI: William B. Eerdmans Publishing Company, 2015.

Edwards, James R. *The Gospel According to Mark*. The Pillar New Testament Commentary. Grand Rapids, MI: William B. Eerdmans Publishing Company, 2002.

Eig, Jonathan. *Ali: A Life*. New York, NY: Mariner Books, 2017.

"Essentials Oils Market Size, Share & Trends Analysis Report By Application (Cleaning & Home, Medical, Food & Beverages, Spa & Relaxation), By Product, By Sales Channel, And Segment Forecasts, 2019-2025"; www.grandviewresearch.com/industry-analysis/essential-oils-market (accessed March 26th, 2019).

"Fastest circumnavigating by tandem bicycle (male)"; www.guinnessworldrecords.com/world-records/89969-fastest-circumnavigation-by-tandem-bicycle-true (accessed July 26, 2019).

Feiler, Bruce, "The Art of Condolence"; www.nytimes.com/2016/10/02/style/how-to-express-sympathy.html (accessed January 19, 2020).

Fitzmyer, Joseph A. *Romans*. The Anchor Yale Bible Volume 33. London, England: Yale University Press, 1993.

Fitzpatrick, Frank, "20 Years Since NHL Fatality, Few Bare Heads," *The Washington Post*, January 24, 1988; https://www.washingtonpost.com/archive/sports/1988/01/24/20-years-since-nhl-fatality-few-bare-heads/2bc-7f2a0-09b3-4c99-8fd0-23c3d2d18485 (accessed January 29, 2020).

Flaxington, Beverly D., "Giving Up Complaining"; www.psychologytoday.com/us/blog/understand-other-people/201206/giving-complaining (accessed January 17, 2020).

Foulkes, Francis. *Ephesians*. Tyndale New Testament Commentaries Volume 10. Downers Grove, IL: InterVarsity Press, 1989.

Fowler, Thomas. *The Elements of Deductive Logic*. London, England: MacMillian and Co., 1883.

France, R.T. *Matthew*. Tyndale New Testament Commentaries Volume 1. Downers Grove, IL: InterVarsity Press, 1985.

Frankel, Eddy, "Now even worse: ridiculed bust of Cristiano Ronaldo gets a dreadful do-over"; www.theguardian.com/artanddesign/2018/apr/03/cristiano-ronaldo-emanuel-santos-new-sculpture (accessed July 30, 2019).

Francis, Enjoli, and Noll, Eric, "Child calls 911 for help with math homework: 'I'm sorry for calling you but I really needed help'"; abcnews.go.com/US/5th-grader-calls-911-math-homework-im-calling/story?id=60712570 (accessed July 23, 2019).

Freedman, David Noel. *The Anchor Bible Dictionary*. New York, NY: Doubleday, 1992.

Garcia, Justin, "Sexual hook-up culture"; www.apa.org/monitor/2013/02/ce-corner (accessed April 17, 2019).

Giacosa, Ilaraia Gozzini. *A Taste of Ancient Rome*. Translated by Mary Taylor Simeti. Chicago, IL: The University of Press, 1992.

Giang, Vivian, "13 Of The Most Ridiculous Things People Have Ever Seen Coworkers Do"; www.businessinsider.com/the-most-ridiculous-stories-about-co-workers-2012-6 (accessed July 22, 2019).

Grant, David, "Alexander's Siege of Tyre, 332 BCE"; www.ancient.eu/article/107/alexanders-siege-of-tyre-332-bce (accessed July 19, 2019).

"The Great Escape from Alcatraz"; www.alcatrazhistory.com/alcesc1.htm (accessed July 11, 2019).

"Great Hurricane of 1780"; www.history.com/topics/natural-disasters-and-environment/great-hurricane-of-1780 (accessed August 16, 2019).

Green, L. *The Letters to the Thessalonians*. The Pillar New Testament Commentary. Grand Rapids, MI: William B. Eerdmans Publishing Company, 2002.

Green, Michael. *2 Peter and Jude*. Tyndale New Testament Commentaries Volume 18. Downers Grove, IL: InterVarsity Press, 1987.

Grudem, Wayne A. *1 Peter*. Tyndale New Testament Commentaries Volume 17. Downers Grove, IL: InterVarsity Press, 1988.

Grudem, Wayne. *Systematic Theology: An Introduction to Biblical Doctrine*. Grand Rapids, MI: Zondervan, 1994.

Guthrie, Donald. *Hebrews*. Tyndale New Testament Commentaries Volume 15. Downers Grove, IL: InterVarsity Press, 1983.

Guthrie, Donald. *The Pastoral Epistles*. Tyndale New Testament Commentaries Volume 14. Downers Grove, IL: InterVarsity Press, 1990.

Goldman, Tom, "Reggie Bush To Give Up Heisman Trophy"; www.npr.org/templates/story/story.php?storyId=129865279 (accessed August 21, 2019).

Hale, Ron F, "'Puff Graham'- Finding the Favor of God"; christianindex. org/puff-graham-finding-the-favor-of-god (accessed August 7, 2019).

Gupta, Neha, "Top 10 Toughest Exams In the World"; finance.yahoo. com/news/top-10-toughest-exams-world-163825127.html (accessed January 19, 2020).

Hansen, G. Walter. *The Letters to the Philippians*. The Pillar New Testament Commentary. Grand Rapids, MI: William B. Eerdmans Publishing Company, 2009.

Harvard Health Publishing, "The gut-brain connection"; www.health. harvard.edu/diseases-and-conditions/the-gut-brain-connection (accessed June 21, 2019).

Heimbuch, Jaymi, "5 fascinating facts about redwood trees"; www.mnn. com/earth-matters/wilderness-resources/blogs/5-fascinating-facts-about-redwood-trees (accessed July 8, 2019).

Heitler, Susan, "Can You Spot 10 Signs of a Childish Adult"; www.psychologytoday.com/us/blog/resolution-not-conflict/201603/can-you-spot-10-signs-childish-adult (August 1, 2019).

"High-Profile $1.9 Billion Defamation Case Settles"; www.cornerstone. com/Publications/Press-Releases/High-Profile-Defamation-Case-Settles# (accessed April 7, 2019).

The Holy Bible: English Standard Version. Wheaton: Standard Bible Society, 2016.

Homer. *The Odyssey with an English Translation by A.T. Murray, PH.D. in Two Volumes*. Medford, MA: Cambridge, MA., Harvard University Press; London, William Heinemann, Ltd., 1919.

Hytrek, Nick, "Breaking: BPI settles defamation with ABC"; siouxcity-journal.com/news/local/breaking-bpi-settles-defamation-suit-with-abc/article_397f35af-b70b-5998-94c0-c46deddf58bf.html (accessed April 7, 2019).

"How Many Is a Googol"; www.wonderopolis.org/wonder/how-many-is-a-googol (accessed July 28, 2019).

Jansen, Bart, "NTSB: Miami bridge that collapsed and killed 6 had design errors"; www.usatoday.com/story/news/2018/11/15/ntsb-miami-bridge-collapse-design-errors/2012020002 (accessed August 19, 2019).

Jebb, R.C., trans. *The Characters of Theophrastus*. London, UK: Forgotten Books, 2018.

Joel, Billy, "Billy Joel – Q&A: Tell Us About 'We Didn't Start the Fire'? (Oxford 1994)"; Filmed [1994]. YouTube video, 4:09. Posted [October 22, 2013]; www.youtube.com/watch?v=Dx3T8pbDcms (accessed June 23, 2019).

Jussim, Matthew, "How 15 NFL Players Train and Get Shredded for the Football Season"; www.mensjournal.com/sports/how-15-nfl-players-trained-and-got-shredded-2017-season/3-david-johnson (accessed August 21, 2019).

Kasner, Edward and James Newman. *Mathematics and the Imagination*. Mineola, New York: Dover Publications, Inc., 2001.

Kelly, Jon, "Who, What, Why: Who was Leonidas of Rhodes"; www.bbc.com/news/magazine-37033910 (accessed January 20, 2020)

Kids Discover, "11 Awesome Facts About Lightning"; www.kidsdiscover.com/quick-reads/11-awesome-facts-lightning (accessed August 5, 2019).

Kittel, Gerhard, G. W. Bromiley, and Gerhard Friedrich. *Theological Dictionary of the New Testament*. Grand Rapids, Mich: Eerdmans, 1964.

Köstenberger, Andreas J., L. Scott Kellum, and Charles L. Quarles. *The Cradle, the Cross, and the Crown*. Nashville, TN: B&H Publishing Group, 2009.

Kottke, Jason, "The World's Loudest Sound"; kottke.org/14/10/the-worlds-loudest-sound (accessed July 1, 2019).

Kruse, Colin G. *2 Corinthians*. Tyndale New Testament Commentaries Volume 8. Downers Grove, IL: InterVarsity Press, 1987.

Kruse, Colin G. *John*. Tyndale New Testament Commentaries Volume 4. Downers Grove, IL: InterVarsity Press, 2003.

Kruse, Colin G. *The Letters of John.* The Pillar New Testament Commentary. Grand Rapids, MI: William B. Eerdmans Publishing Company, 2000.

Kruse, Colin G. *Paul's Letter to the Romans.* The Pillar New Testament Commentary. Grand Rapids, MI, William B. Eerdmans Publishing Company, 2012.

Kuizon, Kimberly, "Officer shows how small spark can become wildfire"; www.fox13news.com/news/local-news/officer-shows-how-small-spark-can-become-wildfire (accessed July 7, 2019).

Lamb, Christopher, "Number of exorcisms in Italy triples"; www.thetablet.co.uk/news/8622/number-of-exorcisms-in-italy-triples (accessed January 18, 2020).

Lafranzo, Julie, "Scientific explanation for butterflies in your stomach"; timesdelphic.com/2019/02/scientific-explanation-for-butterflies-in-your-stomach (accessed January 20, 2020).

Liacopoulou, Ivy, "All You Need to Know About Greek Baklavas"; www.kopiaste.org/2019/01/all-you-need-to-know-about-greek-baklavas (accessed January 20, 2020).

Liddell, Henry George and Robert Scott. *A Greek-English Lexicon.* Oxford, UK: Oxford University Press, 1996.

"Lightning"; www.nationalgeographic.com/environment/natural-disasters/lightning/#close (accessed August 5, 2019).

Louw, Johannes P. and Eugene A. Nida. *Greek Lexicon of the New Testament Based on Semantic Domains Vol. 1.* New York, NY: United Bible Society, 1989.

Lowry, Linda, "Christian Persecution by the Numbers"; www.opendoorsusa.org/christian-persecution/stories/christian-persecution-by-the-numbers (accessed January 19, 2020).

Mackey, Aurora, "Mystery of the Dryer Solved Scientifically"; www.latimes.com/archives/la-xpm-1993-06-03-vl-42901-story.html (accessed July 18, 2019).

Mark, Michelle, "The Miami bridge that collapsed, killing 6, was installed in a few hours and considered a 'marvel' of modern construction"; www.businessinsider.com/miami-bridge-collapse-accelerated-bridge-construction-technique-2018-3 (accessed August 19, 2019).

Martin, Ralph. *Philippians*. Tyndale New Testament Commentaries. Volume 11. Downers Grove, IL: InterVarsity Press, 1987.

Maynard, Matt, "Meet the men hoping to be the fastest to cycle around the planet – on a tandem"; www.redbull.com/my-en/tandem-cycling-world-record-attempt-red-bull (accessed July 26, 2019).

McConnaughey, Janet, "Artist turns Oregon coast's plastic trash into big sea-life sculptures – with a lesson"; www.seattletimes.com/nation-world/huge-sea-life-sculptures-made-from-oceans-plastic-trash (accessed March 28, 2019).

McCoy, Terrance, "The inside story of the 'white dress, blue dress' drama that divided a planet"; www.washingtonpost.com/news/morning-mix/wp/2015/02/27/the-inside-story-of-the-white-dress-blue-dress-drama-that-divided-a-nation (accessed July 24, 2019).

McKendry, David Ian, "Is The Exorcist Cursed? Seven Reasons Why Some Think the Film is Haunted"; www.the13thfloor.tv/2015/12/02/is-the-exorcist-movie-cursed (accessed July 3, 2019).

McNearney, Allison, "How They Partied in Baiae, the Las Vegas of Ancient Rome"; www.thedailybeast.com/how-they-partied-in-baiae-the-las-vegas-of-ancient-rome (accessed January 19, 2020).

McNeilly, Hamish, "Man who led police on 720-kilometre car chase around South Island pleads guilty"; www.stuff.co.nz/national/86215738/man-who-led-police-on-720km-wide-car-chase-around-south-island-pleads-guilty (accessed June 26, 2019).

Moo, Douglas J. *James*. Tyndale New Testament Commentaries Volume 16. Downers Grove, IL: InterVarsity Press, 1985.

Moo, Douglas J. *The Letters to the Colossians and to Philemon*. The Pillar New Testament Commentary. Grand Rapids, MI: William B. Eerdmans Publishing Company, 2008.

Moo, Douglas J. *The Letter of James*. The Pillar New Testament Commentary. Grand Rapids, MI: William B. Eerdmans Publishing Company, 2000.

Morris, Leon. *1 Corinthians*. Tyndale New Testament Commentaries Volume 7. Downers Grove, IL: InterVarsity Press, 1985.

Morris, Leon. *1 and 2 Thessalonians*. Tyndale New Testament Commentaries Volume 13. Downers Grove, IL: 1984.

Morris, Leon. *The Epistle to Romans*. The Pillar New Testament Commentary. Grand Rapids, MI: William B. Eerdmans Publishing Company, 1988.

Morris, Leon. *The Gospel According to Matthew*. The Pillar New Testament Commentary. Grand Rapids, MI: William B. Eerdmans Publishing Company, 1992.

Morris, Leon. *Luke*. Tyndale New Testament Commentaries Volume 3. Downers Grove, IL: InterVarsity Press, 1988.

Morris, Leon. *Revelation*. Tyndale New Testament Commentaries Volume 20. Downers Grove, IL: InterVarsity Press, 1987.

Moulton, James Hope and George Milligan. *The Vocabulary of the Greek Testament*. Grand Rapids, MI: Wm. B. Eerdmans Publishing Company, 1930.

National Geographic Staff, "Tornadoes, explained"; www.nationalgeographic.com/environment/natural-disasters/tornadoes (accessed August 6, 2019).

Newsom, John, "Ironman 101: A Six-Month Training Plan"; www.ironman.com/triathlon/news/articles/2013/05/six-months-to-ironman-a-basic-training-program.aspx#axzz5tBZljP3Y (accessed June 28, 2019).

Ng, Alfred, "Cristiano Ronaldo was built of nightmares and bronze"; www.cnet.com/news/cristiano-ronaldo-statue-was-built-of-nightmares-and-bronze (accessed July 30, 2019).

Nix, Elizabeth, "6 Daring Double Agents"; www.history.com/news/6-daring-double-agents (accessed April 9, 2019).

O'Kane, Caitlin, "Mystery man pays off all layaway items at a Walmart in Vermont"; www.cbsnews.com/news/mystery-man-pays-off-all-layaway-items-at-walmart-in-derby-vermont (accessed August 20, 2019).

O'Neill, Maggie, "This Is the Happiest Time of the Day"; www.good-housekeeping.com/health/wellness/a32015/happiest-time-of-the-day (accessed January 19, 2020).

Osborne, Hannah, "Huge Reservoir of Fresh Water Discovered Hidden Deep Beneath the Ocean Off the U.S. East Coast"; www.newsweek.com/hidden-reservoir-fresh-water-us-coast-1445500 (accessed June 29, 2019).

"Oskar Schindler, a rescuer of the Jews during the Holocaust"; www.auschwitz.dk/schindler2.htm (accessed August 22, 2019).

Peterson, David G. *The Acts of the Apostles*. The Pillar New Testament Commentary. Grand Rapids, MI: William B. Eerdmans Publishing Company, 2009.

The Phrase Finder, "Makes your hair stand on end"; www.phrases.org.uk/meanings/makes-your-hair-stand-on-end.html (accessed July 10, 2019).

"Poseidon (Earthshaker, Dark-haired one, Neptune)"; www.greek-gods.org/olympian-gods/poseidon.php (accessed July 17, 2019).

Pratt, Devin, "Top 10: Lottery Tragedies"; www.askmen.com/top_10/dating/top-10-lottery-tragedies.html (accessed July 6, 2019).

Pruitt, Sarah, "Jefferson & Adams: Founding Frenemies"; www.history.com/news/jefferson-adams-founding-frenemies (accessed July 21, 2019).

Renzulli, Keri Anne, and Connley, Courtney, "Here's what the average NFL player makes in a season"; www.cnbc.com/2019/02/01/heres-what-the-average-nfl-players-makes-in-a-season.html (accessed January 17, 2020).

Rivas, Christine, "15 Facts about the Curious Case of Phineas Gage"; www.therichest.com/shocking/15-facts-about-the-curious-case-of-phineas-gage (accessed July 13, 2019).

"Robert Hanssen Fast Facts"; www.cnn.com/2013/03/25/us/robert-hanssen-fast-facts/index.html (accessed April 15, 2019).

Robertson, A.T. *Word Pictures in the New Testament Concise Edition.* Edited by James A. Swanson. New York, New York: Holman Bible Publishers, 2000.

Seifrid, Mark A. *The Second Letter to the Corinthians.* The Pillar New Testament Commentary Grand Rapids, MI: William B. Eerdmans Publishing Company, 2014.

Shapira, Allison, "Breathing Is the Key to Persuasive Public Speaking"; hbr.org/2015/06/breathing-is-the-key-to-persuasive-public-speaking (accessed July 31, 2019).

Simmons, Andy, "The Dramatic Moment a Man Saved a Stranger from Plummeting Down a Cliff"; www.rd.com/true-stories/survival/car-accident-rescue-story (accessed July 25, 2019).

Smietana, Bob, "Survey: Big drop in those who say being gay's a sin," *USA Today*, January 10, 2013.

Souter, Alexander. *A Pocket Lexicon to the Greek New Testament.* Oxford, UK: Clarendon Press, 1917.

Stanford Prison Experiment, www.prisonexp.org (accessed July 5, 2019).

Starnes, Callie, "Update 2: Man tangled in rope discovered after two days"; www.wrcbtv.com/story/15423293/man-tangled-in-rope-discovered-after-two-days (accessed June 22, 2019).

"State of the Bible 2018: Seven Top Findings"; www.barna.com/research/state-of-the-bible-2018-seven-top-findings (accessed August 18, 2019).

Sterner, C. Douglas, "The Four Chaplains"; homeofheroes.com/heroes-stories/the-brotherhood-of-soldiers-at-war/the-four-chaplains (accessed July 2, 2019).

Stevens, James, "Horse Wanders Town After Escape from Uttoxeter"; www.bloodhorse.com/horse-racing/articles/232587/horse-wanders-town-after-escape-from-uttoxeter (accessed July 18, 2019).

Stott, John R.W. *The Letters of John.* Tyndale New Testament Commentaries Volume 19. Downers Grove, IL: InterVarsity Press, 1988.

Swanson, James. *A Dictionary of Biblical Languages Greek New Testament.* Bellingham, WA: Logos Research Systems, 2001.

Swint, Kerwin, "Adams vs. Jefferson: The Birth of Negative Campaigning in the U.S."; mentalfloss.com/article/12487/adams-vs-jefferson-birth-negative-campaigning-us (accessed July 21, 2019).

SWNS, "Majority of Americans utter curse words when stressed out, study finds"; www.foxnews.com/lifestyle/majority-of-americans-utter-curse-words-when-stressed-out-study-finds (accessed January 17, 2020).

Tanner, Georgeen, "Christian persecution: How many are being killed, where they are being killed"; www.foxnews.com/politics/christian-persecution-how-many-are-being-killed-where-they-are-being-killed (accessed January 18, 2020).

T. Maccius Plautus, *The Comedies of Plautus*. Translated by Henry Thomas Riley. Medford, MA: G. Bell and Sons, 1912.

"Top 10 Most Expensive Auction Items"; content.time.com/time/specials/packages/article/0,28804,1917097_1917096_1917083,00.html (accessed January 20, 2020).

"Top 10 Wizard of Oz Characters"; www.thetoptens.com/wizard-oz-characters (accessed June 24, 2019).

"Two-Thirds of Christians Face Doubt"; www.barna.com/research/two-thirds-christians-face-doubt (accessed August 18, 2019).

"Tyrannosaurus Rex"; www.nationalgeographic.com/animals/prehistoric/tyrannosaurus-rex (accessed January 21, 2020).

Viglucci, Andres, and Nehamas, Nicholas, "FIU had grand plans for 'signature' bridge. But the design had a key mistake, experts say"; www.miamiherald.com/news/local/community/miami-dade/article212571434.html (accessed August 19, 2019).

Walton, John H. *Genesis*. The New Application Commentary. Grand Rapids, MI: Zondervan, 2001.

Wenham, Gordon J. *Genesis 1-15*. Word Biblical Commentary. Waco, TX: Word Books Publisher, 1987.

White, Sarah, "The Science of Disney: Smellitizers"; phdprincess.com/2018/01/15/disney-smells (accessed July 17, 2019).

Wood, Jennifer M., "20 Fascinating Facts About The Exorcist"; mental-floss.com/article/54332/20-fascinating-facts-about-exorcist (accessed July 3, 2019).

"The World Factbook"; https://www.cia.gov/library/publications/resources/the-world-factbook/index.html (accessed May 20, 2020).

Wright, N.T. *Colossians and Philemon*. Tyndale New Testament Commentaries Volume 12. Downers Grove, IL: InterVarsity Press, 1986.

Wright, Pam, "Georgina Tornado Leaves House Seemingly Unscathed"; weather.com/news/news/2019-03-12-georgia-house-left-standing-path-tornado (accessed August 6, 2019).

ABOUT THE AUTHOR

The Rev. Chris Palmer is the founder and pastor of Light of Today Church in Novi, Michigan, and founder of Chris Palmer Ministries. He is host of the popular podcast, *Greek for the Week*, seen on several Internet platforms. His first book with Whitaker House, *Letters from Jesus: Studies from the Seven Churches of Revelation*, comes highly recommended by reviewers.

Chris began in full-time ministry in 2006 and began to preach internationally in 2009, helping many congregations grow, flourish, and expand. His desire for missions is to train and educate pastors, encourage congregations, support the vision of local church, and show the love of God to the culture. For over a decade, he has worked successfully with both traditional churches and the underground and persecuted church in more than forty nations throughout the world, including Europe, Africa, South America, Asia, and the Caribbean.

Chris earned a B.A. in Pastoral Studies from North Central University and an M.A. in Exegetical Theology, magna cum laude, from Moody Theological Seminary. He is a sought-after Greek scholar for his ability to make God's Word come alive from the Greek in a unique way. Chris is often invited to present Greek and hermeneutics workshops at Bible and ministry schools. He is currently working on his Ph.D. in Apocalyptic Studies at the University of Wales, Bangor.

His previous books include *Living as a Spirit: Hearing the Voice of God on Purpose*, *The 85 Questions You Ask When You Begin a Relationship with God*, *The Believer's Journey*, and *Escaping the Haunting Past: A Handbook for Deliverance*. His articles have been published by *Charisma*, *CBN*, *Crosswalk*, and elsewhere.

ENDNOTES

1. Unless the word is idiomatic. Then I introduce it to you the way it is inflected and the way I make use of it in the study; i.e., Study 9, *tetelestai* "it is finished." *Tetelestai* is the perfect tense, the passive voice, and indicative mood. It's not how you would find it in the lexicon. You'd find it under *teleō*. Yet, I have introduced it as *tetelestai* because it is idiomatic and holds a special significance inflected.

2. A "memester" is one who enjoy curating, sharing, and discussing memes.

3. "Meme" can also be a verb. It means to engage in the meme culture by creating, sharing, and even simply, appreciating memes.

4. Richard Dawkins. *The Selfish Gene.* (Oxford: Oxford University Press, 1976), 192.

5. A word family is a group of words that share the same root.

6. Edward Kasner and James Newman, *Mathematics and the Imagination* (Mineola, NY: Dover Publications, Inc), p. 8.

7. There are exceptions; if it is obscene or threatens, defames, incites crime, or endangers national security.

8. Commentators differ on just what exactly Paul was referring to here. Some believe it to be the opposition of Nero, others believe it refers to the persecutions he faced, while still others think it may refer to previous imprisonments. The important thing, however, is the emphasis on God's delivering display of power, as was also the case in Daniel's trial.

9. There were times that it referred to unpleasant smelling things or even neutral smelling things, such as clothes. Despite this, it is best associated with pleasing-smelling things.

10. The "LXX" is the Greek version of the Old Testament.

11. Billy Joel, "We Didn't Start the Fire," on *Storm Front* (Columbia, 1989).

12. Billy Joel Q&A, "Tell Us About 'We Didn't Start The Fire?'" University of Oxford, May 5, 1994 (www.youtube.com/watch?v=Dx3T8pbDcms).

13. See www.thetoptens.com/wizard-oz-characters.

14. The Greek word *genesis*, meaning "to come into being," comes from *ginomai*.

15. While the priest blessed the set and actors, this movie should not have been made in the first place. Disobeying and defying God never yields good results.

16. There is no reason a Christian should be watching *The Exorcist*. This movie dabbles in the occult and is made for entertainment purposes. The subject of demons and demonic possession should never be explored outside of the Word of God and under the leadership and direction of the Holy Spirit, lest the enemy deceive us and take advantage of us through ignorance.

17. The Gospel writers each recorded something different for Christ's last words in order to emphasize something significant about the crucifixion. Matthew and Mark record His last words as *"My God, my God, why have you forsaken me?"* to emphasize Jesus's horrific experience on the cross. (See Matthew 27:46; Mark 15:34.) Luke records, *"Father, into your hands I commit my spirit!"* as Jesus's last words to emphasize that He was united with the Father and was performing His will by being crucified. (See Luke 23:46.) John recorded, *"It is finished"* as Christ's last words to highlight the redemptive aspect of the crucifixion. (See John 19:30.)

18. The perfect tense.

19. In the LXX.

20. "He" is used because it wasn't customary for women to act in Greco-Roman theatre. All roles were played by men, including the roles of women.

21. Or a variation of this title.

22. Psalm 106:16 in our English Bibles.

23. Some modern English Bibles have with ὀργισθείς (*orgistheis*) instead of σπλαγχνισθείς (*splanchnistheis*). This is due to a textual variant found in D. However, σπλαγχνισθείς is a better choice as it is more widely attested (ℵ A B C L W Δ Θ). The UBS5 has σπλαγχνισθείς.

24. Although David Eagleman, a neuroscientist at the Baylor College of Medicine, would disagree. His research suggests that unusual combinations of sounds in a word make people uncomfortable.

25. The Chalcedonian Definition is statement about the person of Christ that was arranged by a church council that took place in AD 451 in the city of Chalcedon near Constantinople. The purpose of the definition was to establish dogma that guarded against the heretical views of Nestorianism, Eutychianism, and Apollinarianism, which were prevalent at the time.

26. Modern medical science would likely disagree with this method today. However, this does not take away from the point about what *anapsychō* means here.

27. Or *tharsei*.

28. See Matthew 9:2; 9:22; 14:27; Mark 6:50; 10:49; John 16:33; Acts 23:11

29. The ESV uses "sympathy" as in "have sympathy." This is the same as saying "be sympathetic." Both convey the adjective, "sympathetic."

30. Some scholars believe that he could have been a well-known Roman official, possibly even related to Emperor Domitian. See B.H. Streeter, *The Four Gospels* (London: Macmillan, 1924), 534–539.

31. In the text (Luke 1:3; Acts 1:1) it is found as *Theophile* because it takes the vocative case. Nevertheless, it is from *Theophilos*.